The Juror's Lonely Quest

LAST CHANCE

FOR

JUSTICE

Laurence H. Geller
and
Peter Hemenway

NCDS
P•R•E•S•S

A Division of the National Center for Dispute Settlement

This book may be purchased for use by educational and professional organizations and institutions. Write to Director of Special Sales, NCDS Press, 2777 Stemmons Freeway, Suite 650, Dallas, TX 75207 for information on discounts and terms or call (214) 638-2700.

Authors' Photograph by Laverne Gonzales (Sacramento)
Edited by Jan Lurie (New York City)

Publisher's Cataloging-in-Publication
(Provided by Quality Books, Inc.)

Geller, Laurence H.
     Last chance for justice : the juror's lonely quest /
  Laurence H. Geller and Peter Hemenway.
     p.cm
     Includes index.
     Preassigned LCCN: 97-65936
     ISBN: 0-9657115-0-1

1. Jury--United States--Popular works. 2. Jurors--United States --Handbooks, manuals, etc. 3. Jury duty--United States--Popular works. 4. Conduct of court proceedings--United States. 5. Simpson, O. J.., 1947- --Trials, litigation, etc. 6. Koon, Stacey C., 1950- --Trials, litigation, etc. 7. Powell, Laurence-- Trials, litigation, etc. 8. King, Rodney. 9. Trials (Police misconduct)-- California--Los Angeles.   I. Hemenway, Peter. II Title.

KF8972.Z9G45 1997   347'.73'75
                          QBI97-40291

1 2 3 4 5 6 7 8 9   GDP   GDP   1 0 9 8 7

To our children Nicholas, Joshua and Vanessa
and to all of the
"impartial judges of the facts,"
namely you, the jurors,
who have the power within you
to make our system of justice work

CONTENTS

PART VI

MAKING JUSTICE WORK

* * * * * * *

* * * * * * *

NCDS PRESS

NCDS Press is a division of the National Center for Dispute Settlement (NCDS).

The National Center for Dispute Settlement is a not-for-profit organization providing a wide range of dispute settlement services including mediation, arbitration, Expedited Dispute Settlement, and training. To date, NCDS has resolved over 125,000 consumer warranty disputes, primarily for the residential construction and auto industries.

NCDS Press publishes and seeks to publish works on traditional and alternative dispute settlement subjects, such as mediation and arbitration.

NCDS Press is pleased to publish *LAST CHANCE FOR JUSTICE - The Juror's Lonely Quest* to enhance awareness and understanding of the critical role jurors play in our diverse society.

Additional copies of *LAST CHANCE FOR JUSTICE*, as well as copies of NCDS Press' audio tape kit: Mediation Skills for the Real Estate Professional, are available through NCDS Press, 2777 Stemmons Freeway, Suite 650, Dallas Texas, 75207, or by calling 214-638-2700.

ACKNOWLEDGMENTS

If we had known five years ago of the time and effort that goes into writing a book, and this book in particular, we probably would have abandoned our project. We naively thought that because we had successfully trained laypersons, lawyers and judges, we could write a book that would explain and then change America's criminal jury system.

We had no idea that separating our writing totally from our full time jobs would cut severely into our evenings, weekends and vacations, limiting our time with family and friends. We owe our loved ones more than we can say for their support as we struggled with this time consuming project.

Without the help we received from another very special group of people, LAST CHANCE FOR JUSTICE would have had little or no chance of being completed. In the legal field, we would like to thank San Diego Superior Court Judge Ronald S. Prager who critiqued one of the earliest drafts, and Judges Kristal Wiitala Knutson, Barry Bernstein and Deborah Smaller for their guidance in making sure our book met their high professional standards. We also recognize Chief Administrative Law Judge John W. Hardwicke (Maryland), former President of the National Association of Administrative Law Judges for his encouragement and support of our work.

We are indebted as well to Dr. David Hemenway, professor at the Harvard School of Public Health, and an author, who made us aware that a few well chosen phrases were far better than an erudite but wordy analysis.

Our very special thanks go to our editor, Jan Lurie of New York City, whose sharp pencil and penchant for clarity kept us on the right track.

We want to express our gratitude to those lawyers and non-lawyers who helped by critiquing our early drafts: former editor Howard Wolff, Maria Obana, Tony Diepenbrock, James F. Heng, Donald J. Fraser, and Sherry Wells (Lawells Law for Laypersons). Thanks also go to the very talented Jennifer Bendahan and Jo Pierce, and especially to Stephanie King Feingold, for their contributions to the design of the jacket. Thanks for the support of Sam Toll of Sacramento's The Electric Page, and some very helpful people at Kinkos in Roseville, CA, Scott Drake, Trevor Smith, Pam Rivera, and Jena Mercer. Thanks also to Scott Pennock.

There are many more people we talked to about their hopes, their concerns, their experiences as jurors, and their frustrations with our criminal justice system. All of their contributions helped provide the framework for this endeavor.

We consider ourselves lucky to have had the astute advice of Martin Davis of Huntington, L.I. New York, and the expertise and guidance of the remarkable Ed Sacks of Chicago, who has been the consultant to this project.

Finally, we greatly appreciate Lester B. Wolff of the National Center for Dispute Settlement for recognizing the importance of our work. We hope to collaborate with him as we work toward making meaningful changes in our jury system, through videos, juror guides, and other teaching avenues.

INTRODUCTION

Not guilty! The white cops who had been captured on video viciously beating Rodney King were off the hook. Within minutes the word was on the streets and within hours, Los Angeles, America's second largest city, was in flames. The much-heralded American jury system had not only betrayed African-Americans again, but all Americans.

From the overwhelming reaction against the verdicts, it was clear that something was radically wrong with our system of justice, or our perception of it.

Was it possible that the jury knew something we didn't? How could Americans explain away what they saw with their own eyes as it was replayed endlessly on the morning and evening news?

After the initial verdicts acquitting the officers, we decided to put aside our feelings of outrage, disappointment and frustration, and to look more closely to see if the results were a travesty of justice or whether they could be explained. The American jury system, and its jurors, were on trial.

This book seeks to present the American criminal-jury system in a new and different light, to demystify jury service in order to empower ordinary citizens so they may serve capably as jurors, and thus make the system work better for everyone.

Our goal is not to substitute our judgment for that of the twelve jurors who heard the case and who failed to convict any of the police officers who participated in beating Rodney King.

Our goal is to present to you the same **evidence*** which was presented to the Simi Valley, California, jury and have you make your own decision.

We ask you to suspend your final decision regarding the accused four police officers until after you have considered the effects of pretrial publicity, until after you have decided whether you have preconceived ideas or biases which make it difficult for you to be objective. We ask you to wait until after you have read most of this book!

We use the first Rodney King beating trial (*People v. Powell et al*) as our main case study because it is an excellent vehicle for understanding the route jurors must travel in their quest for justice. (Although this case is known as *People v. Powell*, three other Los Angeles Police Officers were also on trial in addition to Officer Laurence Powell. They were Timothy Wind, Theodore Briseno and Sergeant Stacey Koon.)

The *Powell* case was unusual in several respects. After the **acquittals**, the Federal Government took what some legal analysts considered the questionable step of retrying the four police officers on Federal **charges**. A second trial was **double jeopardy** in their view. It involved the same beating, but this time Federal civil rights laws were used to prosecute the officers. Many concluded that the new trial was politically motivated, based on the public's outrage and anger with the State verdict.

At the Federal trial, unlike the first trial, everyone knew that if the defendants were not found guilty of at least some charges, there would be a major civil disturbance. As it turned out, two officers (Laurence Powell and Stacey Koon) were found guilty in the second trial and sentenced to prison.

If people were not confused before, they were certainly confused now. The same officers, the same beating, the same videotape and a seemingly more difficult and higher standard for the prosecution to meet in order to win a conviction—and yet two of the officers were found guilty.

Some wondered if the jury sold out to avoid another riot; others conjectured that the second jury, consisting of people from

---

* Words or phrases italicized and bolded appear in the **GLOSSARY**.

a variety of ethnic backgrounds, was able to put aside the first panel's ostensible bias in favor of white police officers and, at last, reach the correct verdict. Were both juries wrong, or both right?

As the Federal Rodney King beating trial was winding down, America faced its most sensational trial in the case of O.J. Simpson, the accused killer. Once again the fairness of the American jury system was put to the test.

Did pretrial publicity stand in the way of a fair trial? And just as troubling was the question of whether jurors' affection for O.J., based on many years of following his outstanding sports career, swayed them as they weighed the evidence. Would they have convicted or exonerated someone who was not famous, rich, and African-American? We focus primarily on the events leading up to the jury trial phase of *People v. O.J. Simpson* to see whether a truly impartial jury was selected, or even whether any jury could have been impartial.

Neither the *Powell* nor the *Simpson* trial occurred in a vacuum. A revolution is going on in America today that exacerbates the pressures on jurors and the jury system. It is symbolized by **three-strikes-and-you're out** laws—in effect, the new American view of crime and punishment.

With the desire to make our streets and homes safe, many states already require longer prison sentences for more crimes, and more severe punishment for younger and younger defendants. As sentences increase and as penalties become "progressive" depending on the number of crimes ("strikes") one has committed, defendants are demanding more jury trials as their first, second and especially their last line of defense.

All of us will have to bear a new burden. It is not just the added costs involved in paying for more judges, constructing more prisons, hiring more correctional officers, prosecutors, public defenders who represent indigent defendants, etc. Ordinary citizens will find themselves being summoned to serve on juries much more frequently because of these new laws.

The District Attorney will have to exercise even more discretion and impose additional limitations on which crimes will be investigated and prosecuted. With fewer guilty pleas, deputy district attorneys will be involved in more trials with even less time to prosecute other crimes, or to prepare a case in a thorough manner. As funds become scarcer, police departments, district attorneys, public defenders, and judges may not be able to devote the time, effort and expense necessary to do the best job they can do.

The public (that's all of us) will have to decide whether to spend more funds to hire more deputy district attorneys and investigators, and to build more prisons, if it wants to convict and incarcerate more lawbreakers for longer periods.[1]

While people now do get convicted of crimes they did not commit, more people may find themselves in this plight if police investigations are not thorough, if funding for public defenders is cut, and if judges become more concerned with moving cases through their courts than protecting people's rights.

The flip side of the coin is also possible. Guilty persons may be acquitted because the police and District Attorney have not been able to expend the necessary resources in the investigation process, or jurors may be reluctant to find a defendant guilty when that means sending a criminal away for life for committing a **misdemeanor** or a nonviolent crime. Incidents of this kind of jury behavior have already surfaced in California.

Our ultimate concern is the trial that is occurring down the street from you, involving ordinary people, in which there has been little or no pretrial publicity. The true test of justice in America is not what happens in the sensational trial but what happens in your county courthouse each and every day.

Jurors hold one of the crucial keys to making this process work. They must first be willing to confront their own belief system, then set aside their prejudices and preconceptions, and use reason in making their judgments. Only then can any of us say, with conviction, that the system worked or failed.

In this book we explain in plain English how our criminal-jury system works and what it strives to achieve. While we refrain from relying on legalese, there are some legal terms that we have to use. Any time there is a high profile trial you'll hear these terms. And after reading this book you will also understand the meaning of these terms whether you hear legal analysts use them on television or read them in the newspaper.

While we started with an obvious bias—that the cops in the first Rodney King beating trial were guilty—that does not mean that we, or those of you who agree with us, cannot take an objective view of the evidence. It is our hope—and belief—that those who believe the police officers did not commit any crime can also put aside their prejudgments, review the facts, and make a determination based on the objective evidence.

It is our goal to provide a framework that will work for *any* criminal trial, including the sensational media events. Once understood, the framework will permit potential and actual jurors to understand their role and appreciate their responsibilities *both before and during* any criminal trial, enabling them to be good "judges of the facts".

We attempt to show that it shouldn't matter if the victim or the person charged with the crime is white or black, rich or poor, educated or uneducated, famous or unknown. Nor should the nature of the crime matter. In each case the defendant is entitled to something called a "fair trial" irrespective of what we know or have seen or heard or think about the defendant, or the crime with which the person is charged.

We will describe circumstances that could lead to not guilty verdicts even when the defendant's guilt appears to be unequivocally established in the media. You might consider those verdicts to be perversions of law and order. Yet a verdict of not guilty in a particular trial may be legally correct, and consistent with our criminal-justice system, despite what the majority of Americans believe.

It may be difficult for any of us to imagine we could be falsely accused of a crime. Many people believe that if someone is arrested and charged, he or she is probably guilty. Yet it's no secret that seemingly honest people make false accusations and actually honest people may incorrectly identify an individual, or may incorrectly remember an event. If you or persons you care for are mistakenly charged with a crime, the only thing protecting you, your child, relative or friend from a lengthy prison sentence may be how the twelve persons who are selected to sit as the jury decide the case.

The questions then become very personal:

What kind of jurors would you want sitting in that courtroom?

And what kind of jurors are you likely to get?

Before going any further, see how you respond to the Impartiality Quiz in Appendix A and see if your answers change after reading the book.

Let us know what you think about *LAST CHANCE FOR JUSTICE.* Visit our website at:

http://www.lastchanceforjustice.com

PART I

SETTING
THE
STAGE

Chapter 1

Rodney King's
Date With Destiny:
March 3, 1991

It was brutal. A fierce stomping. Strike after strike, blow after blow. That's what we saw as we watched TV that March day. Someone had captured on videotape a vicious police beating of an unarmed black man.

This is how America was introduced to Rodney Glenn King. On the ground, batons smashing into him, cops kicking and stomping him.

This was America. This was Los Angeles, a city whose police had lost control.

All videotaped for the world to see. And we didn't see this beating just once. The video was played over and over again on all the TV stations.

People asked how could this happen. Suddenly it didn't matter what Rodney King had done. Whatever he did, he didn't do it on the tape and that is all we had to form our opinion. We saw what the officers did with our own eyes. The saying, "What goes around comes around" finally came home to Los Angeles Police Chief Daryl F. Gates and his police force.

Most of us believed something had gone radically wrong that night in Los Angeles when the police ganged up on that unfortunate African-American man. The thin blue line, whose motto was "to protect and to serve", had exceeded their authority and were exposed as ruthless thugs. These four police officers were going to jail.

Even smooth-talking expensive lawyers wouldn't be able to get them off. The videotape spoke for itself.

Not many people would quarrel with our "dramatization" of America's introduction to Rodney King. Many people would rationalize the riots by saying that the beating was one more racist incident that showed the judicial system just doesn't work for African-Americans. Many others, even those who thought the rioting was unjustified and criminal, still felt that the criminal-justice system had gone awry.

During the next year, the public didn't learn much about what had happened in the Rodney King beating case. There were reports that Mr. King may have been speeding. He may have been drunk or on PCP. He had previous problems with the law. But the media continued to show us that videotape.

Several months before the trial, we did learn about Mr. King's recollections of the beating from a ninety-minute interview with two investigators from the District Attorney's office. Mr. King's attorney released it to the Los Angeles Times.[2] According to Mr. King, the police officers said:

"Lay down, nigger."

"How do you feel now, nigger?"

"What are you going to do now, killer?"

"Shut up, nigger."

The article reported Mr. King as saying that the officer who beat him most savagely had the specter of "death in his eyes." As for running away, Mr. King said that "I had no intention on running until the blow to the head and they said, 'We're going to kill you! Run!'"

This was the gist of Mr. King's expected **testimony**. Some commentators wondered if Mr. King could withstand lengthy verbal battering by defense attorneys as they would try to impeach his testimony by portraying him as a dangerous ex-convict, who was too drugged to either remember the beating or to be able to describe it accurately.

Those were the scenes and recollections embedded in our minds as the trial of the four police officers began. Minimal notice was taken when the case was moved to a small town in Ventura County called Simi Valley, a community with few African-Americans. A state appellate court panel had ruled that political fallout and community divisiveness made it impossible to select an impartial Los Angeles County jury.

At last jury selection was completed. Pretrial publicity, namely the infamous videotape, had helped the public form an opinion about the case. It seemed logical to conclude that *what we saw was what had occurred* in the early morning of March 3, 1991. In a sense, we were all eyewitnesses to the incident, even though we weren't there. There wasn't much other pretrial information to help us form an opinion.

But on April 29, 1992, after six days of deliberation, the jury in *People v. Powell et al* returned verdicts of not guilty on all **counts** with the exception of one count regarding use-of-force by Los Angeles Police Officer Laurence Powell (where the jury reached no verdict).

Reactions of legal analysts to the verdicts were reported in the April 30, 1992 issue of the Los Angeles Times:

- Loyola University law professor Laurie Levenson was shocked because the videotape of the beating was the "most compelling" evidence.

- Burt Neuborne, New York University law professor, concluded that the verdict's integrity would not be accepted because no blacks were on the jury. Further, he noted that the very people who moved away from Los Angeles "to get away from Rodney King" were the same people who sat on the jury.

- Myrna Raeder, a law professor at Southwestern University, said: "In this case, seeing was not believing."

- A former Bronx, New York prosecutor, Ruth Jones, believed that the jurors had a difficult time seeing the police officers as defendants because they "didn't look like what defendants are supposed to look like."

The only juror to discuss the case with the Times said of the police officers: "They're policemen, they're not angels. They're out there to do a low-down dirty job." It was then reported that the juror saw Rodney King "as obviously a dangerous person."

Polls showed that the overwhelming majority of people were opposed to the verdicts. Was this jury, just like the police defendants, part of a conspiracy to keep African-Americans from getting justice on the streets or in the courts? Was this case an aberration in the system, or was racism so institutionalized that these verdicts were just part and parcel of the everyday process?

Our answers lie ahead.

Chapter 2

O.J. Simpson's
Bizarre Journey Begins:
June 17, 1994

First of all, who could believe that O.J. Simpson's former wife, Nicole Brown Simpson and her friend, Ronald Goldman, were murdered during the evening of June 12, 1994? O.J. Simpson was a national hero. Everybody knew of him: his outstanding football career, the movies, the commercials picturing him running through airports to get his Hertz rental car.

Then we saw him on TV, handcuffed on his return to Los Angeles at the request of the LAPD. His lawyer asked that the handcuffs be removed, and they were. But the picture of him, handcuffed, remained in our consciousness.

The LAPD asserted that O.J. was the prime suspect in the case. Everyone waited to see if there would be an arrest.

The media speculated what penalty the Los Angeles County District Attorney would seek. Since two people were murdered, in California it could be a case of *special circumstances* which could result in the death penalty or a life sentence without the possibility of parole. Also, a person charged with special circumstances would not be able to get out of jail on bail after arrest. Thus, even if O.J. were eventually found not guilty, he could spend a year or more in a prison cell before his first opportunity for freedom.

Everybody waited.

Bits and pieces of incriminating evidence were leaked to the press. When, on June 17, the time came to turn himself in

to the police, the unthinkable happened. Instead of surrender-
ing, O.J. fled, taking off in a white Bronco with his close friend,
Al Cowlings, driving.

People wondered about the competence of the LAPD when
it let the accused murderer of two people walk, or more precise-
ly, drive away. People wondered if O.J.'s decision to become a
fugitive meant he had murdered his ex-wife and her friend and
now chose escape rather than surrender.

Then America experienced the bizarre sixty-mile slow-
speed chase on Los Angeles freeways. The police made no effort
to stop the car. In fact, it was reported that O.J. held a gun to
his head, and that he wanted to go to his mother's house.

We watched, but it was hard to believe. California Highway
Patrol (CHP) cars in several rows followed the van on the
highways. Adding to the surreal aspect of the chase was that
drivers of other cars, hearing the news, stopped on the affected
highways. People on overpasses got out of their cars, gathered by
the side of the road and waved, cheering O.J. on.

As the networks televised the chase, they reported that
O.J. Simpson had written notes to family and friends which
could be construed as suicide thoughts, saying good-bye.

Was O.J. going to commit suicide because he had killed his
former wife and her friend? Or was he going to commit suicide
because he knew he could never escape this horrible notoriety
even if he were innocent?

No one knew. But finally the chase ended when he reached
his home. O.J. Simpson was then arrested.

Like the Rodney King beating, this arrest is embedded in
our collective memory. Only days before, O.J. had been a truly
well-loved, successful athlete, actor and TV celebrity. Now we
saw a deeply depressed man whose life had suddenly crumbled.

After June 17, the media engaged in a feeding frenzy.
Leaks gushed from the police, from the District Attorney's
office. Witnesses or potential witnesses were offered thousands
of dollars to tell their stories.

Long before the jury was selected, TV watchers across the
nation were kept "informed" with the latest developments:

- The prosecution apprised the defense and court that it did not have a bloodied ski mask, or any ski mask for that matter. (Earlier it had been reported that this was one of the incriminating pieces of evidence in the possession of the District Attorney.)

- An attendant on O.J. Simpson's flight to Chicago allegedly told the **grand jury** that O.J. had his hand in a bag for most of the trip.

- A male passenger sitting next to O.J. on that flight reported that O.J. did not have his hand in a bag during the trip.

- One of O.J. Simpson's lawyers had said O.J. was at home at the time of the killings. The press reported that O.J.'s housekeeper told the District Attorney that O.J. was not at home at that time. The housekeeper's lawyer denied his client had made any such statement.

- A recorded 911 emergency call (from October 1993) was played repeatedly. A helpless-sounding Nicole Brown Simpson had asked for help from the police because O.J. had broken into her house. In the background, you could hear a man—presumably O.J.— yelling and cursing.

- A storekeeper who sold knives advised a TV show that O.J. had been in his store looking at knives, and had examined one with a fourteen-inch blade. (The murder weapon was alleged to have been a fifteen-inch knife.)

The onslaught of details continued unabated:

- Reports circulated that Nicole Brown Simpson was almost decapitated by the multiple knife wounds.

- A woman testified before the grand jury that she saw O.J. driving around the victim's home about the time of the murder. Her lawyer, however, said she would not testify at the trial.

- Bloodied clothing was supposedly found in the washing machine in O.J.'s home.

- The Los Angeles prosecutor, upset that the tapes of the 911 calls had been released, talked in terms of protecting O.J. and the People's case.

In later weeks, we heard the "inside" story of how two white men had attacked and killed Ms. Simpson and Mr. Goldman; how the cop who found the bloodied glove on O.J.'s property had placed it there because he was a liar, hated blacks, and wanted to frame O.J. Simpson; and how prosecutor Marcia Clark had been on the crime scene illegally before a search warrant had been issued. Here we saw defense counsel working hard to convince the public that their client was innocent.

Was any of this true, credible or even relevant evidence? Did it matter? It sold thousands of magazines and newspapers, filled up time on talk and investigative TV shows and made celebrities out of trial lawyers and law professors turned analysts. Based on these media outpourings, people decided that O.J. was guilty or innocent.

Think back for a moment to that week when O.J. Simpson and his flight first captivated the country in June 1994.

What did *you* believe?

Guilty because:	Innocent because:
☐ He returned from Chicago as soon as the police wanted him to, in order to deflect suspicion.	☐ He returned from Chicago as soon as the police wanted him to, so that he could help in the investigation.
☐ The District Attorney said he was involved in the murder and would plead guilty.	☐ The District Attorney wanted to make a name for himself, so he said O.J. was involved in the murders.
☐ Innocent people don't contemplate suicide, yet he wrote what could be interpreted as suicide notes.	☐ He didn't try to escape the police. The slow-speed chase was the result of a person in pain and turmoil, not the action of a guilty individual.
☐ The fact he had his hand in a bag on the flight to Chicago showed that O.J. had been injured while killing Nicole and her lover.	☐ The fact O.J. didn't have his hand in a bag on the flight to Chicago showed that he was not lying, and that he had not committed the murders.
☐ The fact that he beat Nicole in the past made it likely that he could kill her in a jealous rage.	☐ You just knew in your heart that O.J. Simpson would not do something like this.
☐ There is no doubt he was trying to leave the country when he was spotted in the white Bronco.	☐ O.J. had everything. He would not do anything to jeopardize his fame and fortune.

Soon the word was out that the prosecutor had asked that, if found guilty, O.J. be sent to prison for life without the possibility of parole. Some "experts" immediately declared that the District Attorney's decision not to seek the death penalty was based on the belief that to do so would have significantly reduced any chance of getting a conviction. Others said that considering all the factors, the District Attorney selected the appropriate penalty. Then we learned that a former porno-graphic movie star had information for the prosecution and wanted to cooperate. She and Simpson's friend Al Cowlings had a relationship. Mr. Cowlings allegedly told her that O.J. and he were not driving to any gravesite that day in June.

And then someone who supposedly knew something vital to the case preferred to be held in **contempt of court** and sentenced to jail rather than talk to the grand jury. He had prior run-ins with the law and feared that testifying might be harmful to him.

Friends and family of the victims got involved. Faye Resnick wrote a book titled *Nicole Brown Simpson: The Private Diary of a Life Interrupted* which alleged O.J. Simpson had two faces: the public personality and the cruel wife-beater. The book became an instant sensation.

Members of Nicole Brown Simpson's family were quoted as asking why, if O.J. Simpson were innocent, he needed to hire so many lawyers and pay them millions. He wasn't thinking of his kids, who lost their mother and now could have a bankrupt father as well.

One of Nicole's sisters said she was sure O.J. committed the murder because Nicole had feared for her life. The murder was just O.J. taking his domestic abuse one step further.

It was impossible to keep track of all the **allegations**, the stories in the tabloids, the comments on TV. The public had an insatiable appetite for news, stories, dirt, anything about this case.

And while all this was going on, Los Angeles Superior Court Judge Lance Ito attempted to find an impartial jury.

Pretrial publicity in the *O.J. Simpson* case was a pitched battle for the minds of the public that would not stop. Even after the jury was **sequestered** (isolated from media information about O.J. Simpson and limited in contacts with their own families and friends) beginning on January 12, 1995, the pros-ecution revealed numerous instances of alleged spousal abuse by O.J. Simpson against Nicole Brown Simpson. The D.A.'s office even reached back some seventeen years to paint a picture of O.J. Simpson, the wife-beater, who had allegedly beaten his first wife.

The defense argued that this information should not be allowed before the jury because it was too removed in time. But on the very next day, the defense argued that the jury should hear statements allegedly made fourteen years earlier by the police officer who found the incriminating glove on O.J. Simpson's property. Evidently the defense felt that this purported evidence was not too remote for the jury to consider.

Noteworthy developments early in the case included the dismissal of two jurors, apparently for providing inaccurate or incomplete answers to the questions posed to them; the publication of *I Want To Tell You* by O.J. Simpson in which he proclaimed his innocence in writing and on audiotape; and Opening Statements marred by strident accusations of improprieties on the part of the defense and prosecution.

Did the prosecution, as it continually stated, want to assure that O.J. Simpson received a fair trial or did it want a victory? Did the defense really want the jury and the American public to know "the truth", or did it want to get O.J. acquitted even if he committed the murders?

All the pretrial publicity had been great theater, but was it likely to produce justice?

CHAPTER 3

PRETRIAL PUBLICITY:
TRUTH OR TEASER?

It is common knowledge that Americans have the right to form opinions about cases, about the individuals involved and whether the defendants are guilty or innocent of the charges against them. But there remains a significant challenge to our system of law if those very same opinions result in a defendant being denied the right to a fair trial. And that is the problem of pretrial publicity. There are two very important rights guaranteed by our United States Constitution which collide—the right of all persons to free speech and a free press, versus the accused individual's right to a fair trial by an impartial jury.

The First Amendment[3] to our Constitution guarantees the right to free speech and a free press. Thus, there are few constraints and limits which can lawfully be imposed on the statements made by the trial participants. In the *O.J. Simpson* case, lawyers representing the press argued for the release of information based on the First Amendment.

But the Sixth Amendment[4] guarantees "...a speedy and public trial, by an impartial jury of the State and district wherein the crime shall have been committed... and [the accused] to be informed of the nature and cause of the accusation; to be confronted with the witnesses against him; to have compulsory process for obtaining witnesses in his favor, and to have the assistance of counsel for his defense."

None of the provisions of the Bill of Rights are absolute. Although freedom of speech is guaranteed, there are laws which enable persons to recover monetary damages if they have been **libeled** or **slandered**. The United States Supreme Court has held that freedom of speech does not allow one to shout "FIRE!" in a crowded theater.

The Sixth Amendment guarantees an impartial jury in the district where the crime was committed. If there is concern that an impartial jury cannot be obtained in the district where the crime occurred, the parties might request a change of location or what the law calls a **change of venue**.

In some cases, judges have issued gag orders to stop attorneys from discussing the case with the press, but these orders are generally limited. By the time the case is before a judge and the gag order is issued, the public may have already read or seen or heard the inflammatory material. In the *Powell* case, everybody had seen the video which was the extent of the pretrial publicity. But who needed any more when "A picture is worth a thousand words." There, the pretrial publicity favored the prosecution. However, the *O.J. Simpson* case presented a totally different picture. Each side attempted to establish its version of the murders before a judge had even been selected to try the case, before Mr. Simpson had been formally charged, and before the start of the jury trial. And these attempts continued through the trial, and continue even after the verdict.

In California, some restrictions have been placed on what lawyers can say. But if laws were passed forbidding all public comments by those involved in criminal trials, the tension between free speech rights and the rights of the accused to a fair trial would be put squarely into play.

It's important to be aware that in making comments about a case, the prosecution and defense are simply trying to establish an uneven playing field. They hope to create a jury pool sympathetic to their side. Thus, Los Angeles County District Attorney Gil Garcetti proclaimed shortly after O.J.'s arrest that O.J. would plead guilty with an explanation. Was this simply a lie, or did Mr. Garcetti know something that nobody else did?

Or did he think, based on his expertise, that the case was not one of "who done it?" but "why did he do it?"

We now know that his statement was not an accurate prediction. O.J. Simpson, when asked at his July 22, 1994 **arraignment** (reading of the charges) how he pleaded, responded "Absolutely 100 percent not guilty." Although the statement by Mr. Garcetti was not true, it accomplished a very important purpose for the prosecution because it attuned the public to see O.J. as an acknowledged murderer.

The major difference between the *Simpson* case and the garden variety murder trial is that O.J. was both rich and famous. His attorneys, most of whom were also rich and famous, received as much or more media attention than did the District Attorney.

A free press would have no meaning if Americans were obligated to impose upon themselves self-censorship before they read, listened or looked at anything involving a criminal charge simply because they might be called as jurors.

So should prospective jurors bury their heads in the sand when they are bombarded with pictures, comments, leaks, analyses, stories and gossip and refuse to form any opinion?

Suppose you had decided before either trial had begun that the police officers who beat Rodney King were guilty, and O.J. was innocent. Or vice versa. Regardless of which side you took, ask yourself three questions:

1. Why did you decide what you did?

    In other words, what did you see, read or hear that caused you to form your opinion? Or was your decision just a gut reaction?

2. If new or different information were presented to you, could you form a different opinion?

    If you were told that you couldn't use the information you obtained initially in forming your final opinion, could you later disregard it?

3.   Once you formed your "new" opinion based on the information that had been added or subtracted, could you stick to that opinion?

Could you do this even if you were subject to criticism from others, and even though your opinion required you to reach a decision that conflicted with what you previously had believed was fair or reasonable?

Let's see how this might work. Suppose you determined, based on the videotape, that Rodney King was beaten without provocation on his part and that he was hit repeatedly with police batons. Clearly, the police officers were unjustified in their actions, and were guilty of all crimes.

Could you be convinced that perhaps there was more to this story than what you saw on videotape, that maybe the police had reason to believe their lives were in jeopardy?

Could you say to yourself: "I had no idea what this man did before the police had stopped his car and I had no idea how Rodney King was behaving."?

Could you then say to yourself: "Maybe the police officers' behavior was not as out of line as I originally thought."?

Could you believe that if a police officer acted the way Officer Powell did, when he repeatedly struck Rodney King with his police baton, that he could be acting in a reasonable way, in a manner that was permissible under LAPD rules and regulations? And if you decided that your initial opinion had been wrong, could you stick to your new opinion even if you disliked cops in general and LAPD cops in particular?

Could you say that police Sergeant Stacey Koon and Officer Powell were not guilty of a crime even though they seemed to be two cocky and arrogant individuals whom you would want to avoid under any circumstances? Would you consider changing your mind if other jurors attacked your opinion, or if you knew that your bowling buddies would think you were a sellout if you took such a position?

Or, suppose you initially decided O.J. Simpson was too nice a guy to have committed murder. You sincerely believed that he would not have risked his wealth, his freedom and his hard-won reputation, and possibly his life, by killing Nicole Brown Simpson and Ron Goldman. Moreover, he didn't have time to kill them and still leave on the plane for Chicago. And nobody could have been that calm after brutally killing two people, one of whom he had greatly loved.

Could you ever be convinced that O.J. wasn't such a nice guy, or that even nice people may kill? That he had beaten and threatened his wife before? That there was enough time for O.J. to have killed, and still have taken the limousine to the airport? That an actor, as O.J. was, can learn to mask his emotions? That what you see may not be what is?

And would you be willing to adhere to this new opinion even it meant that O.J. might be incarcerated for life? Or if you knew that the people you hung out with would consider you a racist if you were white or an Uncle Tom if you were an African-American who voted for conviction?

The dilemma that one faces when there is a great deal of pretrial publicity is that we all do form opinions based on the little we know. We are human. But once in the jury box, we are asked to set aside our initial opinion and decide the case fairly. Yet there will be countless others who decide the case based solely on their initial opinions, because they are not exposed to the evidence presented at the trial.

Once you are on a jury, why shouldn't you be allowed to rely on what you have learned before you became a juror? Isn't it valuable and reliable information?

In the Rodney King beating, the one memory that sticks in all our minds is the infamous videotape. The most vivid images are the fifteen or twenty seconds during which we see two police officers (Powell and Wind) beating King, over and over, with their batons and kicking him as he lay on the ground.

No one denied that King was hit repeatedly. Officer Powell testified at his trial that he struck King numerous times. But jurors at that trial were not asked to determine whether a beating occurred. They were asked to determine whether the four police officers were guilty of the specific crimes with which they were charged.

Although the videotape is a critical piece of evidence, it is only a part of the case. It is a scene in a movie, a chapter in a novel. It's as if you read only that part of the Bible in which Moses caused the waters to engulf the Egyptians, and on that basis decided that Moses was a cruel killer.

The pretrial publicity was much more pervasive before the O.J. trial, and much more varied than in any recent case. But again, each story you read, accusation you heard, or interview that was held may not be relevant to the whole picture. It may end up being discounted, because, for example, the person who supplied the information was paid to sell his or her story. Or you may hear one expert say on TV that the blood on the glove or at the scene of the murder is O. J.'s, while at the trial there may be other experts who say it isn't, or that the testing was so sloppy no one could tell. Or the person who gave an interview may say something different when under oath and subject to **cross-examination**; it may turn out that the person who "saw" O. J. near the crime scene was nowhere near the area at the time the murders were occurring; or the person providing the alibi information may be a notorious liar. Or the "fact" may not even be admitted into evidence at trial, for reasons which will be discussed in later chapters.

In the *Simpson* case, we not only heard the sound bites and the interviews, and read the exclusive articles, we also saw evidence discussed in a courtroom, at the preliminary hearing, and in the courtroom of the judge conducting the actual trial before the jury was ever seated. We saw witnesses being questioned, lawyers arguing their points, and judges making rulings. Even if you agree that other information shouldn't be used because of its unreliability, certainly evidence from these court proceedings was trustworthy.

However, evidence which wasn't introduced or reintroduced at the actual criminal trial to O.J. Simpson's jury could not be considered by the jury. The prosecution might have been unable or unwilling to call witnesses because the witnesses had been shown to be liars, to have been incapable of observing or to be so prejudiced that the prosecution believed that their testimony would harm the prosecution case. The experts might have misanalyzed the blood samples, or not taken the proper precautions to ensure that the **DNA** sampling or testing was untainted.

In any case, if the evidence is "good" it will become part of the prosecution's case and be introduced for the jurors to consider. Likewise, if the evidence is "good" from the defense counsel's standpoint, it also will become part of the record and be introduced by the defense at trial.

Pretrial publicity presents us, the public, with a distorted picture. The picture is based on whatever the media deems most sensational, salacious, tantalizing, or saleable at a particular moment in time. We hear innuendoes, uncorroborated statements from mysterious or unreliable "witnesses", and "expert" commentary and analysis from whomever is willing to appear on TV. As long as we recognize that our opinions are based on this "evidence" we should also realize that any opinion we have must be tentative. Non-jurors should be slow to condemn jurors who base their determinations on a very different body of evidence, that being the evidence which is presented to them during a trial. Many things we non-jurors know will not be revealed during the course of the trial. Again, our "picture" is different from that presented to the jurors.

It is our contention that you can be inundated with information and misinformation and still be a good juror. When called to serve, potential jurors need only to be able to set aside those things they have seen and heard and base their decisions solely on what is presented to them at trial.

PART II

"GUILT" VERSUS "NONGUILT"

AND

THE PLAYERS

CHAPTER 4

ACTUAL GUILT
VERSUS
LEGAL GUILT

While all of us might like verdicts of guilty and not guilty to mean that the truth has been established, our system of justice is not specifically designed to determine the truth. Finding the defendant guilty does not necessarily mean that the person actually committed the crime; finding the defendant not guilty does not necessarily mean that the person *did not* commit the crime. Under our system, a verdict of guilty means that the prosecution has proved its case. A verdict of not guilty does not mean a person is innocent. It simply means that the individual's guilt has not been proven. Remember, O.J. Simpson said he was "absolutely 100 percent not guilty." His acquittal does not establish he was innocent of the charges. It does establish that the jury found him not guilty of those charges. Obviously, the goal of our criminal-justice system is not to punish innocent people or to set people free who have committed crimes, but in some instances, our legal system may do exactly that.

Once a juror has been seated and becomes part of the jury, our system requires you to determine whether the accused is guilty or not guilty based *solely* on the evidence and allowable evidentiary shortcuts that are presented in the courtroom. All prospective jurors and all others who criticize jurors must realize that the only evidence a juror can properly consider is evidence that has been introduced to the jury during the trial. If evidence is not introduced, it cannot be the basis for a verdict.

If you had been sitting on the *People v. Powell et al* jury, you would have heard Los Angeles County Superior Court Judge Stanley Weisberg attempt to help focus the jurors by instructing them as to what the court considered a correct basis for decision.

A NOTE TO READERS

Beginning in this chapter, we will quote portions of the actual jury instructions read to the jury at the close of the trial in *People v. Powell et al.* In pursuit of clarity and understanding, we have designated the jury instructions by number and made the examples easier to follow by separating long paragraphs into segments and integrating them into our discussion. We believe that having the opportunity to read the instructions individually in a relevant context (instead of having them presented at one time) will generate a better appreciation of our points.

Regardless of how they look on paper, the juror's introduction to the instructions is hearing them read by the judge.

Judge Weisberg told the jurors not only what they were supposed to but also how they were supposed to do it:

You must base your decision on the facts and the law (JI-1)[5]

You have two duties to perform. (JI-2)

{1} You must determine the facts from the evidence received in the trial and not from any other source. (JI-3)

{2} You must apply the law as I state it to you to the facts as you determine them and in this way arrive at your verdict and any finding you are instructed to include in your verdict. (JI-6)

You must accept and follow the law as I state it to you, whether or not you agree with the law. (JI-7)

It's pretty clear that jurors don't have a lot of leeway as to what law to apply or not. Further, the court is not interested in whether you agree with the law or not. There is no juror discretion when it comes to the law. However, quite a different situation exists when it comes to evaluating the evidence.

Facts are based on the evidence received in the trial and "not from any other source." Judge Weisberg later added the following points of law to clarify his instruction:

You must decide all the questions of fact in this case from the evidence received in this trial and not from any other source. (JI-31)

You must not make any independent investigation of the facts or the law or consider or discuss facts as to which there is no evidence. (JI-32)

This means, for example, that you must not on your own visit the scene, conduct experiments or consult reference works or persons for additional information. (JI-33)

As a juror, you might wonder why the judge wouldn't want you to find out as much as you could about the issues or evidence in the case. It would seem that more knowledge on your part would help you find "the truth". Yet jurors cannot consult reference works or talk to people who might have additional information, regardless of the possible value. All that should matter is what goes on in the courtroom and the information that is presented there. The phrase "from any other source" also covers jurors' own knowledge (based on their education, employment, or other life experiences). Unless evidence is presented to jurors in court, they cannot use specialized knowledge they may have acquired elsewhere.

At the trial, the prosecution and defense lawyers compete for jury support. They introduce items of evidence, each trying to make its presentation the most believable, while portraying the opponent's side in the worst possible light. So the same items of evidence are frequently described differently. Jurors meanwhile are attempting to keep track of how all the pieces presented fit together into a coherent, accurate representation of what actually happened. As a trial progresses, jurors often discover that conflicting views obscure the hoped-for clarity. While you may wish you had access to more information, the judge tells you (more than once) that the evidence given to you "as is" during the trial is what you must rely on to make your decision.

Under California law (which is similar to that of other states) evidence "means testimony, writings, material objects, or other things presented to the senses that are offered to prove the existence or nonexistence of a fact."[6]

When witnesses make statements under oath at a trial or other judicial hearing they are giving testimony. In *People v. Powell et al*, one of the prosecution's key witnesses, CHP Officer Melanie Singer testified in court that she saw Officer Laurence Powell strike Rodney King in the face. That was the evidence.

When evidence is not presented in the form of testimony, it is "writing, materials or other things presented to the senses." These are items which are tangible—able to be seen, heard, smelled, touched, tasted. These other kinds of evidence, as seen in the *People v. Powell et al* trial, included the police and medical reports; the videotape of the beating; audiotapes of conversations between various officers; the PR 24 batons used by the officers to beat Rodney King; and an electrical device called a taser that was used to shoot electricity into Mr. King to disable him temporarily. Jurors could read the reports, see the videotape, listen to the audiotape, feel and view the PR 24 and the taser.

In the *Simpson* case jurors saw situations captured on videotape, high-tech computer dramatizations, objects such as gloves and shoes. They were permitted to go, under supervision of the court, to the scene of the crime.

If the judge had agreed, the *Powell* jury could have been taken to the scene of the chase, or to where the chase ended.

Evidence is used to prove the existence or nonexistence of a fact. In some instances, facts are established without the use of evidence. Such facts must also be considered by jurors in making the mental collage they will use as they try to figure out what really happened.

One common example of a fact that needs no evidence to support it is a **stipulation**. As Judge Weisberg explained:

A stipulation is agreement between the attorneys regarding the facts. (JI-5)

He later told the jury the evidentiary effect of a stipulation:

... if the attorneys have stipulated or agreed to a fact, you must regard that fact as a conclusively proved as to the party or parties making the stipulation or entering into the stipulation. (JI-23)

The parties could stipulate, for example, that Rodney King had an alcohol blood level in excess of .15 percent at the time of the incident and, as a result, the actual medical test would not need to be submitted to the jury.

Another example of a fact with no evidence offered occurs when the court takes **judicial notice**. These judicially noticed facts are so commonly known and accepted that they are recognized as accurate by everyone. The judge can take judicial notice of the fact that water boils at 212° Fahrenheit without requiring a demonstration to be performed. Or the judge can take judicial notice of the day of the week as represented on a calendar so that counsel need not call in experts to testify that June 17, 1994, the day of O.J. Simpson's drive with Al Cowlings, was a Friday.

It is not common beliefs or prejudices that are judicially noticed; only facts susceptible to specific measurement or scientific testing. You cannot take judicial notice, for example, that men make worse parents than women, or that women are more emotional than men, even if many people believe those statements to be true.

An important evidentiary substitute which may be used to make factual findings once **circumstantial evidence** is presented at the trial is called an **inference**. Both of these terms have special legal meaning and they will be discussed in detail in Chapters 13 and 14.

And so, while a determination of actual guilt or actual innocence could theoretically be based on everything known about a crime, that's not how our system works. Remember, legal guilt or legal nonguilt is based only on what is introduced in the court and then only evidence or evidentiary substitutes that the judge permits the jury to consider.

Thus, there may be instances when the accused has committed the act as charged, but the jury returns a verdict of not guilty, because the prosecutor is incompetent, or incriminating evidence is kept from the jury because the judge rules it is **inadmissible**. On the other hand, innocent people have been convicted because witnesses have been mistaken or police officers have perjured themselves (lied under oath), because of overzealous or dishonest prosecutors, because of ineffective assistance of defense attorneys, or simply because exonerating evidence was not available or not obtained at the time.

Now, let's look more closely at some of the things which keep jurors from getting at "the truth".

The Exclusionary Rule

The rationale for the **exclusionary rule** is to deter unlawful police conduct. In America, the Constitution's Fourth Amendment[7] protection against illegal search and seizure has been interpreted by the U.S. Supreme Court to require that items obtained through an illegal search and seizure be kept from the jury. In other countries, such as Great Britain, unlawfully obtained evidence is admitted but the police officer may be subject to disciplinary action.

In the *O.J. Simpson* case, the defense made a **motion** to suppress evidence obtained at O.J. Simpson's home because there was no search warrant issued prior to the time of the search. If the defense established that the search was unlawful, the evidence obtained during that search would be excluded. The prosecutor then would have been unable to introduce the evidence at the trial, regardless of how damaging it might have been to the defendant.

For example, say the police had discovered bloodied clothing in the washing machine, and tests revealed that the victims' blood as well as O.J. Simpson's blood was on the clothing. The clothing could not be introduced if it had been obtained in an illegal search.

Let's go one step further and pretend that the murder weapon, a bloodied knife with the victims' blood on it, was found in O.J. Simpson's hamper with his fingerprints on it. Not only were his fingerprints on the knife, but they were on the knife in places one would hold a knife if one were stabbing someone. The knife, in effect, is the "smoking gun". Everyone agrees a conviction would result. But if the judge determined that the knife was found during an illegal search, it would not be admitted. The exclusion of these items of evidence might result in a twelve-person jury finding that O.J. Simpson was not guilty of the crime he clearly committed in this theroretical scenario.

There are other reasons to exclude evidence. Sometimes lawyers have not complied with their responsibility to share evidence with the other side. In other words, one side fails to meet its duties under the state's **discovery** rules. In that case, the judge could sanction the offending party by ordering the particular evidence excluded.

Sanctity of a Privileged Communication

Los Angeles County Superior Court Judge Lance Ito excluded statements O.J. Simpson made to a minister which were overheard by a sheriff's deputy. Apparently, O.J. Simpson became distraught, threw down the phone in which he had been communicating with Rosey Grier (ex-football player turned minister) and shouted at him through the glass dividing them at the jail.

The loud remarks were overheard by the guard who was some distance away. Although we were not told the precise words used, the statements were reputedly very damaging to O.J. Simpson. The prosecution wanted the statement to be made a part of the record. The defense objected, arguing that statements made by a penitent to his minister are **privileged communications**, and thus inadmissible.

The prosecution argued that notwithstanding the privilege, O.J. Simpson lost any protection he might have had when he chose to raise his voice and communicate so loudly that another person could hear his remarks. Judge Ito ruled for the defense, and prevented the guard from testifying.

Thus, jurors may have been prevented from learning "the truth" because the statements may have been an acknowledgment of guilt. But whatever those words were, no matter how relevant to the determination of guilt, they were not heard by the jury because they were, in the eyes of the law, "privileged".

The rationale for protecting privileged communications is that society has determined it is important to encourage openness between people in a fiduciary or trusting relationship. Thus, admissions made by a person to certain other people in confidence are protected, even from disclosure by someone who overhears the communication. The privilege that existed between O.J. Simpson and Rosey Grier is called the "priest-penitent" privilege. Other common privileges include: husband-wife; attorney-client; and physician-patient.

Finally, there is the constitutional privilege against self-incrimination, which prevents statements obtained in violation of that right from being admitted in any criminal case. This privilege is guaranteed by the United States Constitution's Fifth Amendment.[8]

The "Hearsay" Rule

Hearsay is generally defined as an out-of-court statement submitted for the purpose of establishing the truth of the matter asserted. It is generally inadmissible, which means that a lawyer's *objection* can keep it from being allowed into the record for consideration by the jury. Hearsay evidence is thought to be untrustworthy because it is not given under oath and subject to clarification via courtroom questioning and cross-examination because the person who made the statement is not present and therefore cannot be questioned.

There are numerous exceptions to the rule, which allow hearsay to come into the record and be considered by the jury.

This is due to a perception that certain hearsay statements are reliable even in the absence of the cross-examination of the person who allegedly made the statement. The reliability is based on the time the hearsay declaration is made (e.g., a "dying declaration" is admissible because it is felt people generally don't lie just before they prepare to meet their maker) or on the kind of statement made (a statement made against a person's interest is admissible because people generally don't lie to put themselves in a bad light).

A new hearsay exception was recently enacted in California that would allow the diary of a deceased individual to be allowed as admissible evidence.[9] While such a diary could not have been introduced as a hearsay exception at O.J. Simpson's criminal trial because the law did not permit its introduction at that time, it could be introduced at the civil trial brought against O.J. Simpson by the victims' families.

To illustrate how the hearsay rule might affect the result in a particular case, let's suppose that there was an eyewitness who was 100 percent reliable. The eyewitness told the police that O.J. Simpson had been in his home from 9:45 P.M. until the limo driver picked him up. Then O.J. could not have committed the murders. Three days later, this perfect witness died of a stroke. If the prosecution objected to its introduction as hearsay, the information could not be used by the jury to exonerate O.J. Simpson, because the jury would not be allowed to consider the statement.

Actual situations have occurred in which an eyewitness has seen a crime committed, such as murder, reported to authorities that the crime occurred and who committed the crime—and then the witness has been murdered. The statements by the now-deceased eyewitness are hearsay. They were not made at the trial, and they go to the "truth of the matter," which is the identity of the criminal. If defense counsel objected to its introduction as hearsay, the jury would not hear the evidence, and thus could not use it in reaching a verdict. The actual criminal perpetrator could walk.

Incompetence of the Prosecutor or Defense Attorney

When the prosecution goes forward with insufficient or inadmissible evidence to convict, or has the evidence but fails to present it to the jury, then a guilty person may be acquitted. Thus, an acquitted defendant, even one who subsequently bragged that he had committed the crime, and admitted to the world that he got away with murder, could not be retried because to do so would subject that person to double jeopardy. The exception to the double jeopardy rule may occur when there are separate state and Federal offenses for the same acts. Even though the four police officers were acquitted of state charges in the assault on Rodney King, they were still charged with the Federal crime of depriving Rodney King of his civil rights.

If defense counsel fail to obtain evidence, or don't object to inadmissible evidence, a person may be convicted who might otherwise have been found not guilty. Even though the defendant is innocent of any wrongdoing, a conviction may result: if the defense fails to find available witnesses who could testify that the defendant was elsewhere at the time of the crime; if the defense cannot afford or fails to obtain scientific evidence that shows the defendant could not have committed the crime; if the defense decides not to put the defendant on the stand because the defendant "looks" guilty but the defendant's testimony could have led to an acquittal or a **hung jury**; if the defense fails to establish that prosecution witnesses are lying; or if the defense is incompetent in other tactical matters.

In some cases, but not in all, the inadequacies of the defense may result in a retrial, or the defendant may be freed. In other cases, the defendant may have been executed or served all or a large portion of time in prison before the true information is obtained.

Bias or Incompetence of the Jury or Judge

If the judicial system breaks down at the level of the fact-finders or legal guardians of the system, innocent people may be convicted and guilty persons acquitted. American history is replete with examples of whites acquitted of killing blacks because all the jurors were white and refused to convict; of judges and jurors who were "bought"; of guilty people who were acquitted because the jurors simply did not like the law under which the defendants were charged; and of people convicted because of how they looked or who they were.

Even if the jurors are unbiased, they may render a verdict that is legally incorrect because they don't understand the evidence or the instructions given by the judge. Or the jurors may understand the evidence and instructions, but because the judge has incorrectly characterized the evidence or given the jury the wrong instructions, the final result is legally incorrect.

In conclusion, these are fairly common examples of situations where there seems to be, and often is, important evidence which is kept from the jurors. As a result, the real criminal goes free or an innocent person is found guilty. In later chapters we will discuss how these types of injustice could be minimized, and the trade-offs involved if the system were to be changed.

Chapter 5

The Prosecutor:
Representative of the
"People"

The District Attorney's office enforces the community's laws, and seeks to protect the community from suspected lawbreakers. This is an important line of defense for all of us. While the police may arrest a suspected criminal, it is only the successful prosecution by the District Attorney which will keep that individual off the streets. Thus, everyone has a stake in criminal trials and a vested interest in having the best possible District Attorney to act on our behalf.

When a case is brought by the District Attorney against someone in California, the case is designated as the "*People*" v. *Simpson* or the "*People*" v. *Powell et al.*

In representing the community, the District Attorney makes a number of critical decisions that significantly affect how our system of justice works. He or she has a tremendous amount of power. That power is in the form of wide discretion.

What Crimes Are Prosecuted?

As a governmental entity, most District Attorneys do not have sufficient resources to prosecute every single crime committed in their jurisdiction. Priorities are established as to which crimes warrant the most time, effort and money. The reason violent crimes are more often prosecuted than nonviolent crimes is because there are not enough deputy district attorneys, or too few investigators, to prosecute all the crimes. So the District Attorney's threshold consideration is whether the crime itself warrants an expenditure of public resources.

Who Gets Prosecuted?

Once the District Attorney decides which crimes will be prosecuted in the jurisdiction, there must be a decision as to which suspects are actually prosecuted and which suspects are not. In making this decision, the District Attorney will also have to decide which specific charges to lodge against the defendants.

Based on information obtained by the police or other investigators, the District Attorney must decide if the evidence can be submitted to the court, and if that admissible evidence is sufficient to support the conclusion that the defendant committed the crime. The District Attorney wants to go into trial confident there is sufficient evidence to convict, because otherwise it would be a waste of taxpayer money to initiate the proceedings.

What Are the Charges?

The designation of the crime is crucial because the charges made against the person will determine what evidence will be needed in order to obtain a conviction. Should the charge be **murder in the first degree**, **murder in the second degree**, **voluntary manslaughter**, **involuntary manslaughter** or something else?

Consider how these decisions affected the Rodney King beating trial and the *O.J. Simpson* case. Everybody saw the police beat Rodney King. Should the District Attorney have selected "attempted murder" as the charge? The prosecution decided the evidence really did not support that charge. Since these were police officers, who are lawfully permitted to use an appropriate amount of force to effect an arrest, the simple **battery** charges, appropriate against ordinary citizens, would not be appropriate against them. And that's the point. The charge has to be appropriate to the law and supported by the available evidence.

As for the *O.J. Simpson* case, recall that shortly after Nicole Brown Simpson's murder, there was speculation that O.J. Simpson would be charged with the crime. Yet a number of days went by before he was formally arrested and charged. During that time, the District Attorney was assembling evidence to determine whether or not to go forward, and under what theory.

The District Attorney's decision to have an individual arrested is important because certain protections are given to arrested persons. One is the right to a **speedy trial**. In the case of *O.J. Simpson*, the defense could have insisted on a trial to begin within sixty days from the date of his arraignment. Both sides must be ready to go forward unless the defense agrees to a delay, waiving its right to a speedy trial.[10]

The person arrested must be charged with a particular offense. In **felony** cases, this means the prosecution must convince the grand jury[11] or a judge at a preliminary hearing that there is enough evidence to proceed with a trial.

Who Decides Whether the Case Will be Presented to the Grand Jury or Go to a Preliminary Hearing?

The District Attorney may seek an **indictment** from the grand jury. In this process, which was used in both the Rodney King beating trial and in the initial phase of the *O.J. Simpson* case, the prosecutor presents evidence to the local grand jury in secret. If the grand jury believes there is sufficient evidence to show that an identified individual may have committed a crime, an indictment will be issued.

When there is no grand jury indictment and the person has already been arrested, the law in California provides that the defendant has the right to a preliminary hearing to determine whether there is sufficient evidence to warrant prosecution. Unlike the grand jury proceeding, this is an open hearing where the press and the defendant's counsel may be present. The District Attorney may be forced to reveal some evidence to defense counsel.

In any case, the prosecution has unfettered discretion to choose the grand jury or a preliminary hearing as the method for proceeding, at least in California.[12]

But even unfettered discretion may have some limits.

In the *O.J. Simpson* case, pretrial publicity apparently was responsible for the decision of the supervising judge of the Los Angeles County Superior Court, Cecil J. Mills, to terminate grand jury proceedings. The judge acted in response to a motion filed by O.J. Simpson's lawyers to stop the grand jury investigation, after the media began playing the recording of a 911 telephone call by a distraught Nicole Brown Simpson. As a result of the judge's unusual action, the indictment was presented at a preliminary hearing and the lawyers representing O.J. Simpson were able to learn *some* of the evidence the prosecution was going to use. The reason the defense saw only some of the evidence was because the District Attorney was not obligated to present all or even the best evidence available at a preliminary hearing.

At a preliminary hearing in California, the prosecution must establish **probable cause** that a crime was committed and the defendant committed it.[13] The magistrate who conducts the preliminary hearing will require the defendant to stand trial in Superior Court if there is evidence which would lead a person of ordinary caution or prudence to believe and conscientiously entertain a strong suspicion of the guilt of the accused.[14] The magistrate does not decide whether the defendant committed the crime, only whether there is some rational ground for assuming the possibility that an offense has been committed and the accused is guilty of it.[15]

That standard doesn't sound like the phrase we associate with criminal cases, which is proof **beyond a reasonable doubt.** That's because the individual's legal guilt or legal nonguilt is not the issue in a preliminary hearing. The determination that the prosecution has met its burden at a preliminary hearing means only the defendant will have to stand trial.

When the Los Angeles District Attorney's Office presented what it thought would be sufficient evidence to support a ruling in its favor, it was correct. If the judge had determined that there was insufficient evidence to meet the strong suspicion standard, O.J. Simpson would have been released.

The District Attorney could still have the person rearrested if better evidence became available. But the District Attorney who continually presses charges against defendants after unsuccessful preliminary hearings is abusing the process. Judges may distrust prosecutors who engage in such tactics.

Who Prosecutes?

The District Attorney must carefully consider which deputy district attorney will prosecute the case for two very important reasons, the second of which has nothing to do with winning the case.

By assigning the best prosecutor to the case, the chances of winning the case are enhanced. If you recall, we didn't hear anything about the two prosecutors involved in the Rodney King beating trial case, other than one of them was African-American. The press did not report they were the best in the office; the media did not say that one or both of them had successfully handled sensational cases in the past. If they had been prosecutorial "stars" that surely would have been news.

The situation was quite different in the *O.J. Simpson* case. The Los Angeles District Attorney put in a top team of outstanding deputy district attorneys. Was the reason because Gil Garcetti really wanted to win this one, whereas the former Los Angeles District Attorney did not really care about winning the Rodney King beating trial? We don't know. We do know that after several notorious stinging defeats (the *Powell* case, the *Damian Williams* case involving the beating of truckdriver Reginald Denny during the Los Angeles riots, the first Menendez Brothers' trial which ended with no verdicts being reached), the District Attorney's Office wanted badly to win the *O.J. Simpson* case, or it would lose much of its remaining reputation for competence.

The second reason for determining who will actually prosecute the case is purely political. In California, and perhaps in your state, the District Attorney for a county is elected to office. If there is to be an extensive and well-covered trial, the deputy district attorney who handles the trial may instantly become a well-known person who receives tremendous free publicity, name recognition and all the political pluses associated with media exposure. If an incumbent District Attorney wants to be reelected and a Marcia Clark is the chief contender for that position, she might not be selected to represent the People in a sensational trial. The popularly elected District Attorney knows that the best deputy may help win a particular case, but the victory may lead to that deputy's election as the new District Attorney. While it may make us uncomfortable to think a District Attorney would sacrifice a potential conviction because of an election, in politics anything is possible.

Other political considerations may also be involved in deciding which deputy district attorney prosecutes. The District Attorney may believe it is necessary to prosecute a weak case because the public is clamoring for a vigorous prosecution of an unsavory defendant and the case is too "hot" to drop. The District Attorney might assign brand-new assistants to the case, or less-experienced staff. Or the District Attorney may play politics and assign the deputy district attorney who is his or her leading challenger so that the challenger will publicly fail.

Race, too, may play a factor. Perhaps the District Attorney believes that an African-American prosecutor should be used if the victim is African-American but the defendants are all Caucasian, as in the Rodney King beating case.

In the *O.J. Simpson* case, the inclusion of an African-American on the prosecution team might have been considered desirable, since there were African-American defense attorneys and jurors.

Many considerations go into the decision to assign one or more particular deputy district attorneys to a case. But the reality is that the choice made by the elected District Attorney frequently may be influenced by factors that have nothing to do with protecting the interests of the People.

What Courtroom Strategy and Evidence Are Used?

Once the trial site is determined and the case is ready to proceed, the prosecutor either will prepare a list of questions for jurors to answer, participate in questioning jurors, or both.

The prosecution tries to remove jurors *"for cause"* (prejudice, unwillingness to follow the law, etc.) if the prosecutor believes they won't convict the particular defendant. The prosecution requests the judge to exclude that juror, and the judge will decide whether removal is appropriate.

If a juror can't be removed for cause, the prosecution may exercise its right under existing law to remove a limited number of jurors without the need to give any reason whatsoever (*peremptory challenges*).

The District Attorney's strategy and decision concerning what evidence should be presented at trial depends on a number of factors. These factors require careful consideration and could include:

- Will the jury understand what the evidence is supposed to show?

- What's the best way the scientific evidence can be presented to the jury so that the jury can understand it?

- Will the evidence convince the jury that guilt has been established beyond a reasonable doubt?

- Will defense counsel be able to destroy the credibility of one or more witnesses and thus hurt the prosecution case?

- Should the victim (e.g., Rodney King) testify if he can be portrayed as an unsavory character by defense counsel?

The prosecutor has to take the case "as-is". If the investigation of the crime has been conducted in a sloppy manner, that has to be considered. The quality of investigation by the police, the coroner, the criminalist and others may seriously impair the District Attorney's ability to obtain a conviction. Key witnesses may be unwilling to testify.

Once strategy and tactics are determined, and the jury selected, the District Attorney will make an Opening Statement. The prosecution attempts to establish rapport with the jurors. The prosecution also hopes to set the tone for the trial by telling a story to the jury that will emphasize those facts and witnesses most favorable to a finding of guilt. Then the defendant's counsel will usually give an Opening Statement.

During the course of the trial, the prosecution will question its witnesses, and cross-examine defense witnesses. Exhibits will be introduced. The prosecution will raise objections, and respond to defense objections.

The prosecution will decide the best tactical way to present all its evidence to illustrate the story it has laid out in its Opening Statement.

At the conclusion of the trial, there will be a Closing Statement, summarizing the People's case. After the Closing Statement by the defense, the prosecution will have an opportunity for *final rebuttal.*

The final responsibility of the prosecution is to prepare proposed instructions for the judge to read to the jury.

What Resources Are Provided to Assist the Prosecution?

Resources, or their lack, may make the difference between a successful and unsuccessful prosecution. Unlike multimillionaire defendants, such as O.J. Simpson, who have relatively unlimited resources, prosecutors find themselves operating on fixed budgets. The District Attorney must decide whether to spend some of those scarce resources on experts, scientific tests, etc., in one case or save the money to use in numerous other cases. These decisions are based on prosecutorial discretion, and may vary from county to county and from state to state.

It was clear in the *O.J. Simpson* case that the District Attorney's Office would spend whatever was necessary to prove its case because it had far too much invested in the outcome to cut corners.

The prosecutor has a duty to the People. One important reason to prosecute and incarcerate guilty individuals is to keep them off the streets so that none of us become their next victim. If the wrong person is convicted or the person who actually committed the crime is found not guilty, the guilty person will go free, and remain a danger to society.

Although we are focusing on two sensational trials, the same strategic and tactical decisions are made and the same monetary and personnel choices come into play with the run-of-the-mill trial which does not make the 6:00 P.M. news.

Chapter 6

Defense Counsel: Representative of the Accused

Since defense counsel are attorneys, and officers of the court, you may think that they are committed to seeking the truth, and have responsibilities to protect the People. If you listened to Alan Dershowitz on *Rivera Live* on December 27, 1994, you were told that the motions filed by the O.J. Simpson defense team were designed to arrive at "the truth."

Most of us suspect that when information is limited or withheld, it is because someone doesn't want us to know the truth. Mr. Dershowitz did not say that if successful these motions would prevent important and relevant evidence which revealed the truth from ever being heard or considered by any jury. After all, wouldn't the truth have been better served if the statement O.J. made to Rosey Grier had been admitted without an objection? Or, better yet, if Mr. Grier or O.J. had testified about it?

There are those who believe that if a defense counsel knows that his or her client actually committed the crime the lawyer should not take the case because, if successful, an actually guilty person will go free. Yet lawyers may know that the person they are defending did commit the crime as charged, and not only do these defense lawyers take the case, they do the very best job they can in preventing society from convicting and punishing a guilty lawbreaker.

So, what are the ethics of defense counsel? How can they look themselves in the mirror and respect what they see, knowing that some of their clients actually committed the crimes with which they were charged and without the defense lawyers' conscientious efforts their clients would have gone to jail.

The attorney representing the defendant has a duty only to his or her client, to prevent the prosecution from proving the defendant committed the charged crime. A defense counsel's ethical responsibility, regardless of the ill-repute of the defendant or the heinousness of the crime committed, is to defend that person to the best of his or her ability.

Ideally, defense counsel want to obtain an acquittal. The next best thing to an acquittal is a hung jury, when the jury cannot reach unanimous agreement as to guilt or nonguilt.

A hung jury forces the District Attorney to determine whether it is worthwhile to retry the case.

When defense counsel believe that they can achieve neither an acquittal nor a hung jury, they may decide to **plea-bargain**. Currently, a plea-bargain may be a less desirable tactic, because of the recent "three-strikes-and-you're-out" legislation. Since defense counsel have a duty to their clients, they have to consider the ramifications of a guilty plea—even to a misdemeanor—if that plea will jeopardize their client in the future and count as one of the "strikes" in a subsequent prosecution.

In some situations, the defendant's attorney knows that the client has committed the crime, that the prosecutor has available evidence to establish guilt and therefore the prosecutor won't plea-bargain. In this scenario, the defense counsel may attempt to show the client's capacity was diminished. The defenses can range from pleas of: total insanity; temporary insanity or **irresistible impulse** (Ellie Nesler's April 1993 courtroom killing of the man accused of allegedly abusing her son); **diminished capacity** (the Menendez Brothers); the **battered-spouse syndrome** claim (Lorena Bobbit); the "Twinkie" defense (Dan White's defense in the November 1978 killing of the Mayor of San Francisco and a San Francisco Supervisor, based on the theory that the excessive sugar in the Twinkies he ate made him unbalanced). These defenses may, if accepted by the jury, lead to acquittals, or to convictions on less-serious charges.

The client needs to confide completely in counsel so that the most appropriate defense can be advanced. To assure the trust that this requires, the attorney-client privilege exists. This privilege between a defendant and his or her lawyer protects confidential communications. Thus, defendants can reveal that they were the perpetrators of the crimes charged, and know that their counsel cannot ethically divulge that information.

The defense counsel's only obligation to society is to refuse to **suborn perjury** (to encourage lying under oath). Defense counsel may try to prevent evidence from being used to convict a client, but they cannot try to get a client off by use of fraud.

After defense counsel talk with their clients, they decide how to proceed. And it's no secret that the options are greater for those defendants with money.

O.J. Simpson could afford to hire the best, or at least the most celebrated and famous defense team. His attorneys were able to get air time to make their case. Big bucks were paid so that topnotch investigators could be hired to pursue any and all leads. People in the neighborhood were interviewed about the killings. World-famous **forensic** experts (scientific examiners of the legal evidence) evaluated blood testing. DNA tests were reviewed. Jury consultants were hired so that a jury *least* likely to convict O.J. could be selected. And, if a conviction had occurred, renowned appellate attorneys, such as Alan Dershowitz, would have pursued appeals to the highest courts.

Indigent defendants may receive excellent legal representation from public defenders, but the indigent defendant will not have the means to obtain the extras that come with money.

Defense counsel aren't paid to be objective or fair. They are paid to win. So in the *O.J. Simpson* case, when Mr. Dershowitz or Mr. Shapiro talked to the press, explaining the misdeeds of the prosecution or the LAPD or the coroner, and proclaiming their client's innocence, you could put the same faith in those statements as in the explanations from tobacco executives as to the safety of their product. Regardless of what these lawyers said or actually believed, regardless of how genuine and sincere they seemed, or how artfully they framed their responses, they were biased in favor of their client. They were doing their job. They were trying to get O.J. off.

As defense lawyers, it would have been unethical for them to remain objective or to say anything that could be damaging to their client. They put out information with the best slant on events. They protected their client's interest when they insisted that the leaks and publicity about the case from the police and prosecutor had to stop in order for Mr. Simpson to receive a fair trial, even as the defense team itself was responsible for their own leaks. They were trying to create a potential jury pool and public sympathetic to O.J.

Once the trial site has been set, and the case is ready to proceed, defense counsel have many of the same choices to make as does the prosecution. A defense attorney will either help to prepare a list of questions for jurors to answer, or participate in questioning those jurors, or both. The defense will try to remove unsympathetic jurors for cause. If this tactic is unsuccessful, the defense will use its peremptory challenges.

When the jury is selected, and the charges are read, the defense attorney may make an Opening Statement after the prosecution has done so. The purpose is to put the jury in a certain frame of mind. Particularly when the case involves notorious defendants, or defendants who have received much negative publicity, the defense needs to emphasize to jurors their duty not to prejudge the defendant or the evidence, and to keep in mind that guilt must be proved beyond a reasonable doubt.

As the prosecution presents its evidence, the defense has to make a number of tactical choices. Counsel must decide when to object, and when to let something slide. They want to protect their client, but they don't want to antagonize the judge or jury.

Defense tactics may include intentionally antagonizing the prosecutorial team. Perhaps Mr. Shapiro knew exactly what he was doing when he uttered "bullshit" loud enough for the prosecutor to hear during a pretrial phase in the *Simpson* case.

The defense will attack the credibility of the People's witnesses. They may try to establish prejudice (Detective Mark Fuhrman in the *Simpson* case), or the inability to perceive (not enough light, witness without glasses) or bad character (prior convictions). At times, cross-examination will be aggressive. Other times there may be little examination of a witness because defense counsel believe the jury may be sympathetic or empathetic with the witness and the jury may react negatively to a perceived attack on the witness.

Cross-examination of an expert will be used to attack the expert's expertise. The expert's training, the published articles, will be scrutinized. If forensic tests were run, they will be challenged. The defense will try to show bias on the witness's part.

Once the prosecution has completed its case, the defense must determine which witnesses to put on the stand. When a defense attorney sees that the prosecution case is weak, fewer witnesses may be called. If the defense believes that the prosecution has totally failed to present a strong case, the defense may decide to offer no evidence of its own, and rest its case.

Defense counsel, like prosecuting attorneys, are responsible for developing the strategy to be used in the case, the line of argument, when and what evidence will be presented to the jury, and what evidence will be consciously kept away from the jury. A defense lawyer might keep apparently favorable evidence away from the jury, if its negative effect on the jury potentially outweighed its positive value.

An example of this predicament is the recurring and significant problem for the defense of deciding whether the defendant should take the witness stand and testify in the trial. Putting the defendant on the stand could result in the defendant's cross-examination by the prosecutor, and that could turn out to be devastating.

At the close of the defense case, the prosecution may put on **rebuttal** witnesses which may, in turn, require the defense to put on its own rebuttal witnesses.

After the prosecution makes its closing statements, defense counsel will make their closing remarks, summarizing the strengths in their case and arguing the prosecution has failed to prove its case beyond a reasonable doubt.

Finally, the defense will submit a list of proposed instructions for the judge to read to the jurors at the close of the trial. These are designed to emphasize the law which both applies to the case and is most favorable to the defendant.

After the verdict is rendered, defense may have further work to do on appeal. But the trial work is over.

CHAPTER 7

THE JUDGE:
SUPERVISOR OF THE TRIAL

A preliminary hearing or a grand jury has determined that there is enough evidence to proceed to trial. A trial date is set and a judge assigned to the matter. A group of jurors is called to appear on a certain day. A random selection of those jurors is sent to a particular courtroom. That's when you, the juror, see the judge for the first time.

In most states, after some preliminary remarks, generally the judge will address the jury, and explain the nature of the charges and their duties as jurors. The judge will ask whether the jurors can fulfill their responsibilities. If they feel that they cannot, and the judge is convinced, they may be released from that particular case.

For example, the alleged crime may involve (as in *People v. Powell et al*) charges against a police officer. Jurors whose past associations and experiences would make them unwilling to render guilty verdicts would be excused by the judge. The judge may also excuse jurors, especially in a lengthy trial, when sitting as a juror would result in a substantial hardship on them or their families.

In some trials, such as *People v. Powell et al* and the *O.J. Simpson* case, potential jurors are required to complete a questionnaire prepared specifically for that trial by the respective lawyers (defense counsel and prosecutors). The judge, however, decides which questions should be included.

Throughout all phases of the trial, the judge is the person who maintains control of the proceedings. At a minimum, he or she does the following:

- Rules on motions and objections made by the attorneys, pretrial, at trial, and post-trial;

- Decides, in some instances, whether the trial should be televised;

- Decides which potential jurors to remove for cause, and which jurors will be excused during the trial;

- Holds participants in contempt, if warranted;

- Decides which instructions are read to the jury.

The judge may be extensively involved in deciding legal motions which occur outside the presence of the jury. In the *O.J. Simpson* trial, there were weeks of pretrial argument, with numerous motions by both the prosecution and defense, which were argued in court and shown on TV with no jurors present.

The lawyers sought rulings from Judge Ito to determine what evidence could be presented and how, and what evidence should be excluded. (An example mentioned earlier was Judge Ito's decision to exclude the testimony of the officer who over-heard O.J.'s statement to Rosey Grier.) The lawyers often need answers before the trial begins. The public saw the critically important role of the judge as Judge Lance Ito made numerous pretrial rulings against, or for, lawyers on both sides in the *O.J. Simpson* case. Each side went forward in accord with those rulings, even when the defense or prosecution believed the rulings were incorrect. (Some rulings may be appealed immediately to a higher court, others only after a verdict has been rendered.)

In addition to making rulings before the jury has been seated, the judge is called upon throughout the trial to make additional rulings and decisions. Sometimes the jury is excused temporarily so the lawyers can argue or discuss the situation in the judge's presence in the courtroom or in the judge's chambers. Many times during a trial, the lawyers gather at the **sidebar** which is adjacent to where the judge sits.

Discussion which occurs there is out of the earshot of the jurors. These sidebar discussions address issues such as whether a particular individual can testify to a certain matter, whether the attorney will be allowed to pose a certain question to the witness and whether or not the judge ruled correctly on a specific motion. The judge will either decide such legal questions on the spot after brief discussion, or the judge will put off the decision until it can be researched.

The judge decides all questions of law as opposed to questions of fact. Questions of law could include deciding whether the evidence one party wants to introduce is admissible, that is, can be presented to the jury. The judge generally rules only on protested motions. If either party objects, or makes a motion, the judge determines what the jury sees and hears, and the way evidence or opinion or argument is presented to the jury.

Under our system of law, the jury is the *sole* judge of the facts. An example of a question of fact is whether the evidence presented to the jury establishes that O.J. Simpson killed Nicole.

In the Rodney King beating trial, Judge Weisberg had to rule on the following:

- Could an expert testify as to whether the police officers were following departmental procedures when they beat Rodney King with their batons?

- Could the experts testify as to what a "reasonable" LAPD police officer would have done?

- Could defense counsel show a videotape to the jury of the route Rodney King drove that night in March 1991 before he was forced to stop, when that tape was made one year after the actual incident?

- Could evidence be introduced showing that Officer Laurence Powell talked on the police radio shortly after the Rodney King beating incident, to prove that the message received over the police communication system was from him?

- Could statements made by Officer Powell shortly before the beating incident be introduced to indicate that Officer Powell was a racist?

In the *O.J. Simpson* trial, Judge Lance Ito had to make rulings on the following:

- Could certain objects, such as the bloody glove, be admitted into evidence?

- Could the jury hear Nicole Simpson's 911 call to the police?

- Could a witness testify if the witness had sold a story about the murder to the media?

- Could evidence which might have great value be excluded because it was highly prejudicial, such as photographs showing the grisly nature of the crimes against these two human beings?

- Could a passenger on the same plane as O.J. testify as to whether O.J.'s hand was cut? Could the witness also testify as to whether O.J. was calm or distraught, when that testimony would be based on the witness's opinion?

- Were DNA tests reliable enough to be introduced as evidence?

Such rulings are generally made *only* when the judge is confronted with this issue: If opposing counsel fails to object, the possibly inadmissible evidence will be put before the jury and may properly be considered by them.

The judge also rules on whether evidence already presented to the jury will be stricken from the record. Again, this depends on whether opposing counsel objects to the question itself, to the witness's response, or to an object or writing placed in evidence. In the *People v. Powell et al* trial, the judge sometimes **overruled** an objection and allowed the answer to stand. At times, the judge told the jury to disregard the evidence stricken by him without a further reminder or explanation. At some points, the judge instructed the jury to disregard the evidence as to one or several of the four defendants, and not the others. Sometimes the judge simply sustained the objection without further comment.

Based on counsel's objections, the judge also determines whether opening or closing remarks include comments which are not permissible. Again, the ruling is based on a motion from the opposing party, and is rarely given by the judge on the judge's own motion.

At the close of the trial, the judge reads the jury instructions. These can be lengthy (more than sixty pages of transcript in the *People v. Powell et al* trial), or they may be rather short. In either case, the judge does not explain the instructions, and is not required to provide a written copy to the jurors unless they request one. In California, the current practice is for most judges to give a copy of the instructions to the jury when they begin deliberations. Most of the instructions are based on submissions by the lawyers as to which instructions should be used and how they should be worded. They are generally standardized in California[16] but are sometimes "customized" by the lawyers to fit the particular facts of the case.

After the judge gives the jury its final instructions, the jury begins to deliberate. During its deliberations, the jury may ask the judge to clarify the instructions, or to give them a copy of the transcript to read. The judge determines whether the instructions will be reread or whether the jury will be provided with the pertinent transcript excerpts.

The judge may sequester the jury during deliberations and in some instances for the length of the entire trial. Jurors are essentially locked up with their fellow jurors, and cannot communicate with or see their family and friends, or can do so only on a limited basis, until a verdict is reached or they are dismissed by the judge.

In the *O.J. Simpson* criminal trial, Judge Ito had instructed the jurors, even before the jury phase of the trial started, not to read newspapers or magazines, not to watch TV, or to listen to the radio during the trial, if stories were related to O.J. Simpson. Jurors were instructed not to form an opinion, or to discuss the trial with others.

Unlike most trials, where sequestration occurs only during deliberations, the *Simpson* jurors were sequestered not only for the length of the trial (January 24 - October 3, 1995) but also for thirteen days before the trial started.

Once a verdict is reached, it is read by the foreperson. If requested by either side, the jury is polled (questioned as to how they voted). The judge then discharges the jurors. He or she may still make other decisions such as determining the sentence, releasing the defendant pending appeal or setting aside the verdict. An instance of this last point occurred when many people were stunned by the developments in the 1996 trial of football player Bennie Blades. He had been convicted by the jury of manslaughter of his cousin. The judge, however, freed him, saying that the admissible evidence could not sustain a guilty verdict.

All judges are not the same. Some are extremely interested in the case before them. Others may seem uninterested, impatient, or even hostile. Some have a wide grasp of the law, while others may not. Some make correct rulings most of the time, while others are more likely to err.

The judge is responsible for keeping order on the playing field. In some situations, the judge may decide the outcome of the case—the game—played out in the courtroom. Thus, a particular ruling may be critical as to which team wins and which loses, as to whether the defendant is convicted or acquitted. As far as jurors are concerned, the judge decides what they get to hear and what they don't. If the judge makes a mistake, the juror is bound to accept that mistake for purposes of that trial. If a judge erroneously rules to exclude critical evidence from the jury, the jury must decide the case without it. If the judge commits a gross error by allowing the jury to consider evidence that should have been excluded, the jury must consider that evidence. In this latter instance, if a conviction resulted, an appeal by defense counsel might cause the guilty verdict to be set aside. But, in general, if the case ends in an acquittal, the mistake of the judge may mean that a guilty person goes free and the prosecution has no right to appeal to a higher court, or retry that individual because of the prohibition against double jeopardy.

The rulings the judge makes may influence the jury's final decision, not only when the judge makes legal errors but also when the lack of clarity in rulings, the incomprehensibility of the jury instructions, or the attitude towards witnesses or counsel lead the jury astray.

Ideally, jurors should leave the courtroom feeling that the judge was helpful without being condescending, clear rather than confusing—and at all times an unbiased umpire.

PART III

IMPARTIALITY?

THE

REAL

TEST

Chapter 8

Jury of Your "Peers"— What Is It?

Every criminal defendant has the right to be judged by a jury of that defendant's peers. A peer is defined as "one that is of equal standing with another... one belonging to the same societal group especially based on age, grade, or status."[17] If a peer means an equal, how does that affect the composition of a jury in a specific case? Does it mean that the only persons who should serve on the Rodney King beating trial are men who are white police officers from Los Angeles? Or that the O.J. Simpson jury should be limited to African-American professional sports stars?

In the same vein, should only doctors serve on the jury if a doctor is charged with criminal medical malpractice, only gang members be jurors when a gang member is charged with extortion, or only other homeless people sit on the jury when a homeless person is charged with being a public nuisance?

Suppose the defendant is African-American and the entire jury is also African-American, but the defendant is uneducated and poor and the jury is comprised of middle-class, professional, educated individuals. Is this a jury of the defendant's peers because they are the same color? Suppose the defendant is white and the all upper-class white jury considers the defendant to be poor white trash. Does similarity of color equate with being a peer?

In the instances above, jurors are part of at least one group which is the same as the defendant. But does that fact alone establish the jurors as peers of the defendant?

The *People v. Powell* jury was attacked as being unrepresentative, because it was not a jury of Mr. King's peers. But when the courts talk about the representative nature of a jury, the point of reference is the defendant, not the victim. Rodney King was the victim, and not the perpetrator, of the attack. Mr. King was not on trial. Four white police officers were. The jury was predominantly white, and no blacks served. Wasn't this therefore a jury of the officers' peers?

These examples raise some serious questions as to what is meant by a jury of one's peers. Let's try to arrive at a sensible way of defining this phrase.

The first decision made in relation to the jury is the venue, the place where the trial will be held. Normally, the trial is held in the locale where the crime occurred. That is logical, since the physical evidence, the victim of the crime and the witnesses are most likely to be there. It is reasonable, in that the defendant is often a resident, either permanently or temporarily, in the area of the crime. It is appropriate, as the particular community is the one that has been most affected by the act. It is not arbitrary, to the extent that it fixes the trial site, and does not give either side the opportunity to **forum shop** (seek a more favorable court and locale). It is consistent with the Constitution's Sixth Amendment.

A change of venue may be requested by either party, but it is the judge who presides in the original site who makes the determination. This determination is subject to review by appellate or supreme courts. In all cases, a change of venue is theoretically made to ensure the fairness of the trial.

If the entire community believes that the defendant is a bad person, and has most likely committed the crime charged, the defendant would be allowed to have the venue changed. If the entire community believes the defendant is a wonderful, charming and innocent individual or the law is a bad one, the State's right to a fair trial could be infringed if the trial were held in that community.

This latter statement may seem self-contradictory since we ordinarily think of the State and People as synonymous. Actually, the State is either the Federal, State or local government which enacts the laws under which the defendant is charged. The State has an interest in seeing that its laws are obeyed and enforced, despite the feelings of a portion of its population. If it's a crime to sell cocaine in California, the belief of the majority of citizens in a particular community that the law is a bad one, or that the individual charged is a terrific person who has given a great deal to the community, should not be allowed to subvert the State's interest in enforcing its laws. In this instance there is a distinction between the "People" who are bringing the charges, and the State which has enacted the laws.

Suppose the original venue is determined to be unsuitable. The question then becomes the suitability of alternative venues. In general, the law requires the trial to be moved to a community as similar as possible to the community in which the crime occurred.

In the Rodney King beating trial, the crime occurred in Los Angeles. But based on a change of venue motion, the trial was moved to Simi Valley, in adjacent Ventura County, a town some fifty or so miles away from the scene of the crime. Although Simi Valley is geographically fairly close to Los Angeles, it is far removed in most respects. It is smaller, more rural, and has far fewer African-Americans.

Could people from such a community, whose life style is very different from the hustle and bustle of life in the big city, judge the Rodney King beating fairly and impartially? Consider whether the people who sat on that jury might have been afraid of Rodney King because he was a large African-American male who had broken the law before he was apprehended. Or perhaps jurors from Simi Valley have such a healthy respect for "law and order" that they would not have found these police officers guilty under any circumstances. Could Rodney King, the victim, and the People get a fair trial in Simi Valley? Would there still have been universal condemnation of the verdicts in this case if the Simi Valley jury had contained a significant percentage of African-Americans?

Certainly no one wants jurors to be unfair to the defendant. But, just as important, the jurors need to be fair to the victim.

In the *O.J. Simpson* case, the trial also was moved away from the scene of the crime. Were the jurors in that case representative of the victims or the people who lived where the victims lived? In a way, the situation was the mirror image of *People v. Powell*. The Brentwood community where the crime occurred was predominantly Caucasian. The victims were white. The defendant was African-American. And the jury in downtown LA had a far higher percentage of African-Americans than did Brentwood.

The venue, in and of itself, cannot assure the State or the defendant of a jury of one's peers.

The next chapter describes the **voir dire** process by which the prosecution and defense attempt to affect the composition of the jury. Both are given the opportunity to pick a fair jury through challenges for cause. They seek to exclude jurors for bias, because of a conflict of interest or because the juror is unable to decide the matter because of an inability to reason.

The lawyers may also exclude jurors by exercising peremptory challenges which are limited in number. Perhaps it's because the prospective juror is too much like the defendant and the prosecutor feels that juror might be too sympathetic. But if the juror is like the defendant, isn't that person close to one definition of a peer? Why have that person removed if the goal is to have a jury of one's peers?

Questions regarding the use of peremptories have been presented to the United States Supreme Court. The Court has ruled that peremptory challenges to certain classes or groups of jurors are unconstitutional. Specifically, lawyers cannot exclude blacks[18], or females[19], if these challenges are designed to exclude those groups.

Will Latinos, people from the Middle East or Asia be given similar protection? That is unknown, but it is certain that there will be judicial scrutiny when members of those groups are subject to peremptory challenges.

Instead of striving to achieve a jury of one's peers, the courts and our laws have made it possible to do the opposite: to select a jury composed of people as unequal to the defendant as possible through changes of venue and peremptory challenges.

We have come to believe that the phrase "a jury of one's peers" has little concrete meaning to most people who hear it or use it. As we see it, an impartial juror is the only kind of juror who truly is a peer of the defendant. So, under our definition, a jury of one's peers is nothing more than a group of twelve persons which has not prejudged the defendant before the trial has started, and which will remain totally impartial during the trial and not be governed by prejudice or emotion. A jury of one's peers will make a judgment once the trial is over on nothing but the evidence presented in the case. A jury of one's peers will presume innocence until guilt is proved beyond a reasonable doubt.

CHAPTER 9

VOIR DIRE:
PUTTING YOU ON TRIAL

We need not ask for whom jury duty calls—it calls for all of us. At least for all of us who are registered voters or possess a driver's license.

But before you are summoned to appear for jury duty, some jurisdictions will mail you a short questionnaire to determine whether you are qualified to serve on a jury. Sample questions sent to Placer County, California, prospective jurors included:

1. Can you read and understand English?

2. Are you eighteen years or older?

3. Have you been convicted of a felony and have your civil rights been restored?

4. Would a physical or mental incapacity prevent you from performing jury service?

5. Must you care for a dependent between 8:00 A.M. and 5:00 P.M.?

6. Have you already served on jury duty within the last twelve months?

7. Is there another reason why you could not serve? (This answer requires an explanation.)

Your answers will determine whether you will be excused from jury duty. If there is no basis for excusing you, you will receive a letter asking you to report for jury duty, although some jurisdictions now ask you to telephone the courthouse to find out if (or when) you need to report.

Once at the courthouse, jurors often begin the waiting game—waiting to be part of a particular jury pool, waiting to be assigned to a particular case, waiting for a courtroom to be available, waiting for the attorneys or judges, waiting for settlements, and waiting to go home.

In some cases you will be required to answer an additional questionnaire as part of the process known as voir dire, literally "to see to say" or loosely, to see what they (the jurors) say.

In the Rodney King beating trial, jurors were required to complete a lengthy questionnaire (102 questions). It was described in the Los Angeles Times[20] as follows:

> The Times has learned that the attorneys are focusing their examination of jurors on three issues: whether, or when or is it appropriate, for a police officer to use force against criminal suspects; how they have been affected by the extensive media coverage; and how their family histories and lifestyles might influence their decision in the case...

> There are 173 possible witnesses. These questionnaires ask the jury pool whether they ever feared the police, and the kind of TV shows they watched. They were asked if they owned a video camera, and if they did, whether it had an automatic focus.

> The questionnaires, prepared by prosecution and defense attorneys, indicate that the lawyers expect to have difficulty in choosing a fair and impartial panel of twelve jurors and six alternates.

> Some of the specific questions dealt with whether jurors believe that people in low-income neigh-

borhoods are treated differently than people in middle to upper income neighborhoods; how they viewed
the police in general, and the role of a police officer;
and whether they were more likely to believe a
police officer's testimony than that of a civilian,
because the police officers are generally more truthful and honest than people in general.

Ten questions explore the amount of force a
police officer should use in an arrest.

There are questions about race, designed to see
if jurors have been exposed to prejudice. The jurors
are told that King, a black man, was allegedly victimized by three white officers and a Latino officer, and
are asked whether that scenario causes them concern.

The jury pool members were questioned as to
whether they had heard of the controversy surrounding the King beating, of the status of LAPD
Chief Daryl F. Gates, and on proposed measures to
reform the Police Department.

The *O.J. Simpson* case took the juror questionnaire to a
new level of complexity and intrusion. Prospective jurors were
asked 294 questions. Before answering them, the potential
jurors were advised:

**"Your answers must be truthful and given without
consulting any other person. Remember that you are
under oath as you complete this questionnaire and that
your responses are made *under penalty of perjury*. Your
answers will be verified and checked for accuracy..."**

Little did the O.J. Simpson jurors realize just how seriously
they should take this last sentence!

With that instruction, the jurors would now begin to appreciate just how different the "Trial of the Century" would be. They
may have wondered why all of these questions were necessary.

The *Simpson* questionnaire addressed the following:

Family History/Background	1 thru 9
Residential History	10 thru 18
Employment	19 thru 30
Education	31 thru 40
Military	41 thru 47
Spouse or Partner's Background	48 thru 55
Parents and Siblings	56 thru 57
Legal/Courtroom Experience	58 thru 77
Media Coverage	78 thru 111
Familiarity with the Area	112 thru 115
Familiarity with Judges, Attorneys, Parties	116 thru 130
Familiarity with O.J. Simpson	131 thru 161
Domestic Violence/Use-of-Force	162 thru 181
Ethnic Prejudice	182 thru 192
DNA	193 thru 200
Religion	201
Political	202 thru 205
"Expert" Witnesses	206 thru 213
Science and Math Courses	214 thru 220
Victim or Witness to Crime	221 thru 234
Contacts with Law Enforcement Agencies	235 thru 238
Contacts with Prosecuting Agencies	239 thru 241
Contact with Coroner's Office	242 and 243
Leisure Activities/Entertainment/ Hobbies/Miscellaneous	244 thru 258
Sports	259 thru 275
Diverse	276 thru 283
Sitting as a Juror on this Case	284 thru 291
Concluding Questions	292 thru 294

These questions were "fill-in," multiple choice, yes/no, or essay-type questions. Among the concerns touched upon:

- Marital status, including whether you were divorced and if you were the person who initiated the divorce

- Work experiences over the past ten years, with a brief description of each job, name of each employer and the length of time you were employed at each job

- Work experience in a laboratory, medical research or testing facility

- Favorite and least favorite subjects in school

- Information relating to your spouse's or partner's background, including place of birth, education, race or ethnic background, employment history and whether person was widowed, separated or divorced

- Service, if any, as the foreperson of a jury

- Exposure to any media coverage of the case

- Potential jurors were then asked to check all areas— an extensive list of TV and radio stations, national and local magazines and newspapers—which described their exposure to the trial, indicating how frequently they had watched, listened or read about the case.

- Impressions of the lawyers for O.J. Simpson and the prosecution

- Impressions of Ron Goldman and Nicole Brown Simpson, based upon what had been reported or published in the news media

- Difficulties in believing the evidence presented if it conflicted with the juror's pre-existing beliefs about O.J. Simpson

- Kind of things that can cause a normally law-abiding person to commit acts of violence

- Feelings about interracial marriage, including how it would feel if a close family member or relative married someone of a different race, and if the jurors themselves had ever dated a person of a different race

- Reliability of DNA analysis to identify a person accurately as the possible source of blood or hair found at a crime scene

- Religious affiliation and how important religion is to the juror

- Political affiliations, including whether jurors are currently registered to vote, and whether they voted in the June 1994 primary election

- Preferred type of books (example: nonfiction, historical, romance, espionage, mystery)

- Groups and organizations to which the juror belongs, either currently or for a significant period in the past (Some examples listed—bowling leagues, church groups, AA, Sierra Club, National Rifle Association (NRA), American Civil Liberties Union (ACLU), YWCA, YMCA, PTA, NAACP)

- Three most admired public figures

What's *your* reaction to these questions? Are the lawyers entitled to know your specific political affiliation, the religion you practice, the fact you are an ACLU member or a volunteer for the NRA? In this era of diminishing privacy, what are the chances your answers will remain confidential? Keep in mind the keen media interest in knowing all the most minute details of the trial, and the fact that the specific information obtained via the questionnaire is shared with jury consultants.

It seems likely that the completed questionnaires were then carefully reviewed by the attorneys and consultants who helped draft the questions. Each side was trying to find jurors who would be helpful to the case, and avoid those jurors who were likely to favor the other side. Which juror would be sensitive or insensitive to this defense, that witness, this issue, that evidence? How would the person's background, the books or magazines the person read, the TV watched or not watched, affect that juror when a piece of evidence was presented?

Do you believe that the lawyers and jury consultants who prepared the questions were seeking jurors who would be impartial, who would get at "the truth" as Johnnie Cochran Jr. and Marcia Clark were telling the media? Consider this: If Mr. Cochran was successful at getting at the truth, and in so doing the truth resulted in a verdict of guilty, he could be reprimanded or disbarred, even sued for malpractice.

The *Powell et al* and *O.J. Simpson* questionnaires were unusually lengthy but questionnaires themselves are not limited to sensational trials. In fact, in California the law requires the judge to allow jury questionnaires unless there is a good reason to forbid them.[21]

In California, potential jurors who have not been disqualified on the basis of the initial screening or the questionnaire will be subject to oral voir dire. Twelve jurors are seated and then the questioning begins. This is called the jury box system. In other states, the entire group may be subject to challenge before anyone is called. In California, the questioning must be conducted by the judge, who may permit the attorneys to supplement the questions if good cause for doing so is established. Other states may allow the attorneys to voir dire the pool of jurors.

The California rule is that whenever practicable, voir dire must occur in the presence of all other jurors. So your dirty—or clean but private—linen is on display. The judge may, however, offer you the opportunity to explain your concerns in a setting apart from the other jurors. Although voir dire is to be used only for the purpose of exercising challenges for cause, the courts give great latitude as to investigations of your attitude.

"For cause" means the judge determines you aren't qualified to serve after listening to your answers. You will then simply be excused by the judge, without further explanation. The judge has determined you cannot be an impartial judge of the facts.

Let's take a look at three generic-type voir dire questions:[22]

- Is it your opinion that law-enforcement officers, by virtue of their training, are better and more accurate witnesses than other people?

- Do you think you might always believe the testimony of the victim and the victim's family?

- Have you ever had an experience with a police officer that might make you dislike or disbelieve one who testified in this case?

As you can see, these questions are not excessively intrusive. But depending on the case, questioning may become more specific during voir dire, especially when there is oral probing of the potential juror's responses in the written questionnaire.

Does voir dire really identify jurors who should not serve on a jury because of their predisposition, beliefs, attitudes, biases? While we don't know the answer, we do know not all members of the jury pool will be candid.

If a prospective juror is not truthful, it is possible no one will know and the juror might be seated. Although people are usually asked to be honest and told it is all right to admit things about themselves, many are unwilling to do so in front of others. Many will deny their prejudices even to themselves.

Judge Ito excused two jurors from the O.J. Simpson trial several days before the jury trial began. No explanation was provided at the time, although it appeared that the jurors might have withheld information during voir dire. Obviously even the most painstaking process may have flaws. Such problems are magnified when the defendant is obscure, being tried at a local court without publicity, and with lawyers and judges who have too many cases and too little time to investigate the responses.

There is another concern about answers given to voir dire questions: If a juror conceals something essential, and the defendant is convicted, the courts *may* set aside the verdict. Conversely, if the juror conceals something—or even if the juror is bribed—and the defendant is acquitted, there will be no retrial because of the provision prohibiting double jeopardy.

Prosecution and defense counsel view voir dire as critical. As they see it, an error in judgment, or an erroneous gut feeling might put someone on the jury who will determine the outcome of the case. If the prosecutors in the Rodney King beating trial permitted a juror to be seated who held out for acquittal no matter what the evidence, the prosecution should conclude that it made a serious mistake. If defense counsel permitted a juror to be seated who was convinced of the four police officers' guilt from day one, and could persuade other jurors of the defendants' guilt, the defense could reasonably infer that it failed to protect the defendant adequately. In either of these cases, the jury might still have reached the correct legal result, but the process would have failed.

But these are extreme situations. More often voir dire is used as a way to try to select jurors who are predisposed to a certain position or who are seen as amenable to being swayed to that position. Neither side wants a juror who is unsympathetic and who appears to be a leader, able to convince others.

The lawyer asking for removal of a prospective juror for cause must set out the basis for that request. The judge will then rule on the motion.

Let's suppose you are still sitting in the jury box after voir dire has screened out potential jurors. The attorneys may still remove you by use of a peremptory challenge. Here is where the jury consultants earn their money because the availability of peremptory challenges permits them to remove jurors without any reasons being given.

A peremptory challenge, as we have said, is one in which the prosecution or defense "excuses" a juror even though there is no showing of prejudice or of an inability to discharge a juror's duties. In general, the more serious the charge, the more peremptories allowed each side. Peremptory challenges are not mandated by the Constitution; they are either based on judicial determinations or on State or Federal law. In the *O.J. Simpson* trial, each side was permitted twenty peremptory challenges.

Attorneys, including both prosecutors and defense counsel, are spending a lot of money these days hiring jury consultants. Gut feelings of lawyers, still common in low-cost trials, are being replaced by sociological studies in high-profile cases, because the sociological evidence is believed to be more accurate in selecting, or challenging, jurors. The purpose of these studies and analyses has nothing to do with getting at the truth and everything to do with obtaining a favorable verdict.

The media reported that the prosecutor in the *O.J. Simpson* trial paid for a mock jury to test its case before the jury was actually selected. But most communities cannot expend resources in this manner. Prescreening of jurors by wealthy defendants (as O.J. was able to do) is designed to increase the probability that the selected jurors will acquit.

Finally, voir dire is completed and challenges for cause and peremptory challenges have resulted in the final selection of a jury of twelve, with generally one to six alternate jurors. (There were ten alternate jurors selected for the *O.J. Simpson* trial because of its expected length.) The alternates hear all of the testimony and evidence in the case but do not vote to acquit or convict, or participate in the jury's deliberations, unless one or more of the original twelve jurors is disqualified, excused or becomes unavailable due to illness or other problems during the trial and must be replaced by an alternate.

So, you haven't been dismissed for cause, and no peremptory challenge has been used to disqualify you. Now you are lucky enough to be able to spend days, weeks or months serving on the jury, possibly away from your work, your home, your friends, your family. The O.J. Simpson jury was sequestered for almost nine months, probably a record. Essentially these jurors were being subjected to a gentle form of imprisonment with certain privileges not accorded to inmates. This wasn't the first time hard-working jurors may have wondered who was on trial!

And imagine the frustration a juror must feel if the defendant is not questioned, or even if a defendant takes the stand and many of the questions the juror has been required to answer are not asked, or if asked, don't have to be answered. The defendant can watch, read, see and hear anything about the case. You can't talk about it, form opinions, or review anything. The defendant isn't the one censored—you are.

Once the jury is finally seated, the trial is almost ready to begin. But there may still be pretrial motions as to what evidence can be admitted, what witnesses can be called, before the trial actually starts. Only then will the jury be called into the courtroom and the charges formally read.

Chapter 10

THE JUROR:
SHEDDING YOUR UNIQUE QUALITIES

Y ou've received your jury summons, and you are prepared to do your civic duty. When you walk into that courthouse to serve as a juror, you, like everyone else, bring with you the following:

- all of your life experiences

- your belief system

- your preferences and dislikes

- your biases

- your intuitive skills

In fact, you bring with you everything that makes you the person you are—a unique individual.

However, if you rely on any of the above to help you decide a case, you move further and further away from your primary task: to evaluate the case as an impartial juror. When you go from private citizen to juror, a change is required, a transformation from a person with deep convictions and opinions to someone who won't let those deeply held beliefs influence your deliberation. You are entitled to live by your beliefs, to encourage others to live by your beliefs. But when it comes time to decide whether someone is going to be found guilty or acquitted, you must prevent the intrusion of your own beliefs into the decision-making process.

Our system bases guilt or nonguilt solely on the evidence introduced at the trial. Your values, belief system, and life experiences are not evidence, nor are they introduced to the jury as evidence in the case. You are asked to rule on the facts and to make findings of fact. Unless you base your thinking on these guidelines, you undermine our system of justice, and you risk acquitting or convicting people because of what you think of the person, rather than what the evidence shows the person has or has not done.

As Judge Weisberg instructed the *Powell* jury:

You must decide all the questions of fact in this case from the evidence received in this trial and not from any other source. (JI-31)

Imagine the following occurred. During jury deliberations, a respectable, articulate and educated female juror says to the other members of the jury, "Let me tell you what I think happened in this case." After this person's statement, other jurors think such a version sounds plausible and agree with that version.

But the juror who convinced the others may have determined what happened because of what she would have done, or what she believes another respectable, articulate and educated person would have done in similar circumstances. She may be applying her life experiences to an uneducated, disreputable male defendant whose own life experiences are so dissimilar from hers that they could have taken place on Mars. Thus, based on extraneous factors, such as the juror's personal experience, her reaction to the kind of crime with which the defendant is charged, the arguments of counsel, or the lack of charm of the defendant, the juror substitutes an individual frame of reference explaining everything in the case in these terms. It would be wrong for any other juror to decide the case on the basis of that first juror's speculation, no matter how reasonable the first juror's theory of the case sounded, unless specific evidence in that particular case had been introduced to support the theory.

Jurors are asked not to substitute or apply their individual or even the community's beliefs, their individual or the community's value systems, or their individual experiences in order to arrive at a verdict. To do so would permit findings to be directly dependent on the particular twelve people who served on the jury.

Regardless of how worthwhile or successful a person you are or may think you are, you must understand that you are not being asked to serve because of those attributes. The fact you are successful does not make you a better juror than your neighbor who has just filed for bankruptcy. The fact you are a college graduate does not make you a better juror than someone who is a high-school dropout. The fact you are married with two nice children does not make you a better juror than someone who has been divorced three times and hasn't seen his or her kids in many years.

Of course, all of us are the sum total of our life experiences so it is impossible to divorce ourselves completely from those experiences. We want to use those experiences which have taught us to analyze, to think objectively, to reason. Your level of education, your common sense, your ability to concentrate, may be very useful because they help you understand more quickly and perhaps more completely what is being presented in the courtroom. However, what you think of the person because of whom he or she is, where he or she comes from, or how he or she looks does not help you resolve the factual issues you need to resolve as judges of the facts.

If evidence is not presented, you cannot incorporate any deeply held beliefs into your resolution of the case as a substitute for the presentation of evidence.

In a criminal case, it is the juror's duty to make a finding of not guilty if the prosecution has not met its evidentiary burden even when the juror feels that the defendant probably committed the crime.

Without using the specific phrase "life experiences," Judge Weisberg told the Rodney King beating trial jurors that they must not use the following emotions in performing their duty to decide whether any of the defendants was guilty or not guilty:

...You must not be influenced by pity for a defendant or by prejudice against him. (JI-9)

...You must not be biased against the defendant because he has been arrested for this offense, charged with a crime or brought to trial. None of these circumstances is evidence of guilt and you must not infer or assume from any or all of them that he is more likely to be guilty than innocent. (JI-10)

...You must not be influenced by mere sentiment, (JI-11)

conjecture, (JI-12)

sympathy, (JI-13)

passion, (JI-14)

prejudice, (JI-15)

public opinion (JI-16)

or public feeling. (JI-17)

At the very beginning of the *O.J. Simpson* trial, Judge Ito told the jurors the same thing.

These instructions from the judge are aimed at eliminating bias, emotion, and public pressure. With the exception of conjecture, the emotional responses are all the result of beliefs based on life experiences. The judge is telling you that you should not use those feelings of sympathy, pity, anger or antipathy to decide the outcome of the case.

Conjecture is guessing or speculating. The reason it relates to life experiences is because life experiences help determine which way someone will guess. For example, some people believe that only guilty people are arrested and charged with a crime.

Let's assume you feel that way. Assume further you feel the defendant is a dirtbag lowlife creep who probably committed the crime. That is your personal opinion. You would be willing to tell anyone so and even bet on it. But you're a juror and the prosecutor has, in your mind, failed to present sufficient evidence to show that this bum committed acts necessary to find him guilty of the particular crime. You shouldn't decide that since the defendant was arrested, and charged with the crime, and is a disgusting person, that the defendant is therefore guilty. That might be a good guess, but it would still be a guess.

Suppose the tables are turned. You like and respect the defendant and believe that the police are out to get people of the defendant's age and ethnic background. But the prosecution presents evidence which is sufficient to convict. You should vote to convict, despite your life experiences.

A juror is not judging the person charged with the crime— a juror is judging whether the prosecution has provided sufficient evidence to establish that the person committed one or more acts, and as a result, should be found guilty of committing the particular crime.

But how does one put aside biases, feelings and values?

When you first see the defendant, if you instinctively feel that this individual is either guilty or not guilty, you have a problem as a juror.

If you discount a witness's testimony because the witness happens to be Italian, and you have had bad experiences with Italians, you have a problem.

If you discredit a woman's testimony as to sexual harassment which she allegedly incurred five years ago but didn't report until now, because you know that if that happened to you, you would have reported it earlier, you have a problem.

If you assume a defendant—a police officer who works in a neighborhood where people are always screaming "police brutality"—is innocent because the police have always been helpful to you, you have a problem.

When you reject scientific evidence because it's all mumbo-jumbo, and the results don't square with your view of what must have happened, you have a problem.

If you believe the defendant, a handsome college professor, could never have been drawn to the ugly, retarded woman he allegedly sexually abused, you have a problem.

When you see the judge frequently criticize one of the attorneys and be sarcastic to one side or the other, and you believe this to be a significant factor, you have a problem.

If you believe the defendant is probably guilty because neither the defense counsel nor the judge had a verbal response when the prosecutor boldly proclaimed "Why else would the defendant have been arrested if he weren't guilty?", you have a problem.

Any time you, as a juror, instinctively know something, ask yourself how you've reached your conclusion. If the conclusion isn't based on the evidence you've seen or heard, you aren't acting impartially, you haven't shed your baggage.

Some people believe it is idealistic or naive to think people can set aside their value systems, and that impartiality can never be achieved in our jury system or anywhere else. All of us are products of our environments, and our values and particular life experiences make us who we are. Our values, they say, can't be checked at the door like a coat when we walk into a courtroom or jury room.

But the law demands this.

There are many sociological and psychological experts who say: People are who they are. Accept them with all their personal baggage, their life experiences. People will use their experience to decide the case anyway, and there is nothing anyone can do about it. That's why jury consultants are necessary. Their goal is to find jurors with certain life experiences which makes them receptive to one side or the other.

It is easy for most of us to say we are impartial because most of us do not examine ourselves, or acknowledge we are prejudiced. And so, when the judge during voir dire asks whether the prospective juror can set aside the initial view of the defendant and change this view if the evidence warrants it, most people answer "yes" and believe this is an honest answer. But can most people really do that?

Being impartial is one of the most difficult things imaginable, and not necessarily because of the subject matter of the case. The real difficulty is that jurors may not understand or recognize their own biases or preferences.

We believe that most people *can* separate their feelings and be objective and impartial and act as trial judges instruct them to act. When they enter that courtroom, regardless of who they are and where they came from or have been, we believe they are capable of becoming impartial jurors, *if they really want to.*

You can be an arch conservative or a flaming liberal in your political views. You can believe African-Americans are good or bad or that white people are superior or devils. It doesn't matter. Regardless of what you believe, the great equalizer in our system of justice is that those beliefs must not interfere with your effort to be impartial. If you let life experiences intrude into your decision-making, you really are not impartial in the way the law wants you to be. What's the point then of a jury trial? It's simpler, less time-consuming, and cheaper, to convict the bastard or acquit the nice guy, rather than go through the formalities of a predetermined trial.

We believe that most Americans want to and can perform jury duty in a responsible manner because most Americans want to be fair. However, to be fair, one must start by acknowledging that a problem exists.

No one can solve or eliminate the problem of societal racism or bias. And that is not the purpose of this book. But we are saying that jurors must consciously, continuously and vigorously strive not to use their values, biases, and life experiences in making decisions in the courtroom. Everything you as a juror need to know can be learned by listening and observing attentively, understanding what is going on in the courtroom, and applying your intelligence and analytical skills to that information.

There are no shortcuts.

For those of you who are still skeptical of either the ability to, or the desirability of, shedding the juror's life experiences at the door, consider the comments of many legal experts during the *O.J. Simpson* trial.

There was much talk about the African-American jurors' life experiences regarding the conduct of the LAPD. These jurors were expected to see the police action through their particular lenses. The commentators evidently assumed the jurors would believe allegations of a police conspiracy, and would also assume that police officers, the coroner, and forensic experts all lied in order to convict O.J. Simpson. The jurors were going to substitute their life experiences in lieu of evidence. O.J. Simpson would be acquitted because he was African-American and much of the evidence against him was gathered by incompetent or racist Los Angeles police officers.

The prevailing view was either that it was acceptable for African-American jurors to use these life experiences or, if it were unacceptable, they would use them anyway. Thus, many correctly predicted O.J. Simpson would not be convicted.

Is this acquiescence to the use of, or acceptance of the applicability of, life experiences something African-Americans in particular, or people in general, really want to be the determining factor in the American jury process? Is it acceptable for Caucasians or Asian-Americans to filter the evidence through the lens of their bad experiences with African-Americans, or to use their prejudices to judge all black people? Aren't these life experiences just as valid and important as the African-American jurors' life experiences or beliefs about the LAPD?

Consider the Rodney King beating trial in Simi Valley. The verdicts resulted in riots, deaths, arson and looting in Los Angeles. Should the jurors in Simi Valley, none of whom were black, have used their life experiences in evaluating the evidence against the four police officers? Maybe they did. Should the African-American jurors have used their experiences to determine O.J. Simpson's nonguilt? Maybe they did. If it's acceptable in one case, then it's all right in the next case.

There is a growing movement on the left and the right which argues that jurors are not bound by the evidence or the law. This movement advocates *jury nullification*. Although we will look more closely at what we consider a misguided approach to empowering jurors in Chapter 25, a brief discussion is appropriate here. Adherents of jury nullification contend, through their literature, a toll-free number, and in speeches, that the judicial system cannot and should not restrict jurors in any way in making their decisions.

In our view, this would be a great system for those in the majority, and a disaster for those in the minority. Do we really want the United States to revert to a time when a white could shoot a black before scores of witnesses and be acquitted, and a black man could look at a white woman in a way she found offensive and be convicted of attempted rape? Or will black jurors always acquit black defendants because they are black even when other blacks are victims of the crime charged? Will people who favor unpopular causes, such as the freedom riders, people who are Pro-Life or Pro-Choice, be punished because jurors can and should use their personal beliefs to decide cases?

It might seem sensible to use nullification when there's a stupid law that's being enforced. But who decides the law is stupid? Groups of twelve people at a time in hundreds of thousands of individual cases? Hopefully not!

So to those readers who believe in empowering jurors *in this way*, consider if that's what you really think is right and moral, and whether that's the system you want used to judge you, your friends, your family. We ask these critics to consider and explain how a system based on personal beliefs and prejudices leads to fairer jury verdicts and justice than a system based on an objective view of the actual evidence presented.

We do not advocate dismantling our legal system through jury nullification, or through juror elimination, or through the use of professional jurors. The American jury system can work. However, we believe that jurors need to understand the system and understand their extremely critical role in making American justice work for all persons, not just those who can buy the best legal help. Our primary concern is equal justice for all people.

Ordinary people need not be intimidated by the law. Jurors should be expected to understand their role and what they are supposed to do. We believe that they can do it, independent of education or status, as long as they can reason analytically and make the effort to judge impartially.

Chapter 11

THE JUROR'S OPTIONS

Most people realize that jurors have only three options: to vote to find the defendant guilty, to vote to find the defendant not guilty, or to agree that a verdict can't be reached. Being an impartial juror is yet another kind of option, a vote you can exercise to make our criminal-justice system work better.

If prejudices are so much a part of your existence you feel you cannot discard them, then you should not be a member of a criminal jury and you must have the courage to communicate that to the judge. Your failure to make your limitations known could result in your selection as a juror. You could do tremendous harm by finding a person guilty when that has not been proven, by acquitting a guilty person, or having a mistrial declared because of a hung jury.

Let's return now to the concept of legal guilt or legal nonguilt. From 1994 to 1996, the nation followed the case of Polly Klaas, the young girl from Petaluma, California, who was kidnapped from her home and killed. The accused and now convicted killer was the one who directed police to the girl's body. No one doubted that the defendant was guilty of the murder.

But suppose at the trial of this defendant, the prosecutor had erred and failed to present important evidence. Should members of the jury use their prior knowledge from the publicity associated with the case to overlook the prosecutor's failure to present critical evidence and find against the defendant anyway? In other words, should publicity about a case be used to decide the matter when evidence which has a direct impact on the case is not introduced?

Once again the answer is that the juror must decide the case based on the evidence presented. It is improper to use non-record evidence or information. Thus, the juror is asked to ignore and disregard something he or she "knows" in order to perform as a juror should.

You may think the result is outrageous. This is a hard concept to swallow. It significantly limits the juror and the tools he or she uses to make a decision, but it is the first building block towards impartiality, for it forces you to function in a way you personally may not like.

Judge Weisberg told the Rodney King beating trial jurors:

You must decide separately whether each of the defendants is guilty or not guilty. If you cannot agree upon a verdict as to all of the defendants, but you do agree upon a verdict as to any one or more of them, you must render a verdict as to the one or more as to whom you agree. (JI-155)

Each of the defendants is entitled to the individual judgment of each of the jurors. (JI-156)

Notice that Judge Weisberg did not tell the jurors that they had to agree one way or the other. The juror's responsibility is to render an individual judgment.

If the members of the jury all agree on one of these alternatives, the defendant will either be found guilty or will be acquitted. There are significant consequences to a jury finding of not guilty since that usually bars another prosecution for the same offense. A finding of guilty will frequently mean a loss of liberty and result in imprisonment, if not death in some states.

When we read in the paper that a verdict of guilty or not guilty cannot be reached because there is a hung jury, many people think that means the jury failed to do its job. Not so. Jurors must understand there is no obligation to agree on a verdict. Jurors are there to do their public service by rendering a decision to the best of their ability.

The reason a hung jury is important in our jury scheme is that it may indicate something significant. While it certainly shows jury members could not agree, it may also mean that the prosecutor had an inadequate case and should not have proceeded until better evidence was obtained. It shows that the evidence presented was insufficient to convince one or more jury members of the defendant's guilt or nonguilt.

A more troubling possibility is that a hung jury may indicate one or more jurors had prejudged the case and would not change that prejudgment notwithstanding the evidence presented in the case. A juror who has prejudged the case, and who refuses to consider anything new, undermines our system of justice.

The public must understand that a hung jury does not necessarily mean that a particular jury or juror was deficient in any respect. In fact, it might mean that one or more jurors evaluated the evidence properly while the rest of the jury did not. If the holdouts were correct but went along with the crowd, injustice might have resulted.

Remember, the result of a hung jury is to continue the defendant's status as not guilty in the eyes of the law. The defendant is presumed innocent until proven guilty. The jury instruction given by Judge Weisberg was as follows:

A defendant in a criminal action is presumed to be innocent until the contrary is proved, and in case of a reasonable doubt whether his guilt is satisfactorily shown, he is entitled to a verdict of not guilty. (JI-110)

When a judge orders a jury back to the jury room to work harder to try to reach a verdict, a juror must understand that he or she *is not required* to come to a decision with which all members agree, even though the judge may exert pressure to reach an agreement. For the judge, it often doesn't matter how the jury decides, as long as the jury can agree. Regardless of what the judge wants, no judge can force agreement to something a juror does not believe and no juror should be coerced by the judge.

If you are a juror in a sensational murder trial and the jury cannot agree on a verdict because you believe the evidence does not establish guilt, the municipality will likely, at tremendous taxpayer expense, retry the defendant on the same charges. Even in this situation and even though you are also a taxpayer, you must put your convictions first and maintain your integrity if you remain unconvinced of the defendant's guilt after all of the discussion in the jury room.

Jurors cannot allow administrative convenience or taxpayer expense to become a consideration in their deliberations. The rights of any defendant must outweigh these concerns if our jury system is to preserve any of the credibility it still enjoys.

When insufficient evidence is presented to convict someone of a crime you should vote not guilty. Likewise, when sufficient evidence is introduced to establish that the defendant committed the crime, you should vote to find the defendant guilty. Impartiality requires making those tough decisions.

Clearly, serving on a criminal jury will be an experience that will not be easy to forget. To serve in the manner the law requires will require much introspection by the juror at all stages. But no one said being a juror was easy.

To summarize, the good juror is someone who acknowledges his or her unique nature with all of its strengths and weaknesses. Prejudices are confronted and acknowledged. There exists a conscious and persistent awareness that biases, either pro or con, have no place in jury work.

The good juror is a fact-finder. The outcome of the case is based solely on the evidence actually introduced at trial.

The question remains:

Can you do all that is expected of you?

PART IV

EVIDENCE:

WHAT
YOU
NEED
TO
KNOW

CHAPTER 12

FOCUSING ON EVIDENCE

Only a minuscule number of jurors are lawyers or law students. Yet our system of justice expects jurors not only to understand important evidentiary concepts in the law, but also any evidence introduced during the trial. Regardless of complexity or of its scientific nature, jurors are supposed to be able to evaluate evidence as it is presented during the course of the trial and then to consider that evidence and the pertinent law in reaching a verdict.

At a typical trial, jurors are told what evidence is *after* all the evidence has been entered. In most courtrooms, jurors are given only an inkling of what they are supposed to use to decide the case prior to the conclusion of the trial, when the judge reads the instructions to the jury. Thus, most jurors will go through the entire trial not really knowing *how* they are supposed to evaluate the evidence in the case.

Everybody else in the courtroom—the judge, the prosecutor, the defense counsel and the defendant—know what is happening. Yet the persons who will decide the facts in the case—the jurors—are deliberately kept in the dark.

Compare this situation to a trial by a judge when the parties have waived their right to a jury trial. There are no limitations placed on the judge, whose legal knowledge is used to evaluate the evidence as it is presented. He or she is able to follow and understand what the lawyers are doing.

Contrast this with what the system asks from jurors. Jurors are expressly told:

You must not discuss this case with any other person, except a fellow juror, and you must not discuss the case with a fellow juror until the case is submitted to you for your decision and only when all the jurors are present in the jury room. (JI-34)

Jurors are not told what is happening as the trial unfolds. They aren't given the tools—the jury instructions which explain what they are supposed to do and the reason for certain courtroom procedures—until the end of the trial.

What our system *knowingly* guarantees is that through no fault of their own, the jurors are not equipped to do what they are asked to do: to judge.

We want to examine important evidentiary aspects of a trial from the juror's standpoint, not at the conclusion of the trial, but as the trial unfolds. We believe it is important for jurors to understand what is going on as it is happening, as evidence is being presented which must be evaluated, as jurors observe the demeanor of the people in the courtroom, listen to the experts, and consider the attorneys' argument. Our goal is to lay a foundation that will work for any trial in any state. Once a foundation is established, jurors will be able to put themselves within that framework. Jurors will use this knowledge to put the pieces of the puzzle together as they sift through and study all of the different images that have been presented as the evidence in the case.

It sounds impressive to say jurors are the judges of the facts. But which facts should they be judging? What evidence is crucial to a correct verdict, and what evidence can be disregarded? Jurors need to concentrate on the facts which are crucial in order to make the ultimate decision as to guilt or nonguilt. To do so, they need to know what key facts are at issue in the case, so they can focus on those facts. Those facts are the "relevant evidence," defined in California as follows:

"Evidence, including evidence relevant to the credibility of a witness or hearsay declarant, having any tendency in reason to prove or disprove any disputed fact that is of consequence to the determination of the action." [23]

To understand the concept of relevance, you must consider the four parts of the definition.

1. Evidence, as noted earlier, "means testimony, writings, material objects or other things presented to the senses that are offered to prove the existence or nonexistence of a fact."

2. As you see, the relevance definition uses the word relevant itself. Such a definition isn't helpful. Why not say: "including evidence *used in determining* the credibility of a witness or hearsay declarant."

3. The phrase "having any tendency in reason to prove or disprove any disputed fact" indicates one should use reason, rather than gut feelings or emotion. But what kind of reason can you use? You can't make an investigation of the facts or law. You can't consider facts as to which there is no evidence. You can't visit the scene, or conduct experiments or consult reference works. Why can't you use those kinds of reason?

4. The last phrase "that is of consequence to the determination of the action" is the most crucial, for it tells us that if it's not useful in determining the result, it is not relevant. And if it's not relevant, it's irrelevant and you don't have to worry about judging that fact.

An illustration of facts "of consequence to the determination of the action" can be seen from the following excerpt from Judge Weisberg's instructions describing one of the crimes the four defendants in *People v. Powell et al* were charged with:

...Every person who commits assault upon the person of another with a deadly weapon or instrument or by means of force likely to produce great bodily injury is guilty of the crime of violation of 245 (A)(1) of the Penal Code. (JI-125)

In order to prove such crime, each of the following elements must be proved:
One, a person was assaulted; and
Two, the assault was committed with a deadly weapon or instrument or by means of force likely to produce great bodily injury. (JI-126)

So now the juror knows the two relevant facts that have to be proved in order to find someone guilty of this particular crime. If these facts do not exist, the person is not guilty. If these two facts are found to exist, then the person is guilty if the evidence meets the beyond a reasonable doubt test. But as a sitting juror you might wonder what the phrase a "deadly weapon or instrument" means as well as "by means of force likely to produce great bodily injury." Certainly you would need to understand these terms in order to make a correct finding.

In an ideal judicial system, only relevant evidence would be presented to the jury, so all evidence would be significant. Unfortunately, that doesn't happen in the real world.

Irrelevant evidence may be admitted for several reasons. The evidence looked as if it would be relevant, but wasn't. For example: A witness testifies that the defendant was one block from the murder scene at 10:00 P.M. The evidence is expected to show the murder occurred at 10:05 P.M. In fact, the evidence later establishes that the murder was committed at 1:00 A.M. The witness's testimony is no longer relevant to place the defendant at the scene of the murder.

Or perhaps evidence presented was never relevant, but opposing counsel did not object. Or the judge erroneously admitted the irrelevant evidence over objections. Examples of irrelevant evidence admitted due to error of counsel or the judge occur regularly. It is not up to the juror to worry about whether the system has failed. But if you know which facts must be proven to show that the crime charged was committed, you will spend little time thinking about the irrelevant evidence.

Now let's look at how evidence is actually introduced in a courtroom. Frequently, what you might think would only take a brief period of time will be protracted over hours or days. The unfortunate result for the juror can be unbelievable boredom, and the concomitant problem of attempting to stay alert and focused on that which is relevant.

Lawyers can't cut to the chase to speed up the process. They can't start showing the Rodney King beating videotape or tell the jury, in easily understandable language, what the testimonial evidence is going to be. They must go through the laborious task of eliciting testimony by questioning witnesses.

Before the evidence (in *People v. Powell et al*, the videotape) can be presented to the jury, there must be a foundation laid; it must be established that the videotape is authentic, and that it is trustworthy evidence. Thus, George Holliday was the first witness for the prosecution because he filmed the Rodney King beating. Since the tape was the central piece of evidence in the case, Mr. Holliday's testimony was necessary to show: the videotape which would be played was the one he made, when he made the tape, and how he made it.

There is a great deal of evidence introduced which goes to points that have to be established in order to allow other relevant evidence to be introduced. That is called foundation evidence. Foundation evidence really has little or nothing to do with the case except as a lead-in for the important evidence.

Another example from *People v. Powell et al* occurred when the prosecution wanted to introduce a statement allegedly made by Defendant Powell over the police communication system and recorded onto a tape by that system. Much time was spent during the trial explaining how that system worked, how tapes were recorded, numbered and dated to lay the foundation so that the few words spoken by Officer Powell could be introduced. The prosecution simply wanted the jury to hear Officer Powell say "Right out of Gorillas in the Mist" when describing an African-American suspect.

If the lawyer could prepare a statement and just tell the jury that this is what a particular witness will say, and then have that person concur, it would significantly reduce trial time. Instead, the lawyer must obtain testimonial evidence by asking the witness questions phrased so that no guidance is given to the witness; and the witness must supply his or her own words to answer the question. Furthermore, lawyers cannot, in most instances, ask witnesses they call to the stand any "*leading questions*".[24] These are questions drafted so that the lawyer puts words—the desired answer—into the question being asked. An example might be: "Officer Singer, isn't it true you saw Defendant Powell strike Rodney King with six full power blows?"

Even though the lawyer wants Officer Singer to present evidence to the jury that Officer Powell did strike Rodney King with six full power blows, and believes that Officer Singer would so testify, the lawyer calling Officer Singer has to ask a series of questions in order to get that evidence into the record.

Sample questions to accomplish this might go like this:

Question: Officer Singer, when you got out of your car, what did you see?
(Witness answers)

Question: Officer Singer, describe the officers you saw?
(Witness answers)

Question: Officer Singer, what was Mr. Powell doing?
(Witness answers)

Question: Officer Singer, would you describe how Officer Powell was striking Mr. King?
(Witness answers that Powell used "full power" strokes)

Question: Officer Singer, could you please show and demonstrate what you mean by full power strokes?
(Witness answers by physically demonstrating movements)

Question: Officer Singer, could you describe in
             detail for the record what you just
             demonstrated?
             (Witness answers with detailed
             description of each movement.)

Question: Officer Singer, were these strokes all
             the same, or were some different?
             (Witness answers)

Question: Officer Singer, how many times did
             you see Officer Powell strike Mr.
             King?
             (Witness answers)

While this process ensures that the answer is in the witness's own words, it takes a long time to elicit even the simplest facts by asking question after question.

Now back to the question of what relevant evidence a juror should use to determine guilt or nonguilt. Not all relevant evidence is of the same value.

Some relevant evidence is more significant than other such evidence. The term **probative value** describes this situation. Ask yourself: "Does the offered evidence tend to prove that the fact occurred or did not occur?" Does it prove what the lawyers are trying to show?

A term that jurors may hear frequently during the trial is **weight of the evidence**. The judge and lawyers will remind jurors that it is they who will decide the weight to be given to the item of evidence. Jurors are told that they are the sole judge of the weight of the evidence. In his instructions, Judge Weisberg told the jurors:

Both the people and the defendant have a right to expect that you will conscientiously consider and weigh the evidence, apply the law and reach a just verdict regardless of the consequences. (JI-18)

Judge Weisberg told the jurors of their responsibility and authority to weigh the evidence as it pertained to different types of evidence introduced at trial. The following weight instructions have to do with determining credibility and are similar to the additional eleven instructions that dealt with the jurors' weighing of the evidence:[25]

> **Every person who testifies under oath is a witness. You are the sole judges of the believability of a witness and the weight to be given the testimony of each witness. (JI-60)**

> **You should give the testimony of a single witness whatever weight you think it deserves; however, testimony by one witness, which you believe concerning any fact, is sufficient for the proof of that fact. You should carefully review all the evidence upon which the proof of such fact depends. (JI-83)**

Many people associate the term weight with a quantity-type consideration: the more evidence introduced, the more weight given to the evidence. Thus, if the prosecution has twelve witnesses who will testify in support of its case while the defense only has two, then the prosecution's evidence has more weight *and is therefore better.* That analysis is incorrect. Likewise, the belief that if the prosecution's case is based on a single document which is four pages long while the defense introduces fifty pounds of documents, the defense evidence should be given more weight is false.

Weight refers to the importance of the evidence and its persuasiveness. It has solely to do with *quality* as opposed to *quantity.* Thus, jurors may give more weight to the testimony of one witness than twenty witnesses; one document may be more important and be given more weight than a hundred documents.

For example, suppose there are two witnesses who testify at a trial. One witness, a homeless person, testifies that he saw the man who stabbed the woman. It was daylight. The witness had a good look at the man's face because the man ran right into him as the man was trying to leave the scene of the crime.

The other witness, a college professor, believes that she can identify the same man as the suspect, but she admits she only saw the man running away and never saw his face. She notes that the suspect is about the same height as the man she saw running away. Both witnesses offer relevant evidence, with probative value. The jurors may believe both witnesses are telling the truth. However, much more weight (and importance) should be given to the witness (the homeless individual) who saw the crime committed, and the suspect's face, than to the professor who only saw the back of a person who was running away from the scene of the crime.

When a juror decides that certain evidence is entitled to more weight than other evidence, the juror must also decide how convincing the evidence is. There may be a slight possibility that a particular fact is true, or it may probably be true, or it is very likely to be the case, or it is almost definite, or it shows exactly that something occurred. The stronger the belief that the evidence shows something actually occurred, the heavier the weight of that particular item of evidence. Jurors must constantly be focusing and refocusing on the evidence that is introduced, comparing the weight to be given to some evidence in contrast with other evidence.

Weight and relevance are inextricably tied together. The jury may give great weight to certain evidence at one point in the trial, such as the testimony of witnesses that the officers hit Rodney King with their batons. But, in the end, that evidence was not relevant because Officers Powell and Wind did not contest the fact that they struck Rodney King—they contested whether they were guilty of unlawfully beating him. The weight of the evidence is only important when it is applied to evidence which is relevant to the outcome of the case.

The *O.J. Simpson* jury was presented with evidence that Detective Mark Fuhrman was a racist. They evidently concluded that he was a liar, and discredited his testimony. But if there had been overwhelming evidence that he could not have tampered with the evidence, Detective Fuhrman's lack of credibility should not have harmed the prosecution case, because it would not have been relevant to the ultimate determination of guilt.

Mark Fuhrman denied he ever used the term "nigger." Since he apparently used that term, he lied on the stand. That could have led the jury to disregard his other testimony (see (JI-73) discussed in Chapter 15). But it still would not establish that Mark Fuhrman planted all the incriminating evidence unless he could have tampered with each bloodstain, shoemark, or glove. There may be motive, but there must also be opportunity. Jurors should give no weight to evidence (Detective Fuhrman's racism) unless it is linked to relevant facts. Otherwise, it's simply a ploy to confuse and mislead the jurors.

Conversely, suppose the evidence had established that the detective had no racist tendencies. If the evidence also established that the detective could have planted evidence, this could be directly relevant to a determination that O.J. was not guilty. Opportunity would have been established. The defense would still have to establish motive (e.g., the detective hated O.J. Simpson, the person), or that the glove, bloodstains, or shoemark could have been contaminated by improper handling.

To understand evidence and to focus on relevant evidence and give it the weight it deserves, it helps to know what is *not* evidence. It was not until the end of the trial that Judge Weisberg told the jurors:

> **Statements made by the attorneys during the trial are not evidence... (JI-23)**

> **If an objection was sustained to a question, do not guess what the answer might have been. (JI-24)**

> **Do not speculate as to the reason for the objection. (JI-25)**

> **Do not assume to be true any insinuation suggested by a question asked a witness. A question is not evidence and may be considered only as it enables you to understand the answer. (JI-26)**

> **Do not consider for any purpose any offer of evidence that was rejected or any evidence that was stricken by the court. Treat it as though you had never heard of it. (JI-27)**

Therefore, if jurors in *People v. Powell* had assumed that a question or insinuation was evidence or contained evidence because of its particular words, they had erred. If it had been rejected or stricken, it wasn't evidence. But by the time they learned this, they might have already concluded that a fact had been proved, and the jurors might not remember how they had come to that conclusion.

And so the juror's focus becomes clearer. First, you need to know the key facts that must be determined—the elements of the crime that must be proved by the prosecution if a conviction is going to result. That is the starting point. Then relevant evidence is introduced and you evaluate it to determine whether it helps prove or disprove those facts. You determine how much weight to give to the relevant evidence.

As the trial proceeds, keep in mind those things that are not evidence. An easy task? Far from it. You need all the assistance you can get, as early in the trial as you can get that help. Then you can sharpen your focus during the trial, rather than trying to recall all that was presented and refocus to see what is evidence, what is relevant, and how much weight to give the evidence.

Chapter 13

Direct Versus Circumstantial Evidence: Is One Better?

N ow let's look at the two different kinds of evidence—direct and circumstantial—and see how they affect the weight of the evidence and the predicament each presents to jurors.

At the conclusion of the *Powell* trial, Judge Weisberg told the jurors to consider the following:

A fact is something proved directly or circumstantially by the evidence or by stipulation. (JI-4)

Evidence is either direct or circumstantial. (JI-37)

Direct evidence is evidence that directly proves a fact without the necessity of an inference. It is evidence which, by itself, if found to be true, establishes that fact. (JI-38)

An example of direct evidence in the Rodney King beating trial would be the videotape itself in the following imagined scenario. The videotape is admitted into evidence. Both parties agree that it accurately depicts what happened. The parties also agree that if an officer struck Mr. King in the face, he used unlawful force. If the videotape showed Officer Powell using the baton to strike Mr. King in the face, that segment of the tape would be direct evidence that Mr. King was struck in the face.

Therefore, in our hypothetical example, Officer Powell would be convicted. Once the fact that he struck Mr. King is established, there is nothing more which needs to be proved, nor any inference which needs to be drawn.

The prosecutor in the O.J. Simpson case needed to prove that O.J. killed his ex-wife and her friend. Direct evidence would have been the testimony of a person who actually witnessed the murder. If this person's testimony were believed, the jurors would not have to make any assumptions nor draw any inferences about what happened. They could rely on the testimony, find that the testimony was evidence that O.J. Simpson was the murderer, and on the basis of that evidence, convict him.

In both of these examples, direct evidence could establish the facts that had to be proved. Officer Powell did strike Rodney King in the face, and O.J. Simpson did commit the murders, in our hypothetical scenarios.

But what if, in the Rodney King beating trial, the viewer believed the direct evidence of the videotape established that Defendant Powell struck Rodney King in the head. Yet the medical evidence showed that there was no injury to the face. What then? Or, the person who testified that O.J. committed the crime wasn't wearing his glasses and without them is considered legally blind. What then?

The popular belief seems to be that direct evidence is better than circumstantial evidence. When we think of direct evidence, we frequently think of testimony based on an eyewitness identification. If we believe the eyewitness, there is no need for any circumstantial evidence. The proof is so good. But is the perception accurate?

From a prosecutor's or judge's standpoint, circumstantial evidence is as good as direct evidence, and if the case is based on circumstantial evidence there is no reason why a conviction cannot result. But if you listen to defense counsel or the media, circumstantial evidence is inferior, less worthy evidence, and if that's all the prosecution has, an acquittal should result.

There are numerous problems, in determining the weight to be given eyewitness identification testimony. Here is a partial list of the factors, in addition to the believability of the eyewitness, which bear on the accuracy of the witness's identification :[26]

- The opportunity of the witness to observe the alleged criminal act and the perpetrator of the act

- The stress, if any, to which the witness was subjected at the time of the observation

- The witness's ability, following the observation, to provide a description of the perpetrator of the act

- The extent to which the defendant either fits or does not fit the description of the perpetrator previously given by the witness

- The cross-racial or ethnic nature of the identification

- The witness's capacity to make an identification

- Whether the witness was able to identify the alleged perpetrator in a photographic or physical lineup

- The period of time between the alleged criminal act and the witness's identification

- Whether the witness had prior contacts with the alleged perpetrator

- The extent to which the witness is either certain or uncertain of the identification

- Whether the witness's identification is in fact the product of his or her own recollection

As you can see, even direct eyewitness evidence has its limitations because of the many factors that can mitigate its alleged persuasiveness.

Circumstantial evidence is not direct evidence. There are no eyewitnesses to the crime. There is no direct evidence that would, if believed, establish in and of itself, the key fact that needs to be proved. As Judge Weisberg told the jurors:

Circumstantial evidence is evidence that, if found to be true, proves a fact from which an inference of the existence of another fact may be drawn. (JI-39)

The word inference is then defined by Judge Weisberg:

An inference is a deduction of fact that may logically and reasonably be drawn from another fact or group of facts established by the evidence. (JI-40)

As long as everyone understands what it means to say that a "deduction of fact" can "logically and reasonably be drawn" from one or more facts "established by the evidence," there's no problem.

We say "too confusing." We suggest you think of circumstantial evidence as similar to the web a spider constructs. To make the strongest case possible when direct evidence is not available or needs to be supplemented, the prosecution wants to weave the strongest web of circumstances which tends to establish that a fact occurred or did not occur. The web becomes stronger with each relevant circumstance. The tighter and more secure the web, the harder it is for the defendant (the prey) to fall through it and escape its grasp. The goal is to build such a strong web that the defendant can't escape its snares.

Common examples of circumstantial evidence include fingerprints, testimony as to the whereabouts of the defendant at a particular time, DNA, blood tests, ballistics. This evidence is used to *narrow the range of possibilities* as to who could have committed the act in question, the crime with which the defendant is charged.

If no one sees a killing, but the prosecution can establish that the defendant was at the scene of the crime about the time of the crime, that the defendant's gun was used to commit the killing, that the defendant's fingerprints were on the gun, and that the defendant's hand showed traces of gunpowder, a great many circumstances have been introduced which *tend to* prove that the defendant killed the victim. If no one can establish where the defendant was at the time, and his fingerprints are not on the gun, the circumstantial evidence is less compelling. More guesswork is involved so even though the defendant may have killed the person, the jury may not be convinced by the evidence.

Evidence may be both direct and circumstantial regarding the same act. If the charge is battery, which requires only that one person strikes another, an eyewitness who sees the defendant strike the victim with a brick can give direct testimonial evidence as to that charge. But if the charge is attempted murder, which requires the jury to determine that when the defendant struck, he intended to kill the person, the jury must infer from the facts presented that the defendant had the required intent. The evidence that the defendant struck the victim is circumstantial as to the defendant's intent. The strike itself does not establish that the defendant intended to kill the victim. Additional circumstances are needed.

To compare circumstantial versus direct evidence, let's review what jurors in the Rodney King beating trial were told by Judge Weisberg:

Both direct evidence and circumstantial evidence are acceptable as a means of proof. Neither is entitled to any greater weight than the other. (JI-42)

The following are hypothetical scenarios which help explain circumstantial evidence. The charge against Officer Powell is using unnecessary force in effecting an arrest. The prosecution must prove that Officer Powell struck Rodney King in the face with a baton. Assume no video of Rodney King being beaten exists. Suppose the evidence is:

- Witnesses testify that they saw Officer Powell use "full power body strikes." His baton hit Mr. King. They did not see exactly where the blows landed. From their vantage points, it looked as if the blows struck Rodney King in the shoulder area or above.

- They testify that Mr. King's head snapped back as if he were hit in the face. There is photographic evidence showing Rodney King's face to be black-and-blue. An expert in "use-of-force" testifies that there was serious physical injury to the face, consistent with several powerful baton strikes to the face. Photographs of Rodney King taken several hours before the arrest show no injury to the face.

- Medical evidence from X-rays, and testimony from the treating physician and from a physician expert in dealing with head injuries establish that Mr. King's face was fractured.

Assume further there is no eyewitness who can testify that Officer Powell struck Mr. King in the face. However, based on the above, the prosecution has introduced evidence that shows:

1. Photographs show no injury to Mr. King's face hours earlier;

2. Testimony of witnesses that Defendant Powell struck Rodney King in the shoulder area and above;

3. X-ray evidence showing a fracture of the face;

4. Testimony of a use-of-force expert saying that the baton strike could account for the injury;

5. Medical evidence and testimony of the physicians which establish there was serious injury to the face;

6. The lack of any other evidence which would account for the injuries.

Thus, in our hypothetical, the circumstantial evidence should be sufficient for the jury to conclude that Officer Powell struck Rodney King in the face, even though there is no direct evidence of that fact.

Here's another hypothetical: The charge against O.J. Simpson is murder of two persons.

- Suppose a witness testifies that she saw O.J. Simpson running down the street outside his home at 10:50 P.M. on June 12, 1994.

This circumstance may link O.J. Simpson to the murder, but without other evidence, this fact alone falls far short of establishing that O.J. Simpson killed those two persons.

- Suppose in addition to the witness above, another witness testifies that he saw O.J. Simpson running down Bundy Avenue outside Nicole Brown Simpson's home at 10:40 P.M. on June 12, 1994.

- Suppose a third witness testifies that she saw O.J. Simpson running down Bundy Avenue outside Nicole Brown Simpson's home at 10:40 P.M. on June 12, 1994. O.J. was holding what appeared to be a long, sharp instrument that had red splotches on it.

Combined with the prior testimony, are there now enough circumstances to convict?

- Suppose a fourth witness testifies that he saw O.J. Simpson throw a large red-stained metal instrument into the sewer just before O.J. got into his van and drove away. The police retrieved a large knife from that sewer two days later. The witness identifies the knife as the instrument he saw on June 12th.

Are all these circumstances sufficient to establish O.J.'s guilt beyond a reasonable doubt? No, not even at this point. The web is tightening, but the evidence still doesn't establish that the red stain was blood, or more specifically, that it was the blood of either of the victims or when the murders occurred.

- Suppose the police now examine the knife and after multiple and sophisticated DNA tests report that the blood on the knife matches the blood of Ron Goldman and Nicole Brown Simpson. There are fingerprints on the knife that match O.J. Simpson's. There is medical evidence that the victims died between 10:00 P.M. and 11:00 P.M.

- Suppose there is evidence that O.J. Simpson's hair was found on the clothing of the victims.

Now is there enough evidence to convict, even absent any direct evidence that he committed the murders? We think so. The time element has been established, and there is forensic evidence in terms of fingerprints, blood and hair samples which tie O.J. to the murders.

So despite all of the public denigration of circumstantial evidence by O.J. Simpson's lawyers, by the media, and by his friends, if there had been enough circumstantial evidence, the jury could legitimately have used it to convict him.

Circumstantial evidence consists of proven facts which do not independently establish the ultimate fact, (i.e., that the defendant committed the crime charged). These proven facts must fit together to establish another fact (or prove the nonexistence of a fact). The facts are like pieces of a puzzle. If they can be put together to form a reasonable and logical picture, the jury may properly infer that the picture is accurate and the puzzle complete. The completion of the puzzle is the necessary step in establishing that the fact has been established. In the above two examples, the juror would be drawing an inference that Officer Powell struck Rodney King in the face and that O.J. Simpson committed the act of murder.

It is not always true that in order for circumstantial evidence to support a finding, there must be many circumstances which are established. Like the concept of weight of the evidence, it may only take one circumstance. For instance, suppose the fact that needs to be proven is that the defendant raped a woman. DNA test results show that he could not have been the person who committed the crime. The circumstantial evidence of the DNA test result may by itself cause the defendant to be acquitted, even when there is eyewitness testimony (direct evidence) that the defendant committed the rape.

Circumstantial evidence is often the only evidence. And it may be far more compelling and far more convincing than direct evidence.

CHAPTER 14

THE ELUSIVE CONCEPT OF INFERENCES: CAN YOU GUESS?

Many people—including judges, lawyers and jurors—believe that once some evidence—a circumstance—has been introduced, they are permitted by the law to draw an inference and to use it in making their decision. The problem with inferences is that there must be a certain threshold—a minimum amount of evidence—that is introduced to the jury before an inference can be drawn. If you recall, Judge Weisberg defined an inference as:

"An inference is a deduction of fact that may logically and reasonably be drawn from another fact or group of facts found or otherwise established in the action."

Thus, there are three important limitations:

The drawn fact *must be logical*;

The drawn fact *must be reasonable*;

The drawn fact *must be based on facts established at trial*.

Let's first examine an improper inference. Make the assumption that the only evidence in the *O.J. Simpson* trial was testimony that O.J. Simpson beat his wife and the testimony of Ron Shipp, who reported that O.J. said he had dreamt of killing Nicole Brown. Could one legitimately infer that O.J. Simpson had committed murder?

You could argue that circumstantial evidence was introduced from which you are drawing an inference that O.J. Simpson committed the crime. But is the evidence of beating a wife, and of O.J.'s dream of killing Nicole, sufficiently compelling so that it is reasonable and logical to support a deduction that O.J. killed his former wife?

Even if all your life experiences indicate that wife-beaters and people who fantasize about killing their spouse are highly likely to do so, the answer is no. You may think your analysis is logical and reasonable, but it is not based on facts introduced at trial which establish that your individual life experiences are true as they apply to this particular case.

There are no scientific or psychological studies which have been presented to show that if a husband beats his wife and dreams of killing her, there is an extremely high probability he will kill her. So you are really guessing, speculating, conjecturing. You *may* be right if you guess from the two facts you have that O.J. is guilty, but you are not inferring.

False inferences based on life experiences are not uncommon in our courtrooms. An example occurred when the police officer who telephoned O.J. Simpson about his ex-wife's death relayed that conversation on the witness stand. When examined by the prosecutor, the officer said that O.J. Simpson was very upset upon hearing the news, but he did not ask questions such as: "How was she killed?", "Where was she killed?", "Who killed her?", or "Are my children okay?"

For an entire evening, everyone drew "inferences" from O.J. Simpson's failure to ask these questions. Many people evaluated this lack of inquiry based on their life experiences and their *untested* belief that if they were placed in his situation, they would have responded in a certain way. Since O.J. did not ask certain questions, these individuals inferred that O.J. must have known all about the murder. And if he knew about the murder and hadn't reported it, you could infer that he was the murderer. Had the prosecution selected twelve jurors with those particular life experiences, the jury might have inferred a whole set of actions from their life experiences, and thus have concluded that O.J. Simpson committed the crime.

Suppose there were some people on the jury whose life experiences had actually put them in a similar situation. From their own experience they might know that the shock of being told that a loved one had been killed could cause a person to become totally distraught. The bereaved might not think straight, might not ask the logical, reasonable questions an uninvolved spectator would have asked. O.J. Simpson's failure to ask any of the expected questions would be consistent with their experience of an innocent person's reaction. Would it then be appropriate for them to infer that he did not commit the crime?

You can see from these examples the risk inherent in jurors' using life experiences to come to their decision rather than relying on the evidence in the case. Remember, when it is possible for sitting jurors to consider the same evidence and come to opposite conclusions, they are simply not drawing an inference. They are guessing.

It would have been different if O.J. Simpson had said to the police officer who told him of his ex-wife's death: "It must be horrible to have your throat cut." You could legitimately infer from this statement that O.J. Simpson knew his ex-wife had her throat cut, even though he didn't specifically say so. Since the police had not revealed the details of her death, he had to have obtained that knowledge in some other way. But you could still not legitimately infer that O.J. Simpson killed his wife. He might have heard of the throat slitting from someone else, or he might have seen the body at the scene of the crime, panicked and run away.

If there are two reasonable and logical interpretations of the evidence, and one interpretation supports guilt and the other supports nonguilt, the law, set out below, tells the juror to select the one which establishes nonguilt:

Also, if the circumstantial evidence as to any particular count is susceptible of two reasonable interpretations, one of which points to the defendant's guilt and the other to his innocence, you must adopt that interpretation which points to the defendant's innocence and reject that interpretation which points to his guilt. (JI-45)

The law tells us that if we are going to guess when we should be inferring, guess in favor of the defendant.

In conclusion, the law says to each juror: Don't draw an inference unless it's reasonable, logical, and supported by facts in the case. And even if the inference you've drawn seems to you to meet those three tests, reject that inference if there is another inference you could have drawn which is also reasonable, logical and factually supported when the second inference favors the defendant.

Chapter 15

CREDIBILITY:
WHO'S TELLING THE TRUTH?

The real issue in determining credibility is *why you believe a witness is telling the truth or not telling the truth* when the witness testifies under oath in court.

Believability, or credibility, goes to the very heart of the weight the evidence should be given. But how do you determine when to give the testimony of one witness more weight than the testimony of another? Or give the testimony of one witness more weight than the testimony of a larger number of witnesses on the other side? How do you figure out which scientific test or report is correct, which expert should be believed? Here are some of the factors that cause many of us to disbelieve someone:

- The witness is *being evasive* in his or her answers. The answers are not on point, detour to other subjects, etc.

- The witness's testimony today is *inconsistent* with prior testimony in a courtroom on this day or on a different day, or when compared to statements made by the witness out of the courtroom in reports.

- The witness *cannot remember* what happened. Facts that we think should be remembered cannot be recalled. We know that we would have remembered these facts.

- The witness's testimony is *self-serving*, that is, in the witness's interest.

- The witness is *nervous* on the witness stand—stutters, shakes, repeats things, has difficulty understanding and communicating.

- The witness uses *inappropriate language* in the courtroom setting, *has outbursts of anger*, and does not act the way one normally would or should in a courtroom.

- The witness *never looks into the face* of the person asking the questions, and looks away when giving a direct answer to a question.

- The witness *has no personal knowledge* of what happened.

- The witness *appears to make up answers* as the questioning goes along.

- The witness *seems to have all the answers* even before the questions are asked, and seems prepped with the answers and responds in an artificial and insincere manner.

- The witness *could not have observed the facts* testified to because of a lack of physical capacity, e.g., the witness is blind, or has poor vision and was not wearing glasses, or is hearing-impaired and was not wearing his hearing aid.

- The witness's *story is improbable*.

- The witness *is very dirty, smells* and is otherwise repugnant.

- The witness *is a felon* or a lawbreaker, or simply not an upstanding member of the community.

- The witness *gets defensive* when questioned.

And now some of the factors that cause many of us to believe someone is telling the truth:

- The witness *seems like an honorable person.* The person has a good background, is educated, married, a local high-school team coach, and a member of charitable organizations.

- The witness's *testimony is consistent* with our own frame of reference, experiences and common sense.

- The witness *has no known reason to lie.*

- The witness *is clean-cut, shows respect* and is very polite.

- The witness *thinks carefully before responding* to each question indicating that no coaching has occurred.

- The witness *is calm and not agitated* in delivery, and does not get defensive when asked questions, even sensitive ones.

- The witness *looks directly into the questioner's eyes,* be it the judge or any of the lawyers.

- The witness *responds promptly* to the questions. Answers are direct, sincere, and to the point.

- The witness *acknowledges mistakes.*

- The witness *gives detailed responses.*

- The witness *is a member of our church,* sex, *or ethnic background.*

- There is *no evidence to indicate any inconsistency* between what the person is testifying to in the trial and what that person previously said.

- There is *additional evidence in the case to corroborate* what the witness says.

Now pretend you are the person testifying, rather than the person evaluating. What happens if you are telling the truth but a juror does not believe you? The disbelief stems from the juror's feelings about the kind of person you are, where you are from, your mannerisms, language or appearance. How do you feel about being judged based on the juror's gut feelings?

The question of how much power you as a juror have in determining credibility was answered by Judge Weisberg in the *People v. Powell et al* when he advised the jury:

> **Every person who testifies under oath is a witness. You are the sole judges of the believability of a witness and the weight to be given the testimony of each witness. (JI-60)**

Whenever someone is the sole judge of anything, that represents a tremendous amount of power. No one except you need know how you made your determination. But does being the sole judge mean you have unlimited authority to do anything?

The law provides a guide as to what criteria the State would like a juror to use. Judge Weisberg uses the California standard[27] in his instructions to the *Powell* jury.

> **In determining the believability of a witness you may consider anything that has a tendency in reason to prove or disprove the truthfulness of the testimony of the witness, including but not limited to any of the following: (JI-61)**

> > **The extent of the opportunity or the ability of the witness to see or hear or otherwise become aware of any matter about which the witness has testified; (JI-62)**

> > **The ability of the witness to remember or to communicate any matter about which the witness has testified; (JI-63)**

> > **The character/quality of that testimony; (JI-64)**

The demeanor and manner of the witness while testifying; (JI-65)

The existence or nonexistence of a bias, interest or other motive; (JI-66)

Evidence of the existence or nonexistence of any fact testified to by the witness; (JI-67)

The attitude of the witness towards this action or towards the giving of testimony; (JI-68)

A statement previously made by the witness that is consistent or inconsistent with the testimony of the witness; (JI-69)

An admission by the witness of untruthfulness; (JI-70)

The witness's prior conviction of a felony. (JI-71)

Discrepancies in a witness's testimony, or between his or her testimony and that of others, if there were any, do not necessarily mean that the witness should be discredited. (JI-72)

Failure of recollection is a common experience and innocent misrecollection is not uncommon. (JI-73)

It is a fact also that two persons witnessing an incident or a transaction often will see or hear it differently. Whether a discrepancy pertains to a fact of importance or only to a trivial detail should be considered in weighing its significance. (JI-74)

The last two instructions are important because they tell the juror that the law recognizes misrecollections, that errors can occur and yet the testimony of the erring witness can still be believed as it relates to a specific fact.

Different witnesses see different things even when looking at the same incident. Just because two people differ in what they report does not mean that one is lying. As a juror, you decide not only if a particular witness is telling the truth; you may also have to decide how to choose which truthful witness is more believable.

Sometimes absolutely truthful testimony loses its relevance or importance to the case and is given no weight. For example, all of the defense witnesses who described O.J. Simpson's trip to Chicago and his return the day after the murder, may have been telling the truth regarding how they saw him behave. The jurors may discount the testimony as to Mr. Simpson's distress because it is subject to different interpretations (genuine grief or a clever act) or because there is other evidence which ties in much more directly with O.J.'s guilt or nonguilt.

There is another common jury instruction which was given in the *People v. Powell et al* and played an important part in the *Simpson* case as well:

A witness who is willfully false in one material part of his or her testimony is to be distrusted in others. (JI-75)

You may reject the whole testimony of a witness who willfully has testified falsely as to a material point unless from all the evidence you believe the probability of truth favors his or her testimony in other particulars. (JI-76)

The court here tells the jurors that it is permissible under the law for them to reject the entire testimony of a witness (e.g., Mark Fuhrman) if they find that he was willfully false in an important part of his testimony. It is left up to individual jurors to decide how and what they do when the witness has willfully testified falsely in some aspect.

The judge is telling the jurors that they should distrust the willfully false witness, while an innocent misrecollection (JI-71) does not discredit a witness's testimony.

Judge Weisberg also told the jury in the *Powell* case:

The fact that a witness has been convicted of a felony, if such be a fact, may be considered by you only for the purpose of determining the believability of that witness. (JI-80)

> The fact of such a conviction does not necessarily destroy or impair the witness's believability. (JI-81)

> It is one of the circumstances that you may take into consideration in weighing the testimony of such a witness. (JI-82)

The law gives significant leeway in deciding credibility, but asks that there be a reasoned process, using the tools given in the instructions—objective, legally mandated or sanctioned tools.

If there have been inconsistencies in what the witness says in court compared with an earlier time when the witness was not under oath, you will have to evaluate the inconsistency to see if it is really significant, and therefore diminishes the credibility of the witness. Perhaps the inconsistency was the result of a misunderstanding, or because of boastful or self-ingratiating behavior when the witness was not under oath.

Jurors are told they can disregard testimony when the witness admits untruthfulness. But since no one always tells the truth, there must be a reason to disbelieve the testimony the witness is now giving. Otherwise all witnesses will be discredited.

When the witness lies in one part of the testimony, it is hard to give credence to what is said in another part. If, as it turned out, Detective Fuhrman lied about his use of the term "nigger," why believe him on anything else? Thus, an instruction limiting the "lack of credibility" determination to instances when there is proof of a lie in the witness's testimony, makes more sense than a general rule which undercuts the testimony of any untruthful person.

The witness who is a convicted felon is not necessarily less credible than the witness who has never been convicted of a felony. A person convicted of hit-and-run driving, or manslaughter, may not be a good person, but does that make the felon less credible? Those convicted of refusing to serve in the Vietnam War may have been felons, but to many their integrity was never in question.

A felony conviction may have bearing if there is some relation between the particular felony and honesty. Convicted perjurers, or embezzlers, or stock manipulators, for instance, may in fact have a propensity for disregarding the truth unless it furthers their own interests.

When evaluating credibility, jurors are told they may use cues or indicators—which is what lawyers mean when they talk about "demeanor"—in reaching a conclusion. The juror watches *how* the witness answers the questions; the eye movement or movement of hands, legs, head; eye contact; nervousness; lack of nervousness; respect for the process. All those nonverbal and verbal cues and conduct *supposedly* help the juror decide whether the witness can be believed.

For many of us, our life experiences tell us that people are nervous when they are not telling the truth. Or that someone who is lying won't look you in the eyes. People who tell the truth look you straight in the eye, and are calm.

But consider the person who recently had multi-cultural training, and learned that certain groups never look one in the eye because that is a sign of disrespect in that group's culture. Without training, the person would have interpreted a witness's failure to look people in the eye as an indication that the witness was lying. With the newly acquired information the same witness is now considered credible. The same person, using life experiences at two different points in time, could come to opposite conclusions as to the truthfulness of the witness.

Social and psychological studies of people's ability to discern liars, based on an evaluation of their demeanor, show that people have no such ability. Many people, including judges, law-enforcement personnel and lawyers, believe they have acquired skills which enable them to tell whether someone is telling the truth. What then gives any of us confidence in our individual ability to make such demeanor determinations? Have we ever undergone training or been tested?

If anyone could make judgments as to demeanor, it would probably be successful professional gamblers, or possibly some psychologists. Each is looking for some tip that the person with whom they are dealing is lying (or bluffing). They may be able to get a "tell"—some unconscious quirk, or movement, or habit, which indicates to them that the player/patient is being dishonest. They are trained observers. Their success depends partly on the accuracy of their observations. But even these experts would need lots of time, and the proper situation, in order to make accurate judgments. Do our own life experiences suggest that people who speak in a candid fashion, are actually believable? What of the Reverend Jim Bakker? Surely, a man of the cloth, who spoke with God and to his hordes of parishioners, who could cry and weep for those who suffered was credible, wasn't he?

Is reputation a reliable tool to judge veracity when scoundrels and liars can occupy seats of power and be loved and venerated; when critics of America's Vietnam policy who were denounced and incarcerated and silenced had been telling the truth, while the persons denouncing them, as former Secretary of Defense Robert McNamara finally now admits, were lying?

Jurors are also told that a person's character or reputation can be used to assist them in determining credibility.

Character witnesses often testify as to the solid reputation for honesty an individual has in the community. Does that testimony afford any assurance that this upstanding individual, in testifying, will tell the truth? Or the notorious liar—should testimony by that person be automatically rejected?

To use the standard of character evidence to judge credibility, you must believe either that the community has some reliable knowledge (which it most probably learned from the media) or that the individuals who testify as to their own personal knowledge have verifiable ways of measuring an individual's honesty or its lack.

But even if the common knowledge is correct, how can you know, with some certainty, that this time it won't be different?

Next, let's examine whether the existence or nonexistence of a bias, self-interest or other motive is a helpful analytical tool. If it were, defendants would be told never to testify, because they wouldn't be believed. After all, who has more of an interest in lying than someone who could be incarcerated or executed?

But it's not just the defendant who has a motive. Many, if not all, of the witnesses who testify have a bias, interest or motive to lie.

Consider police officers as witnesses. They certainly may have a motive. They may look good, or receive a promotion if they were the officers who captured a criminal and the District Attorney gets a conviction. They may not look so good, or get a demotion, if the defendant is acquitted. They may know the defendant is a lowlife and a dirtbag. They may know that the defendant committed the crime because they have the evidence to prove it, but the evidence was obtained illegally. If they lie, and the defendant is convicted, justice (at least in some sense) will have been done, a dangerous criminal will be off the streets, and society will be safer.

Or they may simply want to protect one of their own. In the *People v. Powell* trial, a number of police officers testified that Rodney King appeared to be on PCP. None of the LAPD officers testified as to the impropriety of the baton strikes—except Officer Briseno, whose interest it was, as a defendant, to so testify.

Witnesses to a crime may also have an interest in testifying to certain facts. They may feel their standing in the community will be impaired if they change their story, and admit a mistake. They may be plea-bargaining, hoping to get a lighter sentence for themselves. They may be friends or relatives of the defendant, trying to prevent the defendant from going to jail. They may hope—as in the *O.J. Simpson* case—to be able to sell their story to the media. They may have an ulterior motive to lie—they may be in trouble with their friends or family if the true situation comes to light.

Finally, what about the witness's attitude toward the action or the giving of testimony? If the witness feels—as many of the O.J. Simpson witnesses must have felt—that the opposing counsel will malign, criticize, hypothesize or fantasize as to the type of person the witness is—so that giving testimony will only cause self-harm—what is that person's attitude likely to be?

Forget the trial of the century and just think about the unpublicized trial in your community. People, especially low-income or minority or uneducated people, may have totally different attitudes about being a witness and the court process, in general, than a rich, Caucasian doctor. Although they may appear indifferent and perhaps disrespectful, their testimony may be as truthful as the doctor's. And suppose the witness, or the defendant, believes the courtroom is a sham, racist, unfair. What attitude will that person have?

In short, we believe that certain credibility instructions are simply ways of letting jurors decide cases based on whim and caprice, rather than more objective evidence. In the whim and caprice category we include the demeanor of the witness, the person's reputation, and the attitude of the witness. So while a juror can lawfully use these tools in weighing credibility, we urge that they be used only where there is no better way of deciding.

There are better tools to use, if they are used carefully. These include evaluating motive or bias, considering the admission of untruthfulness, and deciding if the felony conviction has a bearing on the truth.

Finally, there are credibility instructions we really like. These are the objective standards which are suggested credibility tools that jurors can use—such as the ability of the witness to perceive those things about which the witness has testified. The juror should be looking to see if the witness was using appropriate hearing or visual aids, if necessary; whether the witness, even if totally flawless physically, was able to perceive (darkness, distance); whether the witness was impaired by drugs, lack of sleep, concentration, etc.. If no such problems existed, the described events are more likely to be accurate.

The witness must be able to relate what he or she saw or heard. This requires memory and the ability to communicate. Memory becomes significant when there is a long time between the act which the witness saw or heard and the trial. It is difficult to remember specific incidents which occurred months or years ago unless there is a reason for remembering those incidents. Some people may suffer memory lapses. Others may be too young or too old to recall accurately what happened.

When the events are fresh in the mind of the witness, the events are more likely to be accurately depicted. The witness will not have been subject to outside effects, which can affect memory. Some of the witnesses in the *People v. Powell* trial could not specifically state whether their testimony reflected what they had initially observed, at the time of the beating, or whether it was based on what they had later seen on the videotape.

This leads to the question of prior consistent, or inconsistent statements. If the person now testifies consistently with what that person reported earlier, greater weight generally should be given to the testimony. The person said it then, and now reiterates the statement was true. An exception to this would be when the person had a reason to lie initially because the person was aware a trial might occur.

When the witness's testimony is inconsistent with what was said earlier, that inconsistency needs to be explained. Was it due to an inaccurate description or misunderstanding at the time the statement was initially made? Or was the testimony revised because of pressure from the prosecution or the defense, or because the witness would like to believe that something different happened than that which was initially reported? Or did the witness simply forget? As a fact-finder you need to be cautious in accepting testimony which is inconsistent with prior statements unless there is a reasonable explanation for the inconsistency.

An excellent tool to use in determining credibility is the use of other evidence to corroborate or undermine the testimony given. Witnesses may be recounting what they believe they saw or heard, but they may be inaccurate.

In the *People v. Powell* trial, the CHP Officers who pursued the King car testified for the prosecution as to what they believed they saw. They had no known motivation to lie or embellish their stories. They were not on trial nor subject to disciplinary procedures. They were testifying against fellow officers whose behavior had shocked them. But the videotape indicated that their testimony as to what happened was not completely accurate.

When defendants or witnesses claim that they were at a particular place at a particular time, there may be other evidence to establish their whereabouts. A person simply cannot be in two places at the same time. So when a witness testifies he was at the scene of the crime, and there is evidence establishing that he was at a meeting in another town, it would be difficult to believe the witness, no matter how honest and upstanding he appeared.

However, on the other hand, if a witness says a fleeing vehicle was a 1989 white Corvette with license plate XYZ 123, and that is the actual license plate of such a vehicle and the vehicle cannot be shown to be someplace else, the witness's testimony is more credible than if there is no Corvette with that license.

If you use the kind of objective criteria just discussed, it is more likely that you will make better credibility determinations. It will also mean that you can say to yourself that you were an impartial judge of the facts.

CHAPTER 16

"EXPERTS":
ARE THEY REALLY?

The general rule in U.S. courts is that those who testify must have personal knowledge of the matter about which they are testifying. A witness may have *seen* an officer strike a suspect with a club or baton, or *heard* an officer tell a suspect to put his hands behind his back, or *touched* a gun and found it warm. Witnesses, in certain instances, may testify as to a person's reputation, habits, or past practices. Again, this testimony is based on personal knowledge of the individual.

But the law makes an exception with a special type of witness. The expert witness need not have any personal knowledge of the individual in order to testify. As Judge Weisberg told the *People v. Powell et al* jurors:

> **A person is qualified to testify as an expert if he has special knowledge, skill, experience, training or education sufficient to qualify him as an expert on the subject to which his testimony relates. (JI-96)**

Sometimes there may be personal knowledge, as when a psychiatrist bases an evaluation of an individual on conversations with that person. More frequently the expert witness has no knowledge of the people involved in the crime. He may have compared fingerprints, or she may have reviewed X-rays or CAT scans. Neither expert may have seen the individual or individuals from whom these samples were obtained.

In other cases, the expert will testify as to what an individual is expected to do in a certain situation, based on the training which has been provided that individual. Thus, if the LAPD has certain rules as to when it is appropriate to use a baton to strike a suspect, the expert may be allowed to testify as to those rules. Further, an expert may be asked **hypothetical questions**, or be presented with real-life situations, and give an opinion as to the proper response to the situation.

The experts give their opinions. They are there to assist the jurors. Judge Weisberg explained that the jurors did not have to accept what the expert said:

You are not bound to accept an expert opinion as conclusive, but should give to it the weight to which you find it to be entitled. You may disregard any such opinion if you find it to be unreasonable. (JI-99)

If the opinion seems unreasonable to the juror it can be completely disregarded. But what is unreasonable? Can you consider an expert opinion unreasonable because you don't think the opinion is correct? Or is the opinion unreasonable only when *nobody* would think the opinion reasonable? Or are there even more gradations?

Experts testify about a wide variety of matters. In criminal law they may give evidence as to ballistic tests, or the cause of death. They may testify as to the amount of alcohol in the blood based on breathalyzer tests or urinalysis. They may identify the type of drug in a person's system or that no drugs were found in the system, or that the white powder obtained during a search of the person's home is, or is not, cocaine.

There were days of testimony from opposing experts in the *O.J. Simpson* case about blood stains, DNA, hair samples, and contamination of evidence collected by the LAPD.

In the *People v. Powell et al* trial, experts testified as to the escalation and de-escalation of force, the appropriate force to use when a suspect behaves in a certain fashion, the kind of force which can be applied, and the training LAPD officers received. The defense experts differed with the prosecution expert as to each of these matters.

Jurors are faced with a major dilemma. You are told by one expert that certain acts are procedurally correct and in accord with police training, and by another expert that the amount and kind of force used exceeded allowable limits. Sometimes there is no middle ground, no areas of agreement. Diametrically opposed expert viewpoints were presented in the Rodney King beating trial in regard to whether the officers followed LAPD procedures during the arrest of Mr. King.

That trial presented an additional problem. Since both the jurors and the experts had observed the videotape and not the actual events, were the experts testifying about matters the jurors couldn't understand themselves? Were the experts more knowledgeable about how to view a videotape? Judge Weisberg recognized the problem and informed the jurors:

> In this case expert witnesses have testified about two types of facts: facts to which they have special qualifications and experience which allow them to testify as expert witnesses and facts on which they have no special expertise. (JI-100)

> In particular, in rendering an opinion as to the use-of-force in this case, one or more expert witnesses expressed an opinion on what physical acts are shown on exhibit 2, the so-called Holliday videotape. Such experts have no more skill than a lay person in viewing the videotape and determining what it shows in this regard. To the extent that you find that the videotape is important to you in your deliberations and decision in this case, you are the sole judges of what physical acts are shown on the tape. (JI-101)

The experts had no greater skills than the jurors did when they testified as to what they saw on the videotape. The experts' expertise lay in their evaluation of the hypotheticals presented, and in their knowledge of LAPD policies.

When determining the credibility of the expert, you need to use the same tools as in other witness evaluations. You must again rely on your logic and intelligence to make an assessment.

Once again, your real-world experiences are, to a great extent, irrelevant. You are viewing a play, seeing and hearing and evaluating only that which is presented by the playwright, the director and the actors. You may know, in your own mind, that to be in a prone position is simply to be lying down, but what if the expert says that for police officers, there is a different meaning to "prone out"?

When expert witnesses testify there are problems for jurors similar to those when non-experts testify. For example, it's easy to confuse outstanding speaking and presentation skills with sound analysis. Some experts are very convincing in style, even when there is little or no substance to their testimony.

Ask yourself if the testimony was consistent with previous statements made by the expert in other trials, or in speeches, or in **depositions**. Was testimony at the trial internally consistent? For example, if the police use-of-force expert initially said there were ten separate escalations and de-escalations of force, did he later change his position to say there were only six incidents?

It's important to consider whether the expert is unbiased. Was she out to get the cops in question, or was he looking to protect the defendants? Experts are being called to testify because they offer a particular view. If the expert does not provide information helpful to the prosecution or defense, the expert will not be called as a witness, even if the expert has been retained, performed examinations, spent many hours on the case and will be paid thousands of dollars for the effort. Rather than call an expert who will harm their case, another expert will be hired who can submit testimony more favorable for the client at the trial.

Experts, just like non-experts, develop reputations. They have an economic incentive to make findings favoring the party which hires them. Thus, there are experts who always work for the same side, either the prosecution or the defense. How objective is such a person?

Experts who sell themselves to one side or the other are frequently considered "whores" of the profession. The problem for jurors is that this group of experts may have honed their presentation skills, may be articulate, interesting and readily understood. What you need to remember is that no matter how knowledgeable or impressive the credentials, these experts are not objective witnesses. They are hired guns. The "non-whore" experts are "straight-shooters"—they testify fairly equally and evenly for both sides and have no particular axe to grind. They too may have outstanding presentation skills, and may be articulate, interesting and readily understood.

Next, how can you tell if the expert knows what she claims to know? Did she know because she had to pass tests to become licensed or certified? Or because she was a recognized authority and the author of any books in her field of expertise? Had she taken courses in the area about which she was testifying, or had she been hired to teach others?

Who should the juror believe when experts, as they often do, reach opposite conclusions from the same facts? Judge Weisberg gave the *People v. Powell* jury the following guidance:

> **In resolving any conflict that may exist in the testimony of expert witnesses, you should weigh the opinion of one expert against that of another. In doing this you should consider the relative qualifications and credibility of the expert witnesses, as well as the reasons for each opinion and the facts and other matters upon which it was based. (JI-109)**

Jurors thus have the additional problem of evaluating the nature, character and extent of the experts' expertise as it relates to another expert or experts. In other words, *just how expert is the expert?* The juror needs to know of the expert's education, training, publications, and reputation. However, the juror will only know that if any of that information has been introduced during the course of the trial.

In all other aspects of the trial and the presentation of evidence, the judge and lawyers are trying to exclude speculation. The expert witness represents a major exception to this general rule. The expert is often there to speculate.

As stated before, the expert is permitted to respond to hypothetical questions prepared by a lawyer. These hypotheticals present facts, some of which may not be substantiated by the evidence. Judge Weisberg explained the hypothetical question to the jury:

> In examining an expert witness, counsel may propound to him or her a type of question known in the law as a hypothetical question. By such a question the witness is asked to assume to be true a set of facts and to give an opinion based on that assumption. (JI-105)

The judge's instruction acknowledges that:

> In permitting such a question the court does not rule and does not necessarily find that all the assumed facts have been proved. It only determines that those assumed facts are within the probable or possible range of the evidence. (JI-106)

Up until now, the court has attempted to limit the introduction of evidence to things that are substantiated or for which a foundation has been laid. Now jurors are told that some of the facts upon which the hypothetical question is based may not have been proven in the case. Judge Weisberg continued:

> It is for you, the jury, to find from all the evidence whether or not the facts assumed in a hypothetical question have been proved. (JI-107)

> If you find that the videotape shows something other than which a particular expert witness assumed to be true for a hypothetical question, you may consider that difference in determining what weight, if any, to give the expert opinion expressed in answering that question. (JI-103)

These instructions are confusing. Since jurors had already been told not to make factual findings until all the evidence was in, the only way to determine whether the answer to the hypothetical was of any value would have been to review each hypothetical question after the conclusion of the trial, and then decide if each assumption had been proved. What a task!

And, there is one final issue concerning expert testimony that needs to be addressed: *Why is a particular individual considered an expert in the first place?*

Does the fact that someone has been employed for many years in a certain field make her an expert? Is the physician who has been practicing twenty years more of an expert— smarter, more careful or more skilled—than the newly interned doctor who has more recent training? Does the fact that the expert has written a book make her a better expert than the person who has not written one, but who has performed far more work in the field? When the expert announces why she is an expert, does the jury have sufficient information to conclude that individual is an expert?

We believe that certain criteria can be helpful in determining the expertise and reliability of the expert:

- The more recent the experience the better

- The more case-specific the expertise, the better

- The more that the expert has testified for both sides, rather than simply the prosecution or defense, the better

- The more acceptance and recognition within the expert community—e.g., awards, articles published by recognized journals, frequent citations by others—the better

- The more clearly the expert can articulate concepts, in a way that's understandable to the nonexpert—the juror—the better

- The more consistent the testimony is in relation to the expert's prior publications and prior testimony, and to testimony given at the current trial, the better

- The more prestigious the educational institutions where the expert has received a degree, or taught, and the more acknowledged the credentials, the better

Your predicament is twofold. You may be presented with little of the information as to the qualifications or bias of the expert at the trial. You may also have to wait until the end of the trial before you can decide whether the facts hypothesized to a particular expert have been proven to your satisfaction. Then you must decide whether the testimony of the more credible expert is even relevant to the guilt or nonguilt of the defendant. We consider it truly amazing that jurors get all this straight as often as they do.

Chapter 17

Argument and Courtroom Theatrics

In all trials, jurors generally are (or should be) told that statements made by the attorneys in the courtroom are not evidence. As Judge Weisberg instructed the *Powell* jurors:

the arguments of the attorneys are not evidence. (JI-28)

the comments of counsel are not evidence... (JI-30)

Sometimes it seems as if lawyers are constantly talking throughout the trial. They may conduct some of the voir dire; they usually make Opening Statements; they ask questions; they raise objections; they introduce items into evidence; and then, at the end of the trial, they make their Closing Statements.

When the lawyers talk, they are not under oath. They are not presenting testimony as to what they have seen, heard, felt, tasted or smelled. They did not prepare the medical reports, use the PR 24 baton, find the bloody glove.

Not one thing the attorneys say during Opening Statements is evidence, even though many jurors may be enthralled by the lawyers, and far too many jurors form their opinion of the case based on what they hear during those statements. But Opening Statements are simply the comments of the lawyers as to what they expect the evidence to show.

If the lawyer states that the evidence will show that the defendant was at home during the time the crime was committed because several witnesses will be called who will testify to that fact, jurors will have to wait to see if the witnesses are called, and if called, what they actually say.

Suppose during Opening Statement, the lawyer goes further and tells the jury that the defendant had an airtight alibi and that witnesses will prove beyond any reasonable doubt that the defendant was at home and therefore could not have committed the crime. The lawyer is arguing the case to the jury, because the lawyer is telling the jurors what conclusion they must draw from evidence that has not yet been presented.

In the *O.J. Simpson* case, Johnnie Cochran Jr. eloquently explained in his Opening Statement to the jury that Rosa Lopez and another witness would provide testimony that would show O.J. Simpson could not be the killer of the victims, because his car was parked in front of his home at the time the murders were committed. The defense did not put these witnesses on the stand before the jury despite what was said in Opening Statements. This does not necessarily call into question the integrity of Johnnie Cochran Jr. At the time he made his statements, he may have believed that these two witnesses would be called. But this example highlights why jurors should not give a great deal of credence to what lawyers say in their Opening Statements.

While the lawyers' statements may be helpful and important in understanding the case, there is no assurance that any evidence will be presented to support their contentions and analysis. Remember, the lawyer is trying to get you to form a picture in your mind before any facts have been presented. Lawyers know that if the jury gets a certain mind-set, it's hard to change.

If verdicts are based on the charm of the lawyer or the argument the lawyer advances, then whichever side can hire the most charming or persuasive attorney will prevail. All the more reason why jurors must wait and see what evidence is actually presented before making even a preliminary decision.

Lawyers are not supposed to argue their cases during Opening Statements. Since judges differ, in some trials lawyers have more leeway to argue the case in Opening Statements than others do.

After Opening Statements, the prosecution presents its **Case-in-Chief** to the jury. Witnesses are questioned in an attempt to establish the facts necessary to convict. The defense in rare cases may not present an Opening Statement. The decision will be based on tactical considerations. And in some cases, the defense may also choose not to present any witnesses because of its belief that the prosecution's case failed to establish the guilt of the accused.

On cross-examination by the defense, counsel try to convince the jury that there are certain facts in evidence by the content of the question, or by the tone of the question. For the unsophisticated juror, the suggestion may work even if the witness answers in the negative, or an objection is sustained and the witness is never required to answer the question.

For example, if the defense is trying to convince the jury that Detective Mark Fuhrman is a racist, the attorney asks: "Isn't it true that you've often used the term 'nigger' to describe African-Americans?" Then, if the answer is "No" the lawyer can look shocked, and ask whether this term wasn't used in speaking to Mr. X on the night of May 5, 1992.

Suppose the answer is "No" but Mr. X is never called. Jurors may still have a seed of suspicion, or even the conviction, that such a conversation occurred and that some obscure legal theory is keeping the actual evidence from them. If the question is stricken, jurors may believe that Mr. X has told defense counsel of such a conversation.

Think about it. Has any evidence actually been presented? Can any inference be properly drawn?

Judge Weisberg so instructed the *Powell* jurors:

> **Do not assume to be true any insinuation suggested by a question asked a witness. A question is not evidence and may be considered only as it enables you to understand the answer. (JI-26)**

It is not only the lawyers' implications which have to be disregarded. It is also the false friendship that the lawyer tries to develop with the jury, while simultaneously attempting to depict opposing counsel as mean-spirited and dishonest.

Again, instructions exist to tell the jury not to fall into the trap. Judge Weisberg noted:

> If in argument any counsel made reference or seemed
> to make reference to the veracity or personal integrity
> of any other attorney, you are to disregard any such
> comment. Such comment should play no role in how
> you decide this case. (JI-29)

Jurors must remember that it is not the attorneys who
are on trial. It is the defendant. When Johnnie Cochran Jr. and
Christopher Darden were trading insults and barbs, that wasn't
relevant to O.J. Simpson's guilt. When Terry White attacked
the defense attorneys in *People v. Powell,* using sarcasm, ridicule, and scorn in an attempt to undermine their case, jurors
should have disregarded the hostility and focused on the evidence. Theatrics are only successful when jurors allow themselves to be manipulated.

The attorney who uses personal attacks against other
attorneys may have "won", if jurors can't put aside the words
they have heard, or the tone and inflection used.

At the conclusion of the trial, the lawyers are allowed to do
what they have been trying to do throughout the case. They get
to argue the case. In fact, the Closing Statements phase of the
trial is sometimes called Argument or Closing Arguments.

Gerry Spence, a well-known defense attorney, has written
a best seller called *How to Argue and Win Every Time.* Consider
what he means. He's saying he can convince you even when his
theory has no merit. If he's right, it's because he—and other
skillful lawyers—are like magicians. And you—the audience—
are looking at the wrong thing. At a trial, you are looking at the
lawyers for guidance and truth, when it is the evidence which
will provide you with that.

That is not to say that argument in the Closing Statement
should be eliminated, or that it's inappropriate. The able lawyer
is using argument to piece together the puzzle, assembling the
evidence in a coherent picture or collage. The lawyer has a
chance to emphasize the evidence which is favorable, and to
attack that which is harmful to the case. Counsel can explain
why one witness is more credible than another, why one expert
has more expertise than the other and why there either is or is
not a reasonable doubt as to the defendant's guilt.

These summations can be very helpful. Jurors can compare the two pictures drawn by opposing counsel, and examine the strengths and weaknesses of each side.

But when the facts asserted by counsel aren't consistent with the evidence, the pieces don't match, the puzzle doesn't fit together.

You can use the lawyers to help get at the truth if that truth has been proven by evidence introduced at the trial and ignore "the truth" which exists only in the lawyers' hyperbole.

If the stakes weren't so high, courtroom theatrics could often be considered entertainment. The give-and-take is sometimes as exciting as going to the theater, as illustrated by some of the sensational trials seen on TV. It is often different for the ordinary trial which gets little or no attention. These trials may be dull and tedious. But in either situation, it is important for jurors to put the proceedings into perspective and not lose sight of their role. You, the jurors, are judges of the facts.

Remember, lawyers are always trying to manipulate the jury, but the jury is often self-manipulated as well. Jurors assume, based on their individual experience, or their contacts with others, that certain groups are more likely to act in one way or another. Cops may be seen either as good guys, or persons trained to lie; people in gangs as liars and no-goods. African-Americans may be considered irresponsible, Asian-Americans as responsible. These are stereotypes which must be avoided because they have nothing to do with what jurors are asked to do.

The same holds true for the attorneys representing the prosecution or defense. If a juror dislikes prosecutor Marcia Clark, while another thinks she is very attractive, that should make no difference in reaching a verdict. If a juror thinks O.J. Simpson's "A" Team is great, that Robert Shapiro and Johnnie Cochran Jr. give off incredible energy, that F. Lee Bailey is a legend—all that has nothing to do with whether O.J. Simpson was guilty of the crimes he was charged with committing. These same lawyers will carry all that energy and charisma with them into any courtroom on behalf of any defendant who can afford their fees.

It is not in the interest of justice for jurors to get attached to counsel, or to consider their negative feelings towards individual lawyers during their evaluation of evidence. You might react negatively to the attorney who is always making objections. You might see that attorney as a whiner, who constantly interrupts the other side in an attempt to keep damaging evidence from the jury. The reality may be that the lawyer asking the questions is intentionally asking improper questions to force the other lawyer to object. That accomplishes the dual purpose of annoying the other attorney and causing the objecting attorney to be seen by the jury as antagonistic.

It is natural to like a lawyer who makes you feel good, has a keen sense of humor, is polite and either pleasant to watch and listen to or dramatic and exciting. It is also natural to dislike a dull, plodding or repetitive lawyer. But the conduct of the lawyer or our personal feelings towards him or her does not establish guilt or nonguilt. Only the evidence establishes guilt or nonguilt. It is the defendant, not the lawyer, who is on trial.

The attempt to create a bond between lawyer and jury is sometimes almost crude. It should have surprised no one that one of the *People v. Powell* prosecutors was African-American, or that the *O.J. Simpson* trial would have a team of prosecution and defense lawyers who were women and men, black and white, old and young.

Recall the hoopla involving the way Marcia Clark looked. At times it seemed as if the most important matter at the trial was whether she wore a symbolic chain, how she coifed her hair, and the outfits she wore. Both sides were subtly trying to influence the jury by convincing jurors they were sympathetic, understanding and the kind of people—by race, gender, dress, empathy—to whom the jurors could relate.

Our advice is to let the commentators comment, the media blather on, the media "experts" run their surveys, and opposing counsel choose any kind of team they wish. But the good juror will fool them all, ignore the trappings and focus on the picture which is being developed through the evidence.

Let's assume you have been able to disregard the lawyers' comments, arguments, innuendoes, and theatrics. You have kept in mind that your feelings towards any of the participants should not affect the verdict you render. That includes your feelings about the defendant.

The jury instructions, given at the end of the trial, make it clear that your like or dislike of the defendant or the lawyers should not affect your verdict. But, in our view, those instructions come too late in the process, after the jurors have already formed their opinions.

In the *O.J. Simpson* case, the jury saw a good-looking, well-dressed, popular, and charismatic defendant. It seems clear some of them liked O.J., particularly the jurors who have spoken or written in his defense, and the juror who gave him the Black Power salute at the end of the trial.

In the Menendez brothers' first trial for the murder of their parents, some jurors developed affectionate feelings for the defendants. Their lawyers wanted the jurors to develop positive feelings for the defendants so that the jurors would disregard the evidence. Were the Menendez brothers less guilty because they wore nice clothes, were young, good-looking, acted politely, and showed sadness or remorse? Exactly what does the appearance of the defendant in a court proceeding, which takes place long after the date the crime was committed, have to do with whether or not that person committed the crime?

Suppose the defendant is not likable. If Sgt. Koon or Officer Powell, defendants in the Rodney King beating trial, were seen as arrogant or cold by jurors, should those factors have been considered in arriving at a verdict?

Have you noticed that the picture of a defendant in a line-up is almost always far different from the defendant you see in court? The line-up picture may show a man with long hair who hasn't shaved for days, wearing a T-shirt and jeans, with a sneer on his face. The man you see in court has short hair, is clean-shaven, wears a suit, and looks as clean-cut, upstanding and middle class as possible. Is that an accident?

Defense lawyers base their presentation on their experience, their intuition, and on paid consultants. They would not alter a defendant's image unless they believed that in doing so they would more likely convince you, the juror, of their client's innocence. You can conclude, then, that either defense lawyers are badly mistaken, or the defendant's looks do make a difference.

So you must look beyond the facade that is carefully constructed for you. Is a man in a business suit more likely to be honest than one in jeans? If you believe so—or if you believe the opposite—you are looking at the image, and not the reality. How a defendant is dressed in court is a matter of costuming for the part the lawyer wants the defendant to play.

This ploy is used not only by the defense nor does it involve only defendants. Prosecution witnesses also have an image of trustworthiness to present, and are encouraged to dress and act accordingly. The investigator who seems gentle and mild-mannered on the stand may have presented quite a different image when grilling the defendant. The cop, clean-shaven and dressed in a conservative suit at trial, may have looked and acted like a dangerous thug at the time of the arrest.

The same cautions also could apply as to how a defendant or witness speaks. The soft-spoken and polite witness may be a loud-mouthed, insensitive bully who has learned or been taught (by the lawyers or jury consultants) to present a more positive and refined image. Remember, image is not reality.

Jurors who have avoided lawyer and/or witness manipulation must also not let themselves be influenced by the judge. Even when the judge seems annoyed at a lawyer, or appears to be dozing when a witness is testifying, jurors should disregard the judge's actions. When a judge nods approvingly at a lawyer, or seems interested in what a witness says, that shouldn't affect your decision. Judges may like certain lawyers better than others, or judges may simply be tired when they are apparently inattentive, or judges may be displaying inappropriate behavior.

Jurors do need to pay attention to the judge's rulings as to when testimony is to be stricken or when a question is improper. Other than that, the judge's reactions to the parties and the evidence is of no consequence.

Judge Weisberg instructed jurors to ignore his behavior:

> I have not intended by anything I have said or done, or by any question that I may have asked or by any ruling I may have made, to intimate or suggest what you should find to be the facts or that I believe or

disbelieve any witness. If anything I have done or said has seemed to so indicate, you will disregard it and form your own conclusions. (JI-172)

Ideally, jurors don't get snowed by attorneys with fancy suits and friendly smiles, and don't let their dislike for a lawyer outweigh the facts of the case. These jurors don't take their lead from the judge's demeanor and don't dote on the lawyers' arguments, unless those arguments are substantiated by the evidence which the lawyers actually introduce.

As lawyers use their art and skill to rise to the height of oratorical eloquence, using ridicule, sarcasm, assumed friendship, bonding, anger, caring, hostility, or feigned or actual disbelief, jurors need to step back and make sure they can distinguish, the dancer from the dance. Otherwise, the words will have an impact that is unwarranted, or the ardor and emotions of the performance will stick in the jurors' minds long after the words are forgotten.

You will be surprised that once you tune into argument, the lawyers' words will jump out at you every time you hear them as mere words, and not as facts to be believed. Once that happens, lawyers will have to rely more on the evidence in the case and their skills in presenting the evidence, and not on their skills in manipulating jurors. That's our goal.

The truly skilled lawyers will still argue the case every chance they can by artfully intertwining their argument with the evidence. It is the sifting of the evidence that is the juror's obligation. The juror's responsibility is simplified when judges or the attorneys focus the juror on the relevant evidence. It is made more complex when the attorney substitutes, with the judge's acquiescence, facial or body gestures, or comment, argument, or implication, for evidence.

The ideal juror will see whether the evidence, and the argument, fit together. Let's hope the next best-selling book about lawyers is called: *How Great Lawyers Argued Brilliantly— and Lost!*

Jurors can and must learn to *outsmart the lawyers.*

CHAPTER 18

OBJECTIONS:

A PRIMER

W hen people watch a trial on TV, they frequently see attorneys object to something the other side is attempting to introduce into evidence. Then the judge makes a ruling. The judge says the objection is **sustained** which means the objection is upheld and cannot be considered by the jurors, or that it is **overruled** which means that the evidence can be admitted.

Objections fall into a number of categories but their purpose is to keep certain questions, responses or evidence from the jury. Objections are made both before a witness answers a question, and after the witness has answered the question. In other words, objections are sometimes made after the jury has heard the answer to the question.

In the *People v. Powell et al* trial, the judge sometimes informed the jury that the response was stricken—that it was not to be part of the record. At other times, he would say nothing other than "sustained." And at other times, after the objection had been sustained, the attorney asked that the answer be stricken and Judge Weisberg would so order.

If a question or answer is stricken, you are supposed to pretend you did not hear the question and the answer. What should you do if the judge sustains an objection, but never tells the jury to disregard the question or answer, or that either or both is stricken? The answers to these questions were only clearly provided by Judge Weisberg at the end of the trial:

If an objection was sustained to a question, do not guess what the answer might have been. (JI-24)

Do not speculate as to the reason for the objection. (JI-25)

Do not consider for any purpose any offer of evidence that was rejected or any evidence that was stricken by the court. Treat it as though you had never heard of it. (JI-27)

There are more than fifty potential objections that can be raised by a lawyer in California. At a minimum it requires a course in evidence, and many years of practice, to understand objections thoroughly. Jurors only need to be aware that there are many different kinds of objections. A partial list of these fifty objections includes: leading; suggestive; irrelevant; nonresponsive; hearsay; no foundation; calls for a conclusion; and speculation.

Some excerpts of objections made at different times by defense attorneys during the testimony of CHP Officer Melanie Singer in the Rodney King beating trial illustrate the variety of possible objections:

Mr. White: (Prosecutor)
> So at that point it was your feeling that you were going to give this person a speeding ticket; is that correct?

Mr. Stone: (Defense)
> *Objection, leading and suggestive.*

The Court:
> *Overruled.* You can answer the question.

* * * * * * *

Mr. White:
> Besides the violation for speed, was it your intent to cite this driver for any other violations of the Vehicle Code?

Mr. Barnett: (Defense)
> *Objection, irrelevant what her intent was.*

The Court:
Overruled. You can answer the question.

* * * * * * *

Mr. White:
Now, at this point or previous to this point had you received any assistance from any other CHP unit?

Answer:
· No, sir. Prior to that incident just—

Mr. Barnett:
Objection. Nonresponsive after "no."

The Court:
Sustained. Everything else is stricken.

* * * * * * *

Mr. White:
What happened next?

Answer:
... The driver of the unit that was to our right nodded his head in acknowledgment.

Mr. Barnett:
I'm going to object. That is hearsay and there is no foundation.

The Court:
All right. The objection is *sustained.*

Mr. Barnett:
Move to strike.

The Court:
The answer is stricken. You may rephrase the question.

Mr. White:
After the—your partner said this to the driver of the other vehicle, patrol vehicle, what did that driver do in response to that?

Mr. Barnett: *(Defense)*
Objection, that calls for a conclusion whether it is in response, and it is hearsay.

The Court:
The objection is *overruled on both grounds.*

* * * * * * *

Mr. White:
If you had relinquished that primary unit status prior to the stop, what would you have done after you relinquished the status as primary unit?

Answer:
After I had relinquished it? Seeing if they need any assistance.

Mr. White:
Would you ordinarily have dropped out of the pursuit at that point?

Answer:
Yes sir.

Mr. Barnett:
Objection. It is irrelevant and speculation.

The Court:
Overruled. The answer will stand.

* * * * * * *

Mr. White:
You were still the agency that was in charge of this situation?

Mr. Barnett:
I'm going to object. That calls for a conclusion without foundation.

The Court:
All right. It goes to her state of mind and she can answer it in that context. You may answer the question.

Mr. Barnett:
For that purpose only, her—

The Court:
Yes, received for that purpose as far as her state of mind at that time.

* * * * * * *

You need not worry about why objections are sustained, or overruled. You need to remember that any innuendo in any question should be disregarded, and any implication in any question is not evidence. Moreover, when an objection is sustained, you should ignore the question itself, any response to a question or any other evidence presented, whether or not the judge specifically says the answer is stricken. You will then be on your way to fulfilling your responsibility to base a decision solely on the *admissible* evidence actually presented to you.

Chapter 19

Beyond A Reasonable Doubt
Just How Sure Is
Very Sure?

At the conclusion of the trial, the judge instructs the jurors as to how much evidence the prosecution must have provided in order to obtain a conviction. In the *People v. Powell* trial, Judge Weisberg read the following two separate times during his lengthy instructions to the jury:

> **A defendant in a criminal action is presumed to be innocent until the contrary is proved, and in case of a reasonable doubt whether his guilt is satisfactorily shown, he is entitled to a verdict of not guilty. (JI-110)**

> **This presumption places upon the people the burden of proving him guilty beyond a reasonable doubt. (JI-111)**

The law in California is that there is a presumption of innocence. The People must overcome that presumption, or there will be an acquittal. While all states have such a presumption, it is not mandated by the United States Constitution. Therefore, it could be changed at any time through legislation so that there would be no presumption at all, or there would be a presumption of guilt rather than one of innocence.

To overcome the presumption of innocence, the People in a criminal trial must produce enough evidence to establish guilt beyond a reasonable doubt. This is called the ***burden of proof.***

In civil trials, such as the wrongful death lawsuit against O.J. Simpson, the general burden of proof is called the "preponderance of the evidence" test. When one party can prove its case by a preponderance—commonly, "more likely than not" or 51% - 49%—that party wins.

The beyond a reasonable doubt standard comes from English common law and from the belief of American legislatures and judicial bodies that a very high burden should be established when the stakes are high, i.e., depriving someone of life, liberty or the pursuit of happiness. It has been considered more important to society to protect the innocent from incarceration or death, than to convict the guilty, even when that might mean a certain percentage of the people who committed crimes go unpunished.

Reasonable doubt was defined in *Powell as follows:*

It is not a mere possible doubt, because everything relating to human affairs and depending on moral evidence is open to some possible or imaginary doubt. It is that state of the case which, after the entire comparison and consideration of all the evidence, leaves the minds of the jurors in that condition that they cannot say they feel an abiding conviction to a moral certainty of the truth of the charge. (JI-112)

This definition raises a number of problems which jurors must resolve. First, on what can reasonable doubt be based? Second, what is mere possible doubt? Third, under what circumstances will the juror know that he or she has what the law calls that absolutely essential abiding conviction?

Most states do not use the word moral in their statements to the jury. In his preliminary instructions to jurors in the *Simpson* case, Judge Ito, in defining reasonable doubt, deleted the phrases "to a moral certainty" and "depending on moral evidence".[28]

The use of the word moral is not helpful because it means too many different things to different people. Some people think abortions are immoral because that involves killing a "person," but killing people in war or executing them for crimes is moral.

Others believe that killing is immoral, but do not consider destroying a fetus to be killing. There are others who believe that any taking of life is immoral.

It becomes even more confusing when "moral" is used as an adjective to modify evidence and certainty. Evidence is simply evidence—it is not moral or immoral.

As to "moral certainty", people with low moral standards theoretically would find it easier to convict than those whose standards were high. Those with low moral standards would be morally certain of the truth of the charges at a lower threshold than those with high moral standards.

Since the phrase "moral certainty" is ambiguous or confusing and the phrase "moral evidence" is meaningless, we think these phrases should be deleted, as Judge Ito did from the instructions given to the *Simpson* jury.[29]

When Judge Weisberg said that everything relating to human affairs is open to some possible or imaginary doubt, he stated a long-accepted philosophical principle. The principle is that the only general statements which are always and invariably true are those which are true by definition. Thus, bachelors will always be unmarried, because that is their status, by definition. But although every ball that has been thrown up into the air by a person has come back to earth, that does not preclude the possibility that a ball will leave earth because either gravity ceases to exist as a force or people become able to throw balls with sufficient velocity to escape earth's gravitational field. So there is a possible doubt that the ball thrown will not, or did not, come down to earth.

That's an example of the "mere possible" or "imaginary doubt" to which Judge Weisberg alludes. It is clear that there can be some doubt, even when jurors find that there is no "reasonable" doubt that the ball returned to earth or that the defendant was guilty. But that does not establish that the doubt is reasonable. The real thrust of the beyond a reasonable doubt standard is that the juror must have an abiding conviction of the truth of the charge.

The courts don't define "abiding," but to us, abiding means that jurors don't have qualms now, when they make the decision of guilt or nonguilt. And they should expect not to lose sleep in the next week, month or year, because of their decision. Abiding represents a belief that exists now and is not expected to change in the foreseeable future.

A "conviction... of the truth" is the belief which results from a comparison and consideration of all the evidence. It is a belief, then, which arises because we have looked at all of the evidence, compared the pros and cons, and then used our reason to arrive at the conviction we now hold to be true. A juror decides Sgt. Stacey Koon is not guilty of the unlawful beating of Rodney King because that's what the evidence shows, not because the juror likes Sgt. Koon, likes cops, or dislikes African-Americans.

There are many levels of conviction. For most educated people, the highest level of certainty results from determinations based on scientific facts. For the large majority of these people, there is an abiding conviction that gravity attracts objects, and that the earth revolves around the sun.

Once forensic evidence has gained general acceptance, it is usually given the same deference. When the defendant's fingerprints are found on a gun, it is accepted by most people that the defendant handled the gun.

Other forensic or scientific evidence, such as DNA and voiceprints, may be less compelling. That is because there is some dispute within the scientific community as to the reliability of that evidence. Jurors will have to be convinced that one set of experts is much more likely to be believed, based on its studies, than the other set of experts.

Let's examine a simple everyday act. You open a sealed carton saying "milk" and pour it into a glass. It is white. Absent any other evidence, you should be able to determine beyond a reasonable doubt that the liquid is milk. It could, of course, be milk of magnesia, or a light white paint, or almost any other chalky liquid. But it is highly unlikely that any of these possibilities is the case, if the only evidence is what has been stated.

But if the white liquid has been poured from a carton without a label, and there was no other analysis of the liquid, you should not have an abiding conviction that the liquid was milk because there would be a number of different possibilities.

If there were evidence that the white liquid, after chemical testing, had none of the elements in milk and if the scientific analysis were sufficiently compelling, you could conclude—have an abiding conviction—that the liquid was not milk.

Let's draw from the Rodney King beating trial. There, the undisputed evidence was that the CHP vehicle driven by the Singers was traveling in excess of 100 miles per hour (mph), and it did not catch up with the Rodney King car. You could infer that the evidence had established, beyond a reasonable doubt, that Mr. King's car was traveling in excess of 100 mph. The inference would be based on the principle that when two objects are traveling along the same path, and object A does not gain on object B, object B is traveling at least as fast as object A.

But suppose Mr. King was charged with driving 120 mph. Would the evidence as stated above be sufficient to establish that fact beyond a reasonable doubt?

It wouldn't. Mr. King should be found not guilty of driving 120 mph. He could have been traveling 120 mph, but the evidence would not be sufficient to give rise to an abiding conviction of that fact.

If more evidence were submitted, such as the exact speed of the CHP vehicle, and the distance between the vehicles at various points, the charge might be proven beyond a reasonable doubt. There would then be objective evidence to establish the charge.

As judges of the facts, jurors need not be concerned with every fact, only the facts comprising the elements of a crime.

If the charge is speeding, and the speed limit is sixty-five mph, then the prosecution has to establish two things:

The vehicle was traveling over sixty-five mph;

and

The defendant was driving the vehicle.

If the charge is assault with a deadly weapon, the prosecution has to establish through its introduction of evidence the following four things:

An assault occurred;

A deadly weapon was used;

The defendant was the person who committed the assault;

and

The defendant used a deadly weapon.

If the prosecution cannot establish *each* of these elements beyond a reasonable doubt, it has not made its case. Jurors might decide that the victim was assaulted, a deadly weapon was used, and the defendant participated in committing the assault. If the jurors did not also feel very sure that the defendant was the one who used the deadly weapon, they should acquit the defendant of that specific charge.

To apply the beyond a reasonable doubt standard, you must understand each element of the crime charged.

Next, you need to consider the evidence presented at the trial by both sides, and to ignore all the other "noise"—the lawyers' comments and arguments, the speculations, the theatrics. Evaluate the evidence in the case. Ask yourself if each element has been proven.

Assume you feel satisfied that each element of the crime has been established to some degree, so you are not ready to acquit at this point. Ask yourself, how sure are you of the defendant's guilt. It may be helpful to "survey" your views much like opinion polls do.

The chart on the next page is an example of what we mean:

	UNSURE	MORE LIKELY THAN NOT[30]	SOMEWHAT SURE	VERY SURE
(ELEMENT 1) A person was assaulted.				
(ELEMENT 2) A deadly weapon was used.				
(ELEMENT 3) The defendant committed the assault.				
(ELEMENT 4) The defendant used the deadly weapon.				

Unless you checked the "Very Sure" box in responding to *each* of the four questions, an acquittal should result. Otherwise you do not have the abiding conviction that is necessary to convict. But just how sure is very sure? Here are some ways to think of that term.

Let's begin by comparing direct evidence from a witness with circumstantial evidence, to see if this affects our determination of beyond a reasonable doubt.

The defendant is charged with forcible rape. The victim positively identifies the defendant as the perpetrator of the rape. Is this testimony better, worse or the same as DNA evidence or semen tests, which purport to show that it was the defendant who raped the victim?

Suppose the experts testify that only one in 100,000 men have DNA similar to that of the defendant, and there are 1,000,000 men in the area where the crime was committed. Suppose, too, there is also expert testimony that shows eyewitnesses are mistaken as often as twenty-five percent of the time.

If you believe the experts, there is a one in 100,000 chance, (ten in 1,000,000) that someone other than the defendant is the rapist. Thus, if the population was 1,000,000 there still could be nine people, in addition to the accused individual, who could have similar DNA. However, as to eyewitness identifications, there is, at least theoretically, a one in four chance (twenty-five percent), based solely on statistics, that the defendant is not guilty if the victim's eyewitness testimony alone is considered. Thus, with the same population of 1,000,000 there could be 250,000 people who could be the rapist and 249,999 of them are not charged with the crime.

Most people would agree that if there were 1,000,000 people in the community, it is really not 25,000 times more likely (250,000 people who could be the rapist based on eyewitness testimony, versus ten people who could be the rapist based on DNA) that the DNA evidence against one defendant is that much better than the eyewitness testimony against another defendant. But the example should make clear, once again, that circumstantial evidence may establish a fact beyond a doubt that most would consider reasonable, while direct evidence by an honest witness may be less convincing.

In either case, there could be—and should be—other factors to consider which may have a direct effect on how the jurors consider the evidence that has been introduced. The eyewitness may have had an unobstructed view, may have totally recalled the situation, and may have specific reasons which support the identification. The DNA tests may have been performed in a careless fashion, or the defendant may have a verified alibi. In each case, the quality of evidence introduced will be crucial to the ultimate finding.

When you are sitting as a juror in a criminal case, it's important for you not to be influenced by the false analysis, however emphatic, of those who insist that direct evidence is better than circumstantial, as well as not to be swayed by the similarly false inference that if one thing is statistically more probable than another, it is always more likely to be true. You can only decide correctly when all the evidence is compared, weighed and analyzed in as objective a fashion as is possible.

The beyond a reasonable doubt standard is confusing for jurors, the media, and sometimes even for lawyers and judges.

During the *O.J. Simpson* trial, over and over we heard that if a forensic scientist was sloppy in handling blood samples, or if one of the cops was a racist, or if the glove didn't fit O.J. Simpson, then there was a reasonable doubt as to his guilt, and the jurors had to acquit. These arguments are fallacious.

To help you understand reasonable doubt and why in some instances doubt about one or more pieces of evidence may not lead to an acquittal, try this exercise: Imagine a "Juror's Table" on which you place boxes (representing the elements of the crime with which the defendant is charged, or put another way, the facts that must be proven by the prosecution) and pieces of paper which represent the items of evidence.

Represent every item of evidence submitted (testimony, baton, glove, sock, etc.) by a piece of paper and place these on the "Juror's Table." If evidence is introduced by the prosecution, mark the piece of paper representing that evidence with a "P"; if introduced by the defense, with a "D."

As the trial progresses and during deliberations, jurors evaluate the pieces of paper on the table. When a juror believes an item of evidence is relevant to one of the facts that must be proved, that piece of paper is then placed in the appropriate box.

In a case of an assault with a deadly weapon, for example, Box 1 will hold the pieces of paper which show that an assault did (or did not) occur. Box 2 will contain papers that show a deadly weapon was (or was not) used; Box 3 will store papers which either link (or do not link) the person charged to the assault committed; and Box 4 will hold papers which establish that it was (or was not) the defendant who used the deadly weapon.

Evidence may be ignored when jurors do not understand what the lawyer or witness is trying to show. The juror cannot figure out into what box to put the evidence. Pieces of paper representing such evidence would be left on the table.

In the course of the trial, some jurors may realize or be persuaded during deliberations that one or more of those pieces of paper left on the table belong in one of the boxes. Similarly, some jurors may realize that an item of evidence previously placed in a particular box really has no value and should be taken out and put back on the table.

Before casting your vote on a verdict, toss the pieces of paper not in any box off the table—they represent irrelevant evidence. You must base your decision solely on the evidence in each box.

As you consider the contents of each imaginary box, you must ask yourself: Do the pieces of paper, either singly or in some combination, establish that the fact needed to be proved by the prosecution was in fact proved?

If you conclude that it was, you must then apply the beyond a reasonable doubt standard. You must ask yourself: Does the evidence from this particular box satisfy the "very sure" test so that I have the necessary abiding conviction that such fact was proved?

If your answer to either or both questions is "No," your vote, regardless of what other jurors argue, should be to acquit.

Let's see how these two questions may actually work and what jurors should do in different situations.

Suppose that at the end of the trial there is a box with no papers in it, or only papers marked with a D. An acquittal should result, because an essential element of the crime has not been proved. The prosecution has failed to establish its case.

But let's suppose that there are initially some papers in each of the four boxes with a P on them. Jurors must review each piece of paper. If the P papers either singly or in some combination represent a fact about which the juror does not feel "very sure"—for example, the witness wasn't credible, the test was performed sloppily, or there's a D paper which sufficiently contradicts the P paper—the "very sure" test has not been met and that particular element has not been established.

If any of the four boxes have no P papers left, acquit the defendant because each one of the elements must meet the "very sure" test.

Finally, suppose that there were initially twenty P papers in each of the boxes. Fifteen of those papers in each box were discarded, because the cop is a liar, the eyewitness could not have seen the defendant, the DNA test rules are highly suspect, etc.

If there are P papers that still remain in each box, and these represent relevant facts which either singly or in some combination provide direct evidence of the ultimate facts, or indirectly prove the ultimate fact through circumstantial evidence, go onto the second question. If you are "very sure" of each of these facts, then you must convict.

You may still have reasonable doubt as to some or much of the prosecution's evidence. That is why you tossed that evidence off your "Juror's Table". But the evidence from the boxes that remains on the table is sufficient to establish guilt.

Turn to Appendix B to try your hand at applying the "Juror's Table" exercise to a hypothetical murder case.

There will always be some doubt as to whether a person is guilty. There may be some—or many—prosecution witnesses you reject. Any time there are reasons—not speculations that it could have, or might have, happened differently—but real reasons based on the evidence, and on solid analysis, that leave you in doubt as to any essential fact, you should acquit. Any time the evidence which remains on the table leaves you with the abiding conviction (meaning it endures after consideration of all of the evidence you have not rejected) that there are substantial and compelling reasons to find that all essential facts have been proven, a conviction should result.

Now step back from all these examples and ask yourself several more questions before you are satisfied that you are very sure or not-so-sure of the fact determinations you made:

Were the facts based solely on the evidence you
had available at the trial?

Did they relate to the specific decisions you had
to make, to the law you had to evaluate?

Did you set aside your emotions regarding this
case and use your reason?

If you decided that a charge was true or the
decision of guilt correct beyond a reasonable doubt,
will you be able to sleep soundly in a week, a
month, or a year from now when you think back
not only on the decision itself, but how you made
that decision?

If you can answer yes to each of these questions, you are
very sure. You have met the ultimate test that confronts a juror
in any criminal trial in which a conviction results.

Before moving on, let's revisit the *O.J. Simpson* criminal
case in terms of its verdict. Do you think that jury used our
"Juror's Table" approach in reaching its verdict? Do you think
jurors discarded the tainted testimony of Mark Fuhrman and all
of the evidence he had gathered at the scene of the crime and
then considered what was left on the table? Or do you think
that they simply found, as Mr. Simpson's lawyers kept telling
them to find, some reasonable doubt about some of the evidence, and then they based their decision solely on that questionable evidence without evaluating and comparing the remaining
credible evidence? In other words, did they ask themselves only
what's bad about the prosecution evidence, rather then ask
what's left after all the bad stuff is thrown out?

Now, let's move to the *People v. Powell et al* case, and see
whether the evidence in the first Rodney King beating trial
warranted guilty or not guilty verdicts.

PART V

THE
RODNEY
KING
BEATING
TRIAL:

A
SECOND
LOOK

Chapter 20

The Charges:
What Must Be Proved

As a juror in a criminal case, you have one very specific purpose: to decide whether the accused should be found guilty of having committed a crime. But each trial is different so that each time you serve you have to determine a different but particular set of facts and then apply those facts to the specific charges against the defendant.

The District Attorney determines the nature of the charges, and those actually selected are the ones which the jury must decide, whether or not they, the media or the public, believe other charges might have been more appropriate.

At the Rodney King beating trial in Simi Valley beginning the morning of March 5, 1992, Los Angeles County Superior Court Judge Stanley M. Weisberg told the jury that prior to the Opening Statements by the attorneys, the clerk of the court would read the indictment—the charges—in this case. The judge reminded the jury that he had read the charges to them earlier, at the beginning of jury selection.

Imagine you were sitting there that morning. Considering the tremendous public attention this trial had received, it is likely that you would not only have been very nervous but you also might have been very eager to begin. And so you look to the court and the judicial system for guidance. You would have heard the clerk read the following, which represents only two of the five Counts read to the jury:

"COUNT I.

"The said Laurence M. Powell, Timothy B. Wind, Theodore J. Briseno and Stacey C. Koon are accused by the Grand Jury of the County of Los Angeles, State of California, by this indictment, of the crime of assault by force likely to produce great bodily injury and with a deadly weapon, in violation of Penal Code § 245 (A)(1), a felony committed prior to the finding of this indictment, and as follows:

"On or about March 3rd, 1991, in the County of Los Angeles, State of California, the said defendants, Laurence M. Powell, Timothy E. Wind, Theodore J. Briseno and Stacey C. Koon, did willfully and unlawfully commit an assault upon Rodney Glenn King with a deadly weapon, to wit, a baton and shod feet, and by means of force likely to produce great bodily injury.

"It is further alleged that in the commission of the above offense the said defendants, Laurence M. Powell and Timothy E. Wind, with the intent to inflict such injury, personally inflicted great bodily injury upon Rodney Glenn King, not an accomplice to the above offense, within the meaning of Penal Code § 12022.7 and also causing the above offense to be a *serious felony* within the meaning of Penal Code § 1192.7(C)(8).

"It is also further alleged that in the commission of the above offense the said defendants, Laurence M. Powell, and Timothy E. Wind, did willfully inflict great bodily injury or torture in the perpetration of the crime, within the meaning of Penal Code § 1203(E)(3).

"COUNT II.

"For a further and separate cause of action, being a different offense of the same class of crimes and offenses as the charges set forth in aforestated count hereof, the said Laurence M. Powell, Timothy E. Wind, Theodore J. Briseno and Stacey C. Koon, are accused by the Grand Jury of the County of Los Angeles, State of California, by this indictment, of the crime of officer unnecessary assaulting or beating any person, a violation of Penal Code § 149, a felony, committed prior to the finding of this indictment and as follows:

"On or about March 3rd, 1991, in the County of Los Angeles, State of California, the said defendants, Laurence M. Powell, Timothy E. Wind, Theodore J. Briseno and Stacey C. Koon, did willfully, unlawfully under color of authority, and without lawful necessity, assault and beat a human being, to wit, Rodney Glenn King, the said defendants being then and there public officers, to wit, Los Angeles Police Officers.

"It is further alleged that in the commission of the above offense the said defendants, Laurence M. Powell and Timothy E. Wind, with the intent to inflict such injury, personally inflicted great bodily injury upon Rodney Glenn King, not an accomplice to the above offense, within the meaning of Penal Code § 12022.7 and also causing the above offense to be a serious felony within the meaning of Penal Code § 1192.7 (C)(8).

"It is also further alleged that in the commission of the above offense the said defendants, Laurence M. Powell and Timothy E. Wind did willfully inflict great bodily injury or torture in the perpetration of the crime, within the meaning of Penal Code § 1203(E)(3)."[31]

Count III and Count IV pertained to allegations regarding the filing of false police reports by two of the defendants. Count V dealt with the crime of **accessory after the fact** and applied only to Stacey C. Koon. (While these three counts are not part of the scope of review of this book, they are set forth in Appendix C so that you can grasp the breadth of the task facing jurors in this case.)

Without any further explanation or clarification, the judge noted that "the indictment has been read and we are now ready to proceed with the Opening Statements."

If you had been a member of the jury listening to the clerk read the charges, wouldn't you ask yourself: "What the hell am I supposed to decide?" You know you have to determine whether some or all the defendants are guilty of having committed one, two, three, four or all of these crimes. But how can you do that if you haven't a clue as to what the charges mean?

Should you conclude that you can use your common understanding of the technical words used in the indictment (a word you may not understand) such as "not an accomplice to the above offense," "serious felony," or "willfully inflict great bodily injury or torture"? If so, is there any assurance that twelve jurors from disparate or even similar backgrounds are going to consider these terms in the same light?

In our view, it is imperative that the court make it easier for jurors to do their jobs by giving them some guidance at this point in the trial. One way to make the jurors' task simpler would be to explain the terms used in the Counts.

For example, for Count I (the crime of assault by force likely to produce great bodily injury and with a deadly weapon):

1. What does "force likely to produce" mean?

2. What does "great bodily injury" mean?

3. What does "deadly weapon" mean?

4. What does "willfully" mean?

5. What does "unlawfully commit" mean?

6. Can a juror consider a baton and "shod feet" a deadly weapon? Don't all people who wear shoes have "shod feet"?

7. How does one have "intent to inflict"?

8. How does one "personally inflict"? Is this different from impersonally inflicting?

9. How does one "willfully inflict" great bodily injury or torture?

10. What is "torture"?

For Count II (the crime of officer unnecessary assaulting or beating any person):

11. What does it mean to say officer "unnecessary assaulting or beating any person"? Are there necessary assaults and beatings?

13. What does "prior to the finding of the indictment" mean? Did someone lose the "indictment"? And what is an "indictment"?

14. What does "unlawfully under color of authority" mean?

15. What does "without lawful necessity" mean?

16. What does "assault" mean?

17. What does "serious felony" mean? Is this to be distinguished from not-serious felonies, frivolous felonies, extremely serious felonies?

The answers to these specific questions would help jurors understand the framework of the case. Other questions remain. Can the jurors find the defendants guilty of some charges and not guilty of others? Can they find some defendants guilty and others not guilty? Why are Laurence Powell and Timothy Wind specifically singled out for doing more than the other defendants if they are all charged under the same counts?

Supporters of the current system may suggest that the trial will become more time-consuming when such information is provided to jurors at the beginning of the trial. These defenders of the status quo might argue that after Opening Statements, the presentation of both the prosecutor's case and the defense counsel's cases, and Closing Statements and the jury instructions, the jury will know what to do and how to do it. Furthermore, jurors will be less likely to prejudge the case when they absorb the whole body of argument and evidence, before focusing on certain facts.

But when the jury is not told what the words used actually mean *before* they hear anything further, how will they know and properly consider what they hear later? Withholding essential knowledge from the jurors does not help them, it hinders them from performing their assigned duty.

If the goal of the criminal-justice system is to have juries which arrive at the correct result, how can it hurt if the jury is more informed rather than less informed? To us, it seems essential that the "judges of the facts" have a clear understanding of which facts are important.

Jurors come from all walks of life, with all ranges of skills and competencies. But most people would be confused after listening to the charges against the defendants in *People v. Powell et al.* Even with a brief explanation of the charges, some jurors are still likely to be confused. But, with our approach, most would have a much clearer picture of the road they had to travel in order to arrive at a correct verdict. That doesn't require every question a juror has regarding the meaning of a word or phrase in a specific charge must be answered. It does mean *making the law simpler to understand*, to sharpen the juror's focus on the puzzle which needs piecing together.

The trial has been in existence for only a few minutes and already there are serious questions as to whether or not the court is helping the process of justice or subverting it.

Chapter 21

OPENING STATEMENTS:
ROAD MAP OF WHERE YOU MIGHT GO

T he jury has been selected, the charges have been read and the trial is ready to proceed. Opposing counsel get ready to make their Opening Statements, an extremely important vehicle for both the prosecutor and defense counsel.

In *People v. Powell et al*, Judge Weisberg described it to the jury as follows:

> "The purpose of an Opening Statement is to give you an idea of what to expect during the course of the trial. It is basically a roadmap to give you a feeling of what the evidence will be as it is presented to you...It is not designed to be all-inclusive and to give detail of all the evidence...."

These brief remarks, which were not emphasized, provided the jurors with a great deal of information. They learned that these Opening Statements:

> *"give an idea of what to expect"* (an overview of the trial)

> *"basically a roadmap"* (the trail to follow to get to the destination, the verdict)

> *"what the evidence will be"* (future tense indicating opening remarks must not be considered evidence, whatever that is)

"not designed to be all inclusive and give detail" (a general story with the specific details to be revealed later)

The Opening Statement is much more than a road map. It is the first opportunity after the jury has been seated for the attorneys to attempt to put their case into perspective so that jurors can follow what happens in the next phases of the trial. It is also the opportunity to plant the seeds either to support a verdict of guilty, if you are the prosecutor, or the seeds that will grow into reasonable doubt and result in a verdict of not guilty, if you are the defense. It is a critical part of the trial and one where a trial lawyer's skills in communication are put to the test.

Even though no evidence is presented during Opening Statements, you need to listen very carefully because the stage is set for the prosecution and defense theories of the case.

There is a problem as to evidence in the Rodney King beating case. The infamous videotape is shown more than once to the jury by different counsel. Isn't that videotape evidence in the case which could be considered by the jury? Actually, it's not evidence, at this point, because it hasn't been introduced at the trial by a witness who could verify that he took it, when it was taken, and that it is the original and not an altered video. Once the video is formally introduced, then and only then is it evidence which the jury can use in making its decision.

During Opening Statements, jurors need to keep two words in mind—"Prove it!"—and think about those words every time one of the lawyers attempts to tell them what the evidence will show. As we review the respective Opening Statements in the Rodney King beating trial, remember those words.

A NOTE TO READERS

Beginning in this chapter we've put our own comments in *italics* to help you focus as you evaluate the evidence, and to indicate what the jurors may have felt as they sat through this trial. As for the statements made by the lawyers, we will either paraphrase their questions and comments or indicate that they are being quoted.

The People Open First

Once the charges and indictment had been read to the jury, the deputy district attorney, Mr. Terry White, gave the People's Opening Statement. After introducing himself and his co-prosecutor, Alan Yochelson, he stated:

> "Just to cut through the legalese as the clerk read it here today, there are five counts in this case. Count I is assault with a deadly weapon, baton or shod feet. That count involves all four defendants. They are all charged in Count I with assault with a deadly weapon."

> "Count II is the charge of excessive force under color of authority... all four defendants are charged in that count."

Mr. White then tells the jury:

> "Those are the charges in this case. Those are the charges that the people believe you will find the defendants guilty of in this particular case."

After making this statement, an attorney for one of the defendants objected to Mr. White's statement:

> "That is improper. That is argument."

Rather than ruling on the objection, Judge Weisberg explains to the jury:

> "This is an Opening Statement, and as I indicated, it is just a preview of what the evidence will be, and as I will say during the course of the trial, ladies and gentlemen, the comments of the attorneys, no matter whether it is Opening Statement, argument or any other time during the course of the trial, is not evidence."

Mr. White then tells the jury:

> "We believe the evidence that is presented in this case will show beyond a reasonable doubt that the defendants

> are guilty of using unnecessary, unreasonable and exces-
> sive force on March 3, 1991, in the arrest of Rodney
> King."

Mr. White then presents what he believes the evidence will
show. He explains that the defendants were employed as police
officers, that they started working at around 11:00 P.M. on
March 2, 1991 and that three of the four defendants, Powell,
Wind and Briseno, were assigned to patrol vehicles and Koon, a
Sergeant, was the field supervisor for all patrol units that night.

He also presents information about Rodney Glenn King,
how he got together with some friends that night, "went to the
liquor store, they got some alcohol, they drank some alcohol."

He states that around 12:30 A.M. on March 3rd, Rodney
King and his friends decided to go for a ride and got on the
Foothill Freeway heading west. Mr. White says:

> "At the time Rodney King entered that vehicle to drive
> the evidence will show he was intoxicated."

He then explains that as CHP Officer Melanie Singer was
driving a CHP car on the freeway (and her husband, Officer
Tim Singer was her partner) she saw a car in the rear-view
mirror that was "approaching her vehicle at a very high rate of
speed." Mr. White indicated that car was driven by Mr. King.
When Mr. King's car slowed down as cars generally do when
they see a Highway Patrol car, Officer Singer exited the freeway
and then got back onto it. He then tells the jury that Ms. Singer:

> "... saw Rodney King's vehicle approximately a half mile
> to a mile ahead of her traveling very fast on the 210, the
> Foothill Freeway. She increased the speed of her vehicle.
> She increased the speed to its top speed of 115 miles an
> hour. In her estimation, however, she was not gaining
> on Mr. King's vehicle."

Mr. White continues:

> "Melanie Singer will testify that she activated the over-
> head lights on her car, the red/blue/white lights on the

California Highway Patrol vehicle, and attempted a traffic stop of Mr. King.

"The evidence will show that Mr. King didn't pull over at that time. He proceeded to the Paxton Street offramp, and got off on that offramp."

He proceeds to describe what happened on local streets, how Mr. King went through a stop sign, a red light, drove down Paxton Street at speeds in excess of seventy miles an hour, stopped for a red light, then again reached high speeds on Van Nuys, in excess of sixty miles an hour. Other police cars from the LAPD and the Los Angeles Unified School District joined the chase at the CHP's request.

"When he [Rodney King] got to the intersection of Foothill and Osborne, he stopped for a red light. He waited there for a few minutes, the light turned green, Rodney King proceeded through the intersection and stopped right about here [pointing to a map], across the street from the Mountainback Apartment Complex.

"The Singers stopped immediately behind him and to his left. The L. A. Unified School District stopped to the rear and the right of Mr. King's vehicle and Unit 16-A23, the unit that held Mr. Powell, Mr. Wind, the defendants, stopped to the left of the CHP vehicle."

Mr. White has set the stage for the beating. He has informed the jury that Mr. King was intoxicated, was driving 115 mph, did not obey the Highway Patrol officers, went through a stop sign, a red light, and drove on surface streets at speeds in excess of sixty and seventy miles an hour before finally stopping. He has told the jurors that Rodney Glenn King would not win any outstanding citizen awards. It also sounds as if Rodney King should have been charged for numerous driving violations. At this point, some jurors may have been wondering why all of this background information was necessary. So what if there was a chase? They were there because the four police officers were accused of beating Mr. King. Other jurors may have thought that if Rodney King was such a dangerous lawbreaker then he deserved a beating.

Mr. White tells the jury that when Highway Patrol Officer Tim Singer's public address system didn't work, he started yelling voice commands to Rodney King to get out of the vehicle. But Rodney King did not exit. One of the witnesses, Bryant Allen, who was also in the car with Rodney King, will testify that Mr. King had trouble getting out of his seat belt.

Mr. White states that another witness, George Holliday, [the individual who videotaped the incident] who lives at the Mountainback Apartments, was looking out his window and will say: "Rodney King got out of his vehicle and put his hands on top... of his car."

Mr. White indicates that Melanie Singer will testify that Mr. King got out of the car and put his hands on top of the car. He says:

> **"Mr. King was being ordered to put his hands in view and to lie down on the ground, but Melanie Singer will testify he wasn't actually cooperating with that, at least not right away.**
>
> **"... she will tell you that Mr. King looked up at a helicopter which was circling the area and pointed at the helicopter and started smiling. He then turned around and did what she will describe as a little dance for a short period of time.**
>
> **"All of this time LAPD and CHP is ordering Mr. King down on the ground."**

Mr. White is revealing these facts to the jury because he would rather have the jury hear them from him than from the other counsel. He wants the jury to know the prosecutor is aware of the events which preceded the beating and Mr. King's erratic behavior.

Mr. White next tells the jury:

"Mr. King eventually did get down on the ground. He got down on the ground in a position where his arms were partially extended, his head was on the ground and his body was—his entire body was on the ground lying flat on his stomach."

When the jury is informed that Mr. King was lying flat on the ground, the prosecutor has differentiated everything which has happened before (and that includes Mr. King's unlawful actions) from what happens next. It is important for the jury to understand when the unlawful police conduct began.

Mr. White says that when Mr. King was flat on his stomach:

"... Melanie Singer approached him to handcuff him to place him under arrest. When she made her approach, Defendant Koon said, 'stop, we'll handle this.'

"... Melanie Singer will testify that Officer Powell and another Officer went to Rodney King each grabbing a wrist.

"She will testify that she believes that it was some type of control move they were trying to place on Mr. King, but it was done in an ineffective manner.

"Mr. King slapped their hands away and stood up.

"... Melanie Singer will tell you that several officers crowded around Mr. King, apparently trying to get control of him, but Mr. King, while he was not actually punching anyone or hitting anyone, was not allowing them to get control of him.

"At that point Sergeant Stacey Koon told the officers to back away, that he was going to use a taser. Now, the taser... is a device which they can shoot fifty thousand volts of electricity through a person. The taser contains cartridges. When the cartridges are expelled, or darts from the cartridges are expelled out, wires are attached to the darts and the cartridge remains in the taser.

When the darts become imbedded in a suspect, they can then shoot electricity through the wires into the suspect...

"The evidence will show, however, that the darts attached to the taser never did become imbedded in Mr. King. That was found out later in the hospital. The taser was not apparently working.

"When it works it is supposed to render a person helpless. They are supposed to just fall down, lose muscular control...

"Now, after the taser becomes... ineffective, Rodney King rose to his feet and you are going to see that on the video when we play the video.

"As the video starts Mr. King is lying flat on the ground. He then rises to his feet. He moves from left to right on the screen in the direction of Officer Powell. This could be either—this could be viewed either as an attack of Officer Powell or running away from Officer Powell."

So, Mr. White here concedes a crucial point: Rodney King's actions could be construed as an attack on Officer Powell but they could also have been an attempt to escape or simply to try to avoid the pain.

Mr. White then focuses on Officer Powell's actions:

"By any interpretation, what Mr. Powell did next, you are going to see on the video, was unreasonable. Mr. Powell struck him a blow to the face with a baton much as a baseball batter would swing at a pitch. He swung that baton, hit Mr. King in the head.

"Melanie Singer will testify that the blow struck Mr. King in the head causing the skin on his cheek to split, blood to spurt out. Mr. King goes down.

"Officer Powell then stands over him and delivers more blows to his head area."

Mr. White then tells the jury about Officer Briseno and the evidence against him:

> "Also during the tape you are going to see another officer, Defendant Briseno, appear to intercede to stop Officer Powell from continuing to strike Mr. King. You are later going to see in the video, however, that Officer Briseno, while Mr. King is on the ground lying on his stomach, as his hands are moving back toward putting them behind his back, Officer Briseno walks over and delivers a stomp to the head and neck area of Mr. King."

Mr. White summarizes what he has presented:

> "The evidence is going to show, ladies and gentlemen, Mr. King was speeding, that he did not stop, that he acted silly, that he did not cooperate initially.

> "The evidence is also going to show that the beating you are about to see on this videotape is unjustified."

The video is then shown to the jury. Mr. White explains and shows Officer's Wind's involvement:

> "... you will be seeing that video a number of times during this trial and... you will see... a man who is down, a man who was not aggressive, a man who was not resisting, yet those blows from Officer Powell and Officer Wind's batons continued and continued and continued for no just reason."

Mr. White then addresses the charges in this case against Officer Powell and Koon regarding their submission of police reports on the incident, reports which are not part of the focus of this book. However, it should be noted that Mr. White used very strong language as he accused them of lying "about every important material fact in this incident in their reports" in order to cover up the beating.

Finally, Mr. White closes his Opening Statement:

"This evidence will show that whatever Rodney King was or whatever he did, it did not justify what you saw on that videotape."

And that basically concluded the People's Opening Statement. It closed as it began, with the People's view of what the evidence would show. It included statements of what other persons were expected to say. As the judge informed everyone at the beginning, the Opening Statement would not mention all of the evidence to be used. Only selected portions would be highlighted. But in this Opening Statement, the videotape on which so much of this case is based was shown.

Before reviewing the next set of Opening Statements, ask yourself how effective, forceful or helpful the Opening Statement by the prosecution has been in presenting the People's case against these four police officers (at least as it relates to Counts I and II)? Is the prosecution off to a good start? Will the evidence actually show what Mr. White says it will? If it doesn't, will the prosecutor's case be seriously weakened?

THE DEFENSE GOES NEXT

Opening Statement for Officer Sergeant Stacey Koon[32]

Darryl Mounger represented Sgt. Stacey Koon. After briefly introducing himself, Mr. Mounger tells the jury that maybe what they think they know about this incident might not be the whole picture:

"...this is the first opportunity that we have to tell not only you, but everybody else, what really happened out there, the way we believe the evidence is going to unfold."

After explaining how evidence will come into the trial for them to consider and what that evidence might be, Mr. Mounger tells jurors the conclusion he believes they will reach after they have considered all of the evidence:

"And all the things that I'm going to tell you will come together at the end and you will see that everything that was done out here on March 3, 1991, was reasonable and necessary based upon the information and the knowledge that Sergeant Koon had at the time he acted."

In a matter of minutes, Mr. Mounger has introduced two critical ideas for the jury to think about. First, the entire world would learn what "really happened" out there. Second, Sgt. Koon acted in a reasonable and necessary manner based on his knowledge and information.

Although Mr. Mounger is technically defending only one police officer, Sgt. Koon, there will be some carry-over effect to the other defendants. If he can show Sgt. Koon's behavior to be reasonable, then perhaps the conduct of Officers Powell, Wind and Briseno was also reasonable.

Mr. Mounger has stated his conclusion, but only the jurors will decide whether the evidence presented during the trial will support what he says it will. He has effectively framed the issues in the case in an attempt to persuade the jurors to view the beating in a different light.

Using Sgt. Koon's experience as a positive factor, Mr. Mounger tells the jury "that Sergeant Koon has been a police officer for fourteen-and-a-half years and you can draw the inference from that he has had a lot of experience." He also mentions that "over thirteen years has been on the street, serving the citizens and dealing with the public."

In other words, Mr. Mounger emphasizes that Sgt. Koon is not only experienced, he works on the street (not at a desk), and he performs public service.

The lawyer then tells the jury about Sgt. Koon:

"... you will not hear testimony that Sergeant Koon struck anyone, but you will hear that he was there in charge of his officers, and remember, with fourteen and a half years... he has more time as a police officer than all these other defendants combined. He is experienced and he is in charge of his officers."

And then Mr. Mounger gets to the heart of his argument:

"But there is a distinction in that the evidence is going to show you that he is not in charge of this situation. There is only one person that is in charge of this situation and that is Rodney Glenn King."

This puts a different spin on the whole episode. Mr. Mounger is claiming it is not the arresting officers, but the arrestee—the suspect/the victim—who was in charge of the "situation," as contrasted with Sgt. Koon, who was in charge of his officers.

"... you are going to hear that at about 12:37 in the morning that the California Highway Patrol did... see a car speeding and they did try to stop it.

"... they asked for more units and... when a police officer asks for more policemen it is because he thinks he has more than what he can deal with.

"And there were three people in that car. You can't forget that... and there were two Highway Patrol Officers and they said, 'we need more help out here' and they didn't have any units available and they said then, 'we need LAPD to come out here and help us' and you will hear this on the tape. They are saying, 'have LAPD find us.'"

Sgt. Koon's lawyer is presenting the same scenario as Prosecutor White, but he is emphasizing that the prelude to the arrest involved a dangerous situation, where CHP needed help because of the perceived danger.

He tells the jurors what Sgt. Koon was thinking when the call for aid came from the Highway Patrol:

"Why don't people stop for the police is in Sergeant Koon's mind What did they do that they don't want me to find out about? Why do they have to get away? Why do you run from the police when you see flashing lights and blaring siren?"

Prosecutor White objects. The court advises Mr. Mounger to confine himself to the evidence and not argue the case. While Mr. Mounger was prevented from pursuing this line, the questions (*really argument*) had been heard by the jury. Mr. Mounger moves on to say:

> "... eventually, after almost an eight-mile pursuit, that this car stopped, and when this car stopped... police officers with their guns drawn were pointing them at the occupants of the car.

> "They ordered the occupants of that car to get down on the ground and to lay in a prone position. And a prone position... is when you are face down with your legs spread apart and your face on the ground so that you can't see the approaching officer.

> "And the reason why police officers put people in a prone position is because it is a taught safe way to approach someone. They don't want to jeopardize themselves."

Mr. Mounger expands upon what Mr. White told the jury:

> "And the two occupants of that car did in fact get out and comply with the officer's orders, but not the driver. The driver displayed bizarre behavior. Sergeant Koon will tell you in his fourteen years of experience that he knows what this means.

> "... Rodney King not only put his hands on the car and waved at a helicopter, but... he reached down and put his hand to his rear, and when Melanie Singer ordered him 'get your hands away from your butt,' Rodney King turned to her and shook [his butt] at her."

And Mr. Mounger goes further:

> "...Rodney King displayed the objective symptoms of being under the influence of something, and Sergeant Koon will tell you, 'I knew he was under the

influence of something. I saw a blank stare in his face. I saw watery eyes. I saw perspiration. I saw that he swayed. I saw that he was slow to follow the command of the officers. I saw him looking through me.'"

Mr. White had told the jurors that "when she [Melanie Singer] made her approach defendant Stacey Koon said, 'Stop, we'll handle this.'" Mr. Mounger presents the situation quite differently to the jury:

"And Sergeant Koon will tell you when he saw this big man not complying getting down on his hands and knees and refusing to go down in this prone position, that he saw Melanie Singer, California Traffic Officer—CHP Officer, approaching Rodney King with a gun in her hand and she got within five feet of Rodney King and Sergeant Koon knew that a gun is the ultimate force that can be used by a police officer and he saw her approaching an individual he knew to be under the influence and someone who was not cooperating and he knew the danger and he ordered her back. He did the only reasonable thing he could do, he did his job, and he said 'Back off, we'll handle this.'"

Mr. White had not told the jury that CHP Officer Melanie Singer's gun was drawn. Mr. Mounger's road map looks very different from that of the prosecution. A new picture is emerging.

After explaining why Sgt. Koon decided to use his officers and not the CHP, Mr. Mounger describes use-of-force and how that relates to escalation and de-escalation of force. His points:

"...it is the suspect who controls what happens on the street.

"That the officer at first will have his uniform presence. He is standing there in his blue uniform with his badge, his gun belt, his handcuffs, and he tells people what to do by verbalizing, 'Get down, get on your face.'

> "But when that doesn't work, there is an array of tools that Sergeant Koon has that his Department requires."

Mr. Mounger uses a chart to explain the escalation of force to the jury and make the jury aware of the tools Sgt. Koon had available that night:

> "You start with verbalization and then you go to the first one which is called firm grip. It may be called pain compliance, but in a sense what it means is that you go in and you grab ahold of somebody, whether it is by the arm, whether you twist the wrist, a wrist lock, a twist lock, but you grab ahold of them with your hands.

> "The next thing is a chemical agent which is like a tear gas or a mace that you use that officers carry on their belt, but that is only used in certain situations. Sergeant Koon would never use that with anybody under the influence and neither would the experts say that it should be used then.

> "The next level up is this taser. It is meant to incapacitate. It shoots fifty thousand volts and it causes most people's motor nerves... to collapse, but it doesn't always work, it is like anything else.

> "But when this doesn't work, the next tool up is a sidehandle baton, a metal baton. It is a tool to protect yourself and to take people into custody.

> "And in addition to that, on the same level with this... there are kicks, but it depends on how you use those kicks, and there will be a lot of time describing them.

> "But when these tools are ineffective, ladies and gentlemen, then you rise to the level of deadly force because all that you have when these tools don't work is a neck hold, whether they call it a carotid, a modified carotid, a bar arm, in some jurisdictions it is a neck hold that could cause death.

"And other than that, you have a firearm, you have guns, you have instruments of death, irreversible, irreversible."

At this point, the judge interrupts and asks Mr. Mounger to confine himself "to an Opening Statement and a review of the evidence you expect to introduce in your argument."

Again, Mr. Mounger was asked to stop speaking after he went through the chart. The jury heard his chart remarks. The jury was not told to disregard anything Mr. Mounger had said.

Mr. Mounger focuses on what he believes happened that night one year earlier:

"... He [Stacey Koon] will tell you that he got his taser and he told his four officers to take Rodney King down to the ground.

"... Larry Powell took one arm, Ted Briseno took another arm. Solano, the probationary employee... took one leg and Wind took the other leg, and while Rodney King was on all fours, Powell, six foot one, 192 pounds, Briseno on the other arm, five-eight and only 135 pounds, arms on his arms, Sergeant Koon observed muscle rigidity. Rodney King's arms weren't moving, but for some reason both arms came right out to the side.

"... Rodney King went face down into the asphalt. At that point Rodney King laughed, he rolled back and forth, pulled his arms away from the officers and pushed himself up, throwing Powell off to one side and Briseno off to the other, leaving Solano and Wind hanging on to the legs and Sergeant Koon, having a back-up plan of the taser, ordered his officers off, 'Back away,' and they did."

More details are added to the defense picture of the attempt to subdue Mr. King than were contained in the prosecution's Opening Statement. They are used to show Mr. King's strength, his laughter even when pinned by four officers.

Mr. Mounger now discusses the taser that was supposed to incapacitate Mr. King:

> "And there is a popping sound that comes with this instrument when it is fired and the popping sound went as Sergeant Koon ordered Rodney King 'Get down or I'm going to shoot you with the taser' and Rodney King started up.
>
> "And bam, the taser went off, and you will hear a clicking sound that goes off with this instrument. That means the juice is going and it is supposed to incapacitate.
>
> "But rather than causing Rodney King to fall down... Rodney King rose up to his feet and groaned, 'Ahh, Ahh' and started advancing toward Koon, and Koon ordered him again 'get down, get down,' but Rodney King kept coming.
>
> "And he shot the taser again and this time hit him in the front and Rodney King dropped down to one knee. At that point Sergeant Koon managed to talk Rodney King down to the prone position spread-eagle on the ground, and ladies and gentlemen, that is when this tape starts.
>
> "And in the first three seconds of this videotape the tone is set for Sergeant Koon's state of mind." Rodney King, "without warning, with no one touching him, rose to his feet and turned, within two seconds to the frame, in a violent charge to Powell."

Prosecutor White had described Rodney King's apparent movement toward Officer Powell either "as an attack of Officer Powell or running away from Officer Powell."

Mr. Mounger challenges that contention:

> "... the evidence will show you that this can only be interpreted as an attack, that there were several avenues of escape that Rodney King could have chosen, but he didn't.

"His actions are clear on the tape and in the photographs and Koon perceived a deliberate attack to Powell and Koon saw Powell react in the only way he had. He took his side-handle baton and he went forward in a chopping motion striking Rodney King, what Koon saw, as across the clavicle.

"And Rodney King went down. And when you watch this tape, Rodney King comes down and appears to make a one point landing right on his face into the asphalt."

Mr. Mounger concludes his Opening Statement with the thrust of his defense:

"... Rodney King and Rodney King alone was in control of the situation because Sergeant Koon is watching the situation. He is watching his officers. He can't see everything. He's not going to tell you he saw every blow, but he will tell you that he was watching Rodney King.

"And that when you are reviewing this tape, if you watch what Sergeant Koon watched... the evidence will show you that when Rodney King is laying spread-eagle in a prone he is not hit.

"But when Rodney King, in the very beginning, in the first six frames of this incident, went from the ground to a charge and when Sergeant Koon will tell you...that once he saw Rodney King rise to his feet and attack at Powell, that in Koon's mind in charge of his officers, that Rodney King has set the tone."

"And any reasonable... doubt or benefit of the doubt that Sergeant Koon would have normally given a suspect Rodney King took away."

Mr. Mounger's Opening Statement was an effort to move Rodney King to the center of the stage and remove the four police officers from the jurors' primary focus. There's no doubt that Mr. Mounger's Opening Statement could have favorably impacted the other defendants in the minds of the jurors.

Opening Statement for Officer Laurence Powell

Michael Stone represented Officer Powell. Mr. Stone tells the jury he would like to introduce them to the defendant: "He is a twenty-nine year-old single man—" but he is interrupted with an objection from Mr. White. The court then asks Mr. Stone to confine himself to the evidence at this point in the proceedings. The court noted that Mr. Stone would have the opportunity to present other material later. Lawyer Stone then states that Powell:

> **"Joined the LAPD as a police reserve officer in 1984 and found that police work agreed with him."**

There was another objection by Mr. White and the court advised Mr. Stone not to "get into that sort of editorializing" and confine himself to the evidence.

Mr. Stone explains Officer Powell's police background:

> **"Graduated from the police academy, started serving on the LAPD as a patrol officer. He was promoted to Police Officer 3, became a field training officer in 1991 and was assigned to Foothill Division as a Field Training Officer.**
>
> **"The job of a field training officer is to instruct new police officers or rookies... in field police work, and... on... the date of this incident, he was assigned as a field training officer and had in his charge Officer Timothy Wind..."**

Then Mr. Stone turns to the events in this case starting with the police chase. After describing some of the events, he points out:

> **"... this entire chase covered a distance of 7.8 miles. Fully four miles of this chase was on surface streets where the speed limits did not exceed thirty-five miles per hour."**

Clearly, defense counsel are focusing on Rodney King's actions before the incident.

"... Mr. Singer, who is the passenger in the CHP car, got on the loud speaker system... and orally ordered King to pull over and stop, repeatedly as they sped down Paxton Avenue.

"... Mrs. Singer will tell you that when Mr. Singer did that, the passenger in the rear of the King automobile reached up and tapped Rodney on the shoulder, but he didn't stop.

"Bryant Allen... one of the passengers, along with Freddie Helms, in the King automobile, and Mr. Allen will tell you that he repeatedly asked or pleaded with Mr. King to pull over and stop, that the police were following him.

"And he will tell you that Mr. King was acting very strange, no response, just looked straight ahead, didn't appear to be nervous at all, but continued to drive."

Mr. Stone provides additional details:

"Suddenly at Terra Bella Mr. King slams on the brakes and the King vehicles [sic] comes to a stop. Melanie Singer swerves to the left to avoid a rear end collision and completely passes the King vehicle...

"Mr. Singer, in the right side of the CHP car, is looking at Mr. King out his right passenger window. Melanie Singer slammed on the brakes of the Highway Patrol Car... and reversed back to the rear of the King car.

"At that point Mr. King took off again... and finally pulling up to the right and stopping because he couldn't go any farther. A truck was stopped ahead of him..."

After noting what happened once the officers were out of their cars, Mr. Stone talks about resistant suspects:

"Now, when those four officers approached Mr. King, they all went for one of the limbs, either the left hand or the right hand, one of the legs, while Sergeant Koon, armed with a taser, instructed them and directed them and he told them, 'If he starts to fight, back off,' because, you see, the training that these officers receive... is that they don't tie up with resistant suspects. You don't wrestle them into handcuffs. That is why they have the taser.

"Well, Officer Powell... went up and grasped Mr. King's left hand with the idea of handcuffing him. He didn't have his baton out. None of the officers did at that point. Nobody had hit Mr. King. They only ordered him down."

Lawyer Stone goes on to describe what happened next:

"And Officer Powell went up, grabbed his wrist and tried to move it back to a handcuffing position, and King began to laugh and suddenly he went into a push-up position and with the full body weight of Officer Powell on his back he pushed up and Powell rolled off and all of the officers scrambled away."

Mr. Stone then directly challenges the prosecution regarding whether or not the taser worked that night or not:

"... the taser works when the darts pierce the clothing at an optimum distance of ten to twelve feet. That is exactly what happened in this case.

"The evidence will be that the taser was working, not malfunctioning."

Everything described so far occurred before the videotape. Mr. Stone explains that the second cassette was fired and the darts land properly... as a result King falters momentarily.

"And you see him at the very beginning of that tape rise up, not slowly, not lumbering, but very quickly rise up, turn and charge Officer Powell.

"In the very beginning of the tape you see Officer Powell is on the right side of the screen and you see Mr. King charging him. You see Officer Powell swings his baton."

Mr. Stone then lets the jury know what they can expect to hear, and that the testimony won't be supported by the medical evidence in the case.

According to Mr. Stone, Melanie Singer will testify:

"... Officer Powell struck Mr. King in the head and in the face and in the hands, as Mr. King covered his face.

"... Officer Powell struck Mr. King five to seven times full power stroke baseball type swings with that metal baton.

"... the medical evidence will be it didn't happen.

"The injuries to Mr. King's face consist of some abrasions and a mild fracture of the right side of the face at the cheek bone level, the zygomatic arch... the fractures are too diffuse to be... caused by a baton.

"There were no head shots, officers are trained not to hit someone on the head, because a strike to the head or a strike to the face can be fatal with this baton."

Focusing now on one of his most important points which relates to the videotape itself, Mr. Stone says:

"One of the things about this tape... is that there is a lot of things that you didn't see at first when you look at the tape and there is a lot of things you see only after examination."

At this point there is a recess and when court resumes, the judge admonishes the lawyers outside the presence of the jury regarding the use of argument in an Opening Statement:

"... as I have indicated, these are Opening Statements, they are not argument, and counsel are not just going to be reminded, but are ordered not to use these as vehicles for argument.

> "And if I find that there are further violations of that, I'm going to intercede rather directly and limit your Opening Statements."

Notice that the judge is so annoyed that he is threatening the attorneys, saying he will act to stop them from using argument even if there is no objection raised.

After the recess, Mr. Stone plays the videotape and freezes the tape so that particular frames can be shown to the jury. He also uses blown-up photographs of the frozen frames to high-light his points. He says:

> "Now... you will see Mr. King sitting on his buttocks and you will see him reach up and put his hands behind his head... and at that point the testimony will be Sergeant Koon says, 'okay, okay, he gives. That's it.'
>
> "And at that point, as the tape goes forward, you will see that there are no more baton blows and Mr. King is handcuffed and taken into custody."

Mr. Stone informs the jury that they will be viewing the videotape at three different speeds in the trial. The first part will be in real time, the actual time. The second is slow-motion and the third will be very slow-motion. Mr. Stone next states:

> "... Los Angeles Police Officers... are trained in the escalation and de-escalation of force and that as the suspect's movement and activities create an increase in the threat to the officer or an increase in the resistance to arrest or an increase in the attempt to escape, the officers are taught to escalate force.
>
> "As the suspect becomes more compliant or ceases the threat or ceases the resistance, the officers are taught to de-escalate the force.
>
> "... practically every level, except excessive force... was used in this case. Every level of force except deadly force.

"Sergeant Koon and the other officers attempted verbalization, tried to get Mr. King to lay down... Sergeant Koon and another [sic] officers are yelling at him, 'get down, get down, hands behind your back. Get down, get down, hands behind your back.'

"He doesn't respond to any of these things. The firm grip... and pain compliance have not worked. They've tried to handcuff him, and in the very beginning of that tape when you see Officer Powell, look down at his back pocket. You are going to see silver handcuffs dangling open.

"... when he [Officer Powell] went up and attempted to handcuff Mr. King and met with the resistance, he just stuck the handcuffs in his back pocket and when he was assaulted he drew his baton.

"... four darts from the taser—two cassettes are fired into Mr. King.

"All the electronics appear to be working. Doesn't faze him. Multiple baton blows don't appear to faze him.

"The conclusion of every officer who was there at the scene was that they had a duster on their hands, a person who was under the influence of phencyclidine, PCP, or angel dust.

"The evidence will be that Sergeant Koon who has had a lot of experience dealing with persons under the influence of PCP and taking them into custody and he has had a lot of experience using the taser, and his conclusion, as well as that of the officers, was that they had a duster on their hands.

"The officer's perceptions are based on their experience and their knowledge and their training and their observations.

"And one of the most important parts of the defense in this case is Mr. King's bizarre behavior from the very moment he was first sighted by the CHP officers through the point that he was finally taken into custody.

"Police officers are trained not to tie up with persons that are violent or possibly under the influence of drugs. In particular, PCP is probably... one of the most dangerous drugs that confronts police officers in the course of their duties."

Mr. Stone concludes his Opening Statement by referring to the charges dealing with the filing of a false police report.

His version of the evidence is different from Mr. White's (no head shots by Powell; the taser did work; King clearly charged Powell; King was apparently on PCP, not alcohol) and adds to Mr. Mounger's defense (the proper escalation and de-escalation of force was part of police procedure). Mr. Stone's version, if accepted, may also exonerate the other defendants.

Opening Statement for Officer Timothy E. Wind

Paul R. De Pasquale represented Officer Wind. He immediately makes a point regarding Officer Wind's experience:

"...in terms of the LAPD, Timothy Wind does not compare in his experience to what you heard about Sergeant Stacey Koon. Timothy Wind had only been out of the police academy of Los Angeles for just about four months at the time of this March, 1991 incident."

This lawyer tells the jury that he's not going to speak to them at great length about the evidence because "you've already heard it discussed by three attorneys from their various perspectives." But he indicates that he wants to make a few points and expand upon a few already made.

"Now, you will hear from Bryant Allen he was trying to get through to Mr. King, getting no response, getting something like a trancelike failure to respond from Mr. King, and the pursuit went on.

"... one of the very first things that happened when Tim Wind got out of the car he was in... with Larry Powell... was that shouted advice, information 'watch out, he's dusted.'"

[Tim Wind] "... had been informed and educated that in dealing with PCP suspects, in dealing with dusters, police officers have been killed."

Mr. De Pasquale then continues:

"It was Tim Wind's awareness, upon hearing this advice, 'watch out, he's dusted,' that not only for police officers, but... even for the person suspected of being under the influence, you have a very dangerous situation, the potential for life-threatening confrontation. That is the state of mind the evidence will show, of Tim Wind. We're dealing with a serious and a dangerous situation."

Mr. De Pasquale is saying what the evidence will show. Is he telling the jurors to expect Mr. Wind to testify? But what if Mr. Wind doesn't testify. How then will Mr. De Pasquale prove the state of Mr. Wind's "awareness"?

Mr. De Pasquale notes:

"...it will be the uncontroverted unopposed evidence that several people were pointing guns at Mr. King and Mr. King was told, 'get your hands away from your pockets,' and in response Mr. King did exactly the opposite at gunpoint.

"At gunpoint he put his hand to his rear end and shook his rear end in the direction of Melanie Singer who was giving the instruction, not an act calculated to make anybody feel secure..."

One of the prosecution lawyers objects that Mr. De Pasquale is engaging in argument. Judge Weisberg says "sustained. Come on, Mr. De Pasquale, let's stick to the evidence here."

Mr. De Pasquale moves on to talk about training:

> "On this night Larry Powell... was Timothy Wind's field training officer. Stacey Koon... was Timothy Wind's Sergeant.
>
> "So Tim Wind was acting under their supervision and under their instruction."

Mr. De Pasquale implies that even if Tim Wind erred, he was doing so with the knowledge and approval of his superiors. Mr. Wind legitimately believed he was acting appropriately, even if it is ultimately determined his actions were excessive. He was just following orders, doing his duty.

Mr. De Pasquale wants his client to be distinguished from the other defendants. Even it is determined by the jury that his actions were inappropriate, Mr. Wind believed that his actions were being sanctioned at the time the blows were being inflicted upon Mr. King. How can he be faulted in that instance.

Mr. De Pasquale then comments:

> "...[the] taser appeared to have an effect, it appeared to have discomforted Mr. King, but it didn't incapacitate him and it didn't stop him."

As for the use of the baton, Mr. De Pasquale states:

> "Timothy Wind got involved in the use of the side-handle baton after the initial charge of Powell. Tim Wind... used the baton. He acted in accordance with his training. He stood and watched when Mr. King tried to rise. Tim Wind moved in, used the strokes, as per his training, and he backed up.
>
> "... Tim Wind trying to keep a distance from Mr. King, but it is his responsibility... to participate and to keep Mr. King from getting up, because according to his training... Mr. King is a much greater threat."

Focusing next on the use of kicks by his client, Lawyer De Pasquale tells the jury:

> "... Tim Wind also uses what's called the front kick. It is also called the departmentally approved front kick.

> "... it is not like a field goal where you are kicking something with your toe or your instep, but it is a process of using the bottom of the foot in a downward motion, departmentally approved. That is what Tim Wind was trained to do.

> "The responsibility was to keep Mr. King down."

Notice how Mr. De Pasquale interjects the words "departmentally approved." He wants the jurors to remember those words because it legitimizes the actions of his client.

And then Mr. De Pasquale returns to a theme already advanced by another defense counsel:

> "At the beginning of the incident... it almost seemed... this thing was going to end almost before it started, because Powell moved in to cuff, the four people moved in before Mr. Holliday turned his video on, and the situation almost stopped before the problems started.

> "But Mr. King resisted, threw these four people off, and the escalation of force became necessary per the training of the LAPD.

> "It was not an appropriate case for chemical agents. Tim Wind was a witness to the use of the taser which appeared to have an effect, didn't stop Mr. King. He did what he was taught to do, which is to use the side-handle baton and the kicks in the departmentally approved fashion.

> "and according to Mr. Wind's training, that should have ended it. Those things hurt. This should be over and it wasn't. Mr. King kept trying to get up.

"Now, you were not in Tim Wind's shoes. You were not at that point at the level where you could employ deadly force and in the LAPD not only is a gun deadly force, but a neck restraint is deadly force.

"There was not justification, as long as he wasn't on his feet engaged with an officer, there was not justification for the use of deadly —"

At this point, the prosecution objected noting that "this is not Opening Statement. This is argument." Judge Weisberg then reiterates his earlier concern:

"All right...let's see if you can control your argument and contain your argument until such time as it is appropriate at the end of the trial."

Finally, Mr. De Pasquale concludes:

"... the evidence will show a situation in which Mr. Wind was using the tools, the tools had not done what they were supposed to, and his situation, you will hear evidence... was one of fear and frustration, not pleasure in inflicting injury."

Mr. De Pasquale has reenforced the idea that either Rodney King was "dusted" or his actions were consistent with someone on PCP. He has reenforced the version of the events which treats the beating and kicking as the "departmentally approved" response. And again, this helps the case of the other three officers.

The morning session is over. The judge gives the jurors the following admonition:

"But again, don't discuss this case with anyone, don't form any final opinions about it.

"All you've heard at this point is what lawyers expect the evidence to be. It will be something that we'll have to wait and see whether their expectations are fulfilled when the evidence... is presented in this trial...

"So at this point you have heard no evidence, there is nothing to even evaluate at this point, just expectations of what the lawyers expect the evidence to be."

Although you would ordinarily expect the defense lawyers to say nothing that would strengthen or support the People's case against a different defendant in the same case, in People v. Powell et al, one of the defendants (Briseno) actually argued the guilt of another defendant (Powell).

Opening Statement for Officer Theodore Briseno

John Drummond Barnett represented Officer Briseno, who was accused of only one act, that of stomping Rodney King. Mr. Barnett began his Opening Statement:

"I'm not going to rehash what the other lawyers have said and I'm sure you are kind of tired of listening to lawyers not argue this case."

Mr. Barnett then delivers his version of the beating, what he believes the evidence will show.

"... Officer Briseno... arrived at the scene where Mr. King was being or attempting to be put into custody, and he saw Mr. King charge at Officer Powell.

"He then saw officer Powell take his baton and with a power stroke smash him [Rodney King] right in the face.

"... after that blow was struck, Officer Powell, in a torrent of blows, continued to hit Mr. King, as Mr. King was ... on the ground and on his knees. He continued to hit him backwards and forward in power strokes.

"And when he [Officer Briseno] saw that, when he saw the torrent of blows, he went over to Officer Powell, who was... poised to strike again.

"And he stopped him. He put his hand out... and he grabs at the baton and he pushes him away.

"... he pushed Powell back... Officer Briseno was afraid... Mr. King was going to be further beaten and so he pushed him away.

"After he pushed him [Powell] away, after he stops this power stroke, behind him, you will see in the film, Officer Wind came in and began power strokes... and immediately thereafter, Powell takes another swing at Mr. King.

"That swing almost hits Officer Briseno in the head. Mr. Briseno has seen what this very baton has done to the face of Rodney King. He has felt and seen the stroke that almost hit him in the head.

"... after that, he [Briseno] walks around the side and he's yelling at Mr. King to stay down, to stay down.

"When there is a break, when the blows cease momentarily, then you will see Officer Briseno step forward and he will lift his left foot... up.

"Officer Wind is poised to strike. Officer Briseno in lifting his foot up, does not want to put his head in the strike area. He doesn't want to get hit with the baton... being wielded by Officer Wind, and so he puts his foot out like this, his weak foot, and he starts to press down.

"He [Briseno] sees a number of things. He sees Wind winding up... He knows Powell is behind his back. He believes... that they're out of control and that he has to be mindful of his own safety.

"And ... he is not stomping, but attempting to place his foot down while keeping his head in an area where he can avoid being hit himself by one of these metal PR-24 batons, and that is what he does...

"And he sees Mr. King is moving. He wants Mr. King flat so that he can cuff him for two reasons: One, so Mr. King can be put safely in custody, and two, so that the actions of these batons will cease."

And with Mr. Barnett's "Thank you," the Opening Statement phase of the trial concludes and the People now can
present their evidence.

*Before moving to the next phase of the trial, let's review
what the jurors sitting in that courtroom have heard and seen.*

*The People spoke once; the defense spoke four times. The
defense, with the exception of Officer Briseno (whose attorney
attacked Officer Powell and, to a lesser extent, Officer Wind)
worked together to emphasize the strong points and to add others.*

*The attorneys spoke for several hours. The jurors were
reminded on several occasions that nothing they heard was
evidence. So was there a difference between what they heard
and saw in the Opening Statements from any of the pretrial
publicity to which they had been exposed? Well, the Opening
Statements were more structured—a road map—but they were
nonetheless argument, opinion, hearsay, speculation. All of the
lawyers' statements would have been the subject of objections if
attempts were made to submit them as evidence because they
were hearsay. It was hearsay because the lawyers were simply
saying what they thought other people (who were not then
testifying) would say.*

*Although Judge Weisberg sometimes explained in response
to an objection that lawyers' remarks are not evidence, at other
times he sustained the objection (e.g., when Mr. De Pasquale
remarked that Rodney King shook his rear end at officer Melanie
Singer) without any instruction to the jury to disregard what the
lawyer said. In fact, Judge Weisberg made a curious remark
when he told Mr. De Pasquale to "stick to the evidence" even
though the judge has previously said that no evidence was being
presented.*

*Thus, as the jury approached the evidence part of the trial,
they had heard lots of lawyer jargon and some instructions from
the judge. But they hadn't heard what certain legal words meant.*

*If you had been on that jury would you now be clear about
what it meant when an objection was overruled or sustained?
Would you know for sure whether you could use the videotape,
charts and diagrams you had been shown to reach your verdict?*

The fact is that the jury has not yet been given a clear explanation of the process they have just "witnessed". Where does the case stand from where they sit?

The lawyers still must: "Prove it!"

Chapter 22

Case-In-Chief:
Putting Evidence
On the Juror's Table

It is time for the prosecution to present their "Case-in-Chief. This is the evidence portion of the trial, and the prosecution goes first since it must prove the case against the defendants. Part IV of this book provides a basic understanding of evidence. But what about the *Powell* jurors? What did they *know*?

Well, Judge Weisberg told the jurors during Opening Statements that they hadn't heard any evidence. So theoretically they knew that the lawyers' statements were not evidence.

But the jurors also heard the judge admonish the lawyers "to stick to the evidence" and not make argument. So it is possible the jury believed that some of the lawyers' statements were evidence.

Mr. Mounger, representing Sgt. Koon, gave his own explanation of evidence at the beginning of his Opening Statement:

> "And the evidence is going to come to you in many ways. It is going to come to you from the witness stand. It is going to come to through exhibits such as the videotape, through still photographs, through documents that have been blown up and documents that will not be blown up and presented to you.
>
> "It will come to you from the court in some instances where you are told that these are an agreed-upon set of

facts, there is no dispute about this, but a lot of things are going to come to you by way of inference, things that you will understand because of other facts. You all know that two plus two is four. If you see two plus two, you don't have to be told that."

The jurors were expected to keep these explanations in mind as they viewed the videotape; looked at charts and diagrams of the police pursuit; saw demonstrations of what happened through physical reenactment of what witnesses had seen. Even the lawyers themselves would become actors, playing the role of participants in the beating.

The jury would also hear testimony from individuals as to what they personally had seen, heard or thought they had seen or heard (testimony based on personal knowledge); testimony from other witnesses as to what others had told them (hearsay); testimony from experts as to medical findings and as to the appropriate use-of-force (expert testimony); testimony as to what the witnesses thought the officers and Mr. King were doing or trying to do (opinion); testimony from the officers as to their state of mind. The jury would also get to see objects, such as the PR 24 baton; hear taped transmissions from the officers; read the police reports.

Jurors must have asked themselves a number of questions as the evidence was being presented to them during the trial: Was all of this evidence? Was all of this evidence really necessary? Was any evidence better than other evidence? Were some experts better than others? Was there any way to determine if a witness was lying?

Now let's look at the evidence presented to the jury in the courtroom in Simi Valley, California.

The prosecution called twenty-one witnesses. What follows is a summary of what they said and how they described what happened. It sets forth what the jury saw and heard, interspersing testimony given on *direct examination* or cross-examination in a more sensible format than the hodgepodge way evidence was presented to the jurors.

THE PROSECUTION GOES FIRST

George Holliday testified that he "saw a gentleman standing by the white vehicle with his hands on the car and some police officers around him." It took him "about a minute" to get his video-camera. He then began filming from his balcony. That videotape is introduced into evidence. Mr. Holliday testifies that it has not been altered or changed. He also stated that he "saw several police officers hitting a man."

He is then subject to cross-examination by each of the four defense attorneys.

This is a positive strategy for the defendants, because each witness can be examined four separate times about any inconsistency or discrepancy so that if one lawyer misses a point, another will catch it. In theory, but obviously not in practice, when evidence was only presented related to the guilt of one or several defendants, only the attorney for that defendant(s) should have been allowed to cross-examine the witness. But remember, unless the prosecution objects, the defense can ask whatever it wants.

On cross-examination (and on direct with a hostile witness) the attorney is permitted to "lead" the witness. Mr. Barnett, representing Sgt. Briseno, uses the tactic of asking leading questions effectively in the following exchange:

Question:
"You don't remember saying it, but by viewing Mr. King that evening from the balcony you formed a couple of conclusions. One was that he was drunk, and two, you were amazed at his lack of response to the batons; is that correct?"

Answer:
I guess so. I mean if I did have the—the—you must have transcripts of all the things I said at the police station. I don't remember exactly what I said, and if I said it, I said it."

This isn't exactly what Mr. Barnett hoped for; he never does get a direct acknowledgment from Mr. Holliday as to his impressions of Mr. King. But Mr. De Pasquale does.

Mr. Holliday testifies that Mr. King was "drunk, yes, or something" and that he was amazed at the time, and is still amazed, at Mr. King's lack of reaction to what was being done to him by the police officers.

Although the prosecution had entered the videotape into evidence, the defense may have successfully conveyed to the jury in cross-examining the first witness that the person who filmed the incident believed Mr. King was drunk and that he had an amazing lack of reaction to the blows from the officers.

Next, a slow-motion version of the video is entered into evidence after stipulations by all attorneys that it is an accurate copy of the first exhibit. The judge explains that a "stipulation is an agreement between the lawyers as far as certain facts that are not in dispute... That means they're proven..."

The jury might still have wondered whether stipulations are evidence, or better than evidence because they are proven.

Bryant Allen was a passenger in the back seat of Rodney King's car during the March 3, 1991 chase. He testifies that he saw the lights and sirens and kept on saying: "Rodney, you know, why don't you pull over." Finally, Mr. King did. Mr. King had trouble getting out of the car because of his seat belt. When he finally exited, Mr. Allen could hear him hollering, screaming. He also answered "Yeah" when asked by one of the prosecution lawyers if he had told the police that he had heard the "sound of batons like bones being cracked."

If you had heard these last words, would you have wondered if Mr. Allen still thinks the sounds he heard were of batons like bones being cracked, why he thought that at the time, whether he actually thought that at the time or whether that is just how batons striking any object sound, and how he knows what bones being cracked sounds like?

The prosecution shows Mr. Allen photos of Mr. King taken after the incident. The bruises, swelling, and leg cast were not observed by Mr. Allen prior to the arrest of Mr. King.

On cross-examination by Mr. Barnett, Mr. Allen testifies that he is about six feet, 198 pounds and that Mr. King is a couple of inches taller and much more powerfully built. Mr. King had consumed a forty-ounce bottle of a strong malt liquor called Old English 800. During the chase, Mr. King was in a trance, acted "weird." Mr. King's actions were so "strange" that Mr. Allen considered jumping out of the car while it was still moving. He testifies that he thought the police might have shot Mr. King as Mr. King was getting out of the car, because of the problems with the seat belt.

Mr. Mounger, representing Sgt. Koon, gets Mr. Allen to acknowledge that he wouldn't know if Mr. King had bruises or other injuries on his legs or chest or shoulders, because Mr. King was wearing shirts and pants.

In answers to defendant Wind's lawyer, Mr. De Pasquale, witness Allen acknowledges that he is a convicted felon.

Robert Ontiveros was the Assistant Day Watch Commander, Foothill Division, on March 3, 1991. He testifies that he saw Sgt. Koon and Officers Briseno, Wind and Powell on the videotape. He testifies that Officer Powell and Wind were together in car 16A23, that officers Solano and Briseno were in 16A53, and Sgt. Koon was in a one-man unit 16L140.

Melanie Singer is a CHP Officer with three years' experience. She was the driver in the car that chased Rodney King. Her husband, Officer Tim Singer, was working with her that night.

She testifies that Rodney King was driving over 100 mph on the freeway. She knew this because she was driving 115 mph and was not catching him. At that point, she intended to pull him over for speeding and for a seat-belt violation as "the parties in the vehicle were not wearing seat belts." The red spotlamp, alternating headlight, and the siren were turned on.

The white Hyundai they were pursuing exited the freeway and a "failure to yield pursuit" was sent to other police units.

The Hyundai exited at about sixty mph. It went through a stop sign at close to forty mph. It cut through an intersection and its speed increased to eighty mph. It slowed down to thirty-five mph, and made a left turn on a red light. It then proceeded at sixty to sixty-five mph. Assistance was requested from the LAPD as there were no CHP vehicles in the area of the pursuit.

The Hyundai driver slammed on the brakes at a red light. Tim Singer picked up the Public Address (PA) system and, using it like a bull horn, told the driver to pull over and stop.

Ms. Singer saw a school district police vehicle pull next to her. The two vehicles pursued the Hyundai when it started again. The Hyundai speeded up to fifty-five mph and ran another red light. At that time an LAPD vehicle joined the chase. The Hyundai then slammed on its brakes.

Again, Officer Tim Singer used the PA to tell the driver of the Hyundai to pull over. The Hyundai instead went through the intersection at twenty-five mph, then fifty mph. It finally "got trapped" behind a Chevy pick up. There was a chain looped from one section of a post to another, and the driver of the Hyundai couldn't go any further because the road was blocked.

Melanie Singer classified this as a "high risk" stop "due to the fact that the vehicle did not stop for us." Her husband was yelling at the Hyundai's occupants because the PA system wasn't working. Tim Singer kept yelling, "Put your hands where I can see them. Exit the vehicle."

There were now seven LAPD vehicles on the scene. Four to six of the police officers were on Ms. Singer's left, with their guns drawn. She saw the driver trying to get out of the car, using a "rocking motion" to do so. He finally got out. She described him as "almost happy, jovial." He was smiling and his arms were by his sides. Tim Singer was yelling at him to step away from the vehicle, to extend his arms, to prone himself out on the ground, to lie face down.

A helicopter was hovering. The driver waved at it. Tim Singer continued to yell at him, telling the driver to get back from the car, prone out. The driver moved away from the car, dropped his arms to his sides, and turned his left side to Melanie Singer. She couldn't see his right hand.

She drew her gun, pointed it at the driver, and told him to get his hand away from his butt. In response, he turned his rear end toward her, grabbed his right buttock with his right hand and shook it at her.

She yelled at him to lie down on the ground and prone himself out. Her gun was pointed at him. He danced around "almost like a pitter-patter."

He finally got on the ground. For the first time, she heard officers other than herself or Tim Singer yelling for the driver to get on the ground. She told him to "lay your chest to the ground, extend your arms. Lay your legs on the ground. Prone yourself out." But he didn't. At "no time did he extend his arms. He kept them bent almost to a push-up position and his legs were bent with his toes in the air."

His right ear was on the pavement. He was smiling. She told him to turn his head away. He lifted up his head, to the right, apparently looking at an LAPD Officer who had walked to the right of him. She then approached the driver with her gun out. Her explanation:

> **"At this time, sir, when I—when he got out of the vehicle, no one had been close enough to detect any weapons, and it is our policy and it is our training to approach the suspect when he is in the prone position with the gun withdrawn. We approach in a position of advantage. We are trained to do this. When you approach, we approach with caution, and that is the way we are trained."**

When she was four or five feet away from his left wrist, an officer, Sgt. Koon, told her to "get back," that LAPD would handle it. She stepped back.

Two LAPD officers moved in and grabbed the suspect by the wrists. They tried to swing his arms behind his back to handcuff him. Officer Powell had his left wrist. The suspect "pulled down with his left wrist, rolled against Officer Powell, pulled his right wrist away from the other officer, rolled against him and jumped straight up."

Then approximately six officers moved towards the suspect. They tried to grab portions of the suspect's clothing or arms. The suspect was slinging his arms wildly trying to throw the officers off him. He hit one officer on the chest with one of these swings, but it wasn't a punch.

Sgt. Koon told the driver to stop resisting or he would shoot the driver with a taser. Then Sgt. Koon told his officers to back away, which they finally did. He told the suspect to get on the ground or he'd shoot him with his taser. The suspect didn't, and Sgt. Koon did. Electrical cartridges from the taser landed in the suspect's right side. The driver screamed, grabbed his side and made a moaning sound, but didn't fall down. Sgt. Koon warned him to get on the ground or he'd shoot again. The suspect was still moving his arms, flailing them wildly.

Melanie Singer did not hear any clicking noise from the taser. The suspect was ten or twelve feet from Sgt. Koon, and moved towards him. Sgt. Koon took two steps back, and fired the cartridge again, striking the suspect in the chest.

Ms. Singer then describes the effect of the taser cartridges which she believed struck Mr. King's chest:

> "...he began to stagger, almost appearing like a monster where he kind of staggered one way and then staggered the other way and then he—he staggered one more time almost towards my location, by the patrol vehicle, and then fell, like all of his body weight just carried him forward to where he almost landed, maybe four or five feet directly in front of me."

The prosecution asks if the suspect appeared to be "running or charging." Melanie Singer says he didn't appear to be running, but it seemed his body weight was carrying him in a certain way. He fell in her direction, hitting his left knee, his right knee, his left hand.

Officer Powell came up to the right of the suspect, and struck the driver with his baton in a power swing "right across the top of the cheek bone splitting his face from the top of his ear to the chin." Blood spurted out.

The driver reached up with both hands, covered his face with his hands, and screamed. Officer Powell moved in a circular motion, striking him in the head five more times. During these strikes, no directions were given to the suspect.

Ms. Singer testified that based on her CHP training, there was no reason for the strike to the head or the five next blows.

The suspect was huddled over about four or five feet from her after these blows. Sgt. Koon said, stop, stop, that's enough, that's enough.

Officer Briseno then used his left palm to push away the baton that Officer Powell had in an upright position, a power-stroke position.

Melanie Singer thought the event was over. She reholstered her weapon, and went to the patrol vehicle where the two passengers were prone on their stomachs. One had already been handcuffed, by the school district officer, and Tim Singer was handcuffing the other. She patted down the handcuffed passenger, Bryant Allen. She saw nothing more of the driver's arrest.

The next time she saw Mr. King he was on his chest, his hands behind his back, his ankles bound. He had blood all over his face, and under his chin. He spoke, but his words were garbled. He didn't appear hostile. No one said to her that Mr. King was on PCP.

She had a conversation with Mr. King at the hospital where he'd been taken. She could understand him. She was filling out arrest forms at the hospital. She was planning to arrest Mr. King for DUI, driving under the influence of alcohol. There were no other violations she considered.

The baton was then introduced as evidence. Ms. Singer gave a demonstration of how the baton was held, and the power swings she had seen. This concluded her direct testimony.

Judge Weisberg had told the jurors, before the first witness was called, that they could take notes if they wished, but not to let note-taking "get in the way of watching the witnesses and looking at the evidence." As a reader, you can't watch the witnesses or look at the evidence, but you can think about what's been said. So far, what's your impression of Mr. King?

What images do you have of him? Has the testimony up until now been consistent with what the prosecution said it would be? What inconsistencies have there been between Bryant Allen's and Melanie Singer's testimony? Has Melanie Singer followed the procedures that she says are CHP policy? Has she correctly described the DUI charge as the only appropriate one against Mr. King?

On cross-examination by Officer Powell's lawyer, Mr. Stone, Melanie Singer testifies that she spoke with Mr. King within five minutes of having seen him struck with a PR 24 baton five to seven times with all the strength that Officer Powell could muster, and that Mr. King could be understood and was perfectly coherent.

She looks at a photo of Mr. King taken after the incident, and the first power stroke, described by her as splitting open the chin from ear to chin, is shown to have resulted in a cut of one inch or less in length. Her answer: "I saw what I saw."

In response to Mr. Stone's question: "Now, you saw the flesh-ripping injury caused by the first power stroke, correct?" Ms. Singer answers, "Yes, sir."

Mr. Stone says to Melanie Singer that she told her CHP supervisor on the morning following the incident that she was unable to tell whether Officer Powell's head shots were intentional. She says she doesn't believe she said so.

Melanie Singer reviews the injuries to Mr. King in photos taken after the incident. She says she saw no external injuries to the left side of Mr. King's head consistent with the blows she described. She has no explanation for this.

Mr. Stone shows the videotape. She says Officer Powell's blows which she described occurred before the tape began. She then says the blows occurred in the blurred beginning of the tape. She testifies that at no time was she standing near Tim Singer. She acknowledges the video appears to show otherwise. She testifies that she sees on the video Mr. King get up from a prone position, turn and move toward an officer in a rapid fashion, but that she didn't see that at the scene.

Melanie Singer demonstrates what she saw by playing the role of Officer Powell. Mr. Mounger plays Mr. King. Mr. De Pasquale describes what is occurring.

She resumes testifying, and reports that she has made 300 to 400 prior arrests, but has never had to point her gun before. She testifies that Mr. King was acting bizarre. She says that she was taught at the academy not to approach high-risk suspects unless they were prone to the ground, but Mr. King never assumed that position.

She approached Mr. King with her left foot forward, her left hand away from her body with her palm open, dragging her right foot, with her gun hidden at her right side. She had her handcuffs in their case, the baton on her ring on her belt. Mr. King was lying on his stomach his arms in a push-up position, his toes pointed up in the air. She believed she had the situation under control. Just at that point Sgt. Koon intervened.

No blows had been struck at that time. Two officers approached, one on each side to handcuff Mr. King. She testified that Mr. King resisted, swinging his arms wildly but not kicking or punching. She also testified that at the hospital she saw the taser darts imbedded in Mr. King's flesh in his chest.

Ms. Singer had written in her report, prepared one or two days after the incident, that: "The subject became almost violent and not faltering at all in his steps but continued to take swings at the officers." Her testimony is that Mr. King was swinging wildly, not punching at the officers. She also described Mr. King as not compliant in her report. He "kept kicking at the officers" during the initial attempt to handcuff him.

Ms. Singer testifies that she and Tim Singer feared that Mr. King might have a gun. This fear would continue until Mr. King was searched, or was immobilized so he couldn't retrieve any weapon he had.

Timothy Singer describes the chase and the situation when the Hyundai came to a stop. CHP Officer Singer got out from the right side of the patrol car with his weapon drawn and pointed down. He told Mr. King to raise his hands. Mr. King stepped slightly away from the car, bent over and put his hand on the roof of the car. He then stepped back from the car, pointed to the helicopter, and waved at it. He started moving his feet and shaking his hips as if he were dancing. He never turned around in a complete circle, so Mr. Singer couldn't see his entire body.

Finally, Mr. King got down on all fours. Mr. Singer then began to order the other passengers. They got out and Mr. Singer approached them with his baton out and his gun reholstered. He then heard someone yelling "get back, everybody get away." There was a popping sound on his left then he saw Mr. King rising from the ground. He heard a second popping sound, and he saw Mr. King standing up, his face vibrating or convulsing.

During cross-examination, Mr. Singer described the convulsing this way: "It appeared that the muscles in his face were going wild and his cheeks were vibrating in and out and his face was in a grimace." Mr. King staggered towards him. Before Mr. King reached him, Officer Powell struck Mr. King with the baton on the right side of his head above the ear. Mr. King continued towards Mr. Singer and Officer Powell struck Mr. King again, this time along the right side of the jaw. Officer Powell struck Mr. King in the head five times. Officers then began to encircle Mr. King. Mr. Singer turned his attention to the passengers again, thinking the situation was under control.

Like his wife, Mr. Singer says he heard no mention of PCP at the time of the arrest. Mr. Singer had arrested eighty to 100 persons under the influence of PCP and didn't consider Mr. King under that influence.

Mr. Singer testified that he was scared because he had seen Mr. King shot twice with a taser, then hit a powerful head blow with a baton, and Mr. King was still advancing towards him.

Mr. Singer describes this part of the action: "...it appeared like a scene from a monster movie." He also testifies that he described it this way to interviewers and had said that "after the monster gets shot he just keeps coming." The "monster" theme is developed by several of the attorneys, including one of the prosecutors on **redirect**.

Mr. Singer acknowledges that in several respects his description of what happened is incomplete or is inconsistent with what he is shown on the tape. He attributes this to tunnel vision, to the excitement of the moment.

Frank Schultz is a CHP Officer who is allowed to answer one question, which is whether Officer Melanie Singer had told him on March 3, 1991 that Mr. King was hit in the head with a baton. He answers yes.

This is hearsay, but it is admitted as a prior consistent statement of Ms. Singer's. Notice that Officer Schultz does not say that Mr. King was hit in the head; he repeats what he'd been told, that Mr. King was hit in the head.

William Rhiel is a communications electrician for the City of Los Angeles, working in the police and fire operations support section. He testifies in detail as to how voice radio transmissions are taped and timed.

Edward Jordan is an LAPD Officer who controls all master audio loggings of all recorded equipment of incoming 911 calls and audiotapes from field officers. He identifies the tape of a transmission—shown to be from Sgt. Koon—which occurred shortly after the incident. The typed message says: "Just had a big-time use-of-force, tased and beat the suspect of CHP big-time."

There is also a message from Officer Powell. It says "Oops" and then goes on to say "I haven't beaten anyone this bad in a long time." Another message from Officer Powell is admitted which says: "I think he [Rodney King] was dusted. Many broken bones later after pursuit."

Officer Jordan's sole function as a witness is to introduce the tapes (he is their custodian) and explain the taping system.

Leshon Frierson is a police service representative for LAPD. He is a dispatcher, the voice that is heard over the police radio. He first describes the system, then the transmissions made the night of the chase. The officers are reporting their location as they pursue Mr. King.

Unit 16A23, the vehicle of Officer Powell and Wind, at the conclusion of the incident calls in and says, "We need an RA [Rescue Ambulance] Foothill and Osborne. Victim of "Ah, Ah" with a voice in the background, "Beating, Yeah, Numerous Head Wounds."

Mr. Frierson testifies that "beating" is not normally a term that officers use. He also testifies that the first officer appears to be laughing or giggling. He couldn't tell which officer was laughing. He didn't assume that the officers had done something wrong (this answer was stricken), but he did not report that he thought something was wrong (this answer was not stricken).

Antonio Mancia is an intensive-care physician in pediatrics, neonatology and emergency medicine. He examined Rodney King on March 3, 1991. He observed that Mr. King had five or six lacerations, or open wounds, on the face.

There was a two centimeter (three-quarters of an inch) "superficial" laceration on the right side of the scalp just above the hairline. Two stitches were given. There was another superficial laceration on a point below the right eye on the cheekbone, three centimeters in length for which Dr. Mancia gave three stitches. There was a five centimeter superficial laceration, slightly deeper, on the right side of the face above the jaw line, for which he gave five stitches. There was a two centimeter laceration in the upper corner of the lip, requiring two stitches. The fifth laceration was inside the mouth, in the oral mucosa, requiring five stitches.

Dr. Mancia testified there were several bruises on the right side of the head, the chest, the back, legs, and the nose was bleeding. He says that his clinical impression was that Mr. King wasn't under the influence of PCP or under the influence of alcohol. But Dr. Mancia had written in his report: "involved in a fight, PCP ingestion, several abrasions." He testified that he had been told this by a nurse.

Dr. Mancia had also written "PCP overdose" as a diagnostic impression. He testifies this was based on the history he'd been given and was not his diagnosis.

Although Dr. Mancia hadn't personally observed these particular manifestations of PCP use, he testifies that the literature indicates that PCP users may exhibit "superhuman strength" and trancelike behavior, may not respond to commands and sometimes are "oblivious to pain."

David Giannetto is an Emergency Room (ER) specialist who examined Rodney King at 6:15 A.M. on March 3, 1991 in the jail ward. He testifies that Mr. King was alert and fully oriented. Mr. King denied that he'd consumed alcohol. Dr. Giannetto explains that he observed the sutures, except for the one inside the mouth. X-rays showed Mr. King had a fracture of the zygomatic arch on the right side of his face, underneath the right eye. Another physician concurred with this evaluation, as well as with the impression that there was blunt trauma to the right side of the face.

Dr. Giannetto also noted an injury to the maxillary sinus, which was probably caused by the incident. There was a fracture (broken bone) of the fibula, the smaller leg bone, probably caused by hitting the leg or the leg hitting another object. There was some blood over the right eye, a subconjunctival hemorrhage. Mr. King appeared to be mildly intoxicated.

Dr. Giannetto reported that Dr. Mancia had called him to discuss the patient he was transferring. Dr. Mancia described Mr. King as possibly under the influence of PCP and that the patient needed to be observed solely for the purpose of possible PCP intoxication.

The only treatment actually rendered by Dr. Giannetto was setting the fracture of the leg.

Richard Di Stefano is an assistant watch commander at the Foothill Station. This LAPD sergeant had given training the evening of March 2,1991 in the use of the PR-24 baton, and Officer Wind had demonstrated the movements with good proficiency. Based on the training, Officer Powell appeared weak and ineffective in his efforts and was asked to repeat the baton swings. The object was to have Officer Powell strike harder, so there would be a greater expectation that the power chop would break bones.

In the training, Sgt. Di Stefano explained the mechanical movement of the baton but did not tell the officers when a baton should be used. He did tell them that the baton was an impact weapon and they must use as much force as possible.

Lawrence Davis was working as a charge nurse in the ER at Pacifica Hospital when Rodney King was admitted at 1:30 A.M. on March 3. Mr. King was accompanied by four to six officers, including Officers Powell and Wind.

Mr. King said that he was an usher at Dodger Stadium. Officer Powell was the only officer to speak with Mr. King. He commented to Mr. King that "we had a pretty good hardball game tonight" and "Yeah, don't you remember the hardball game. We hit quite a few homeruns" to which Mr. King nodded his head in agreement.

At the grand jury hearing, Mr. Davis had testified that it was Mr. King who brought up the "hardball" comment, and that it was then that several officers—not just Officer Powell— answered in the affirmative.

Nurse Davis also testified that the officers told him Mr. King was on PCP. He testified that Mr. King had been struggling with his restraints, and that none of the four tasers had embedded themselves in his skin. He testified that he, too, had joked with Mr. King about his condition.

Nurse Davis asked Officer Wind what Mr. King's face had been hit with. Officer Wind took his night stick out and said Mr. King had resisted arrest. Officer Wind patted his baton.

Carol Edwards is also an ER Pacifica Hospital nurse; she testifies that the tasers were not embedded in Mr. King's skin and that she told Officer Powell and Wind that the taser hadn't worked. She repeats Nurse Davis' version of the hardball statement, as made by Officer Powell.

Glenda Tosti is an LAPD senior police service representative assigned to the Communications Division. After explaining how the police-communication system works, including terms such as emergency board operator (EBO), radio telephone operator (RTO) and area command center (ACC), she testifies as to the statement of "Oops" and "I haven't beaten anyone this bad in a long time" on the Mobil Digital Terminal (MDT) of Officer Powell, as well as the "dusted," "many broken bones" statement. She testifies that the word "beat" means "hit" in certain instances.

She also testifies as to Sgt. Koon's statement, sent at 12:56 A.M. on March 3, 1991 which was, "Just had a big-time use-of-force. Tased and beat the suspect of a CH (sic) pursuit big-time," as well as a message sent back to his vehicle that was, "Oh well, I'm sure the lizard didn't deserve it, Ha, Ha." She testifies that officers are told they are responsible for the messages they send, but not those they receive on the system.

Byung Kuk Yun is a systems programmer with the City of Los Angeles, who has worked with the LAPD MDT System. He testifies as to the typed MDT message from Sgt. Koon's police vehicle at 12:56 A.M. on March 3, 1991 which said "You just had a big-time use-of-force. Tased and beat the suspect of CHP pursuit big-time." The response from the Foothill Division station was, "Oh well, I'm sure the lizard didn't deserve it, Ha, Ha." This was displayed on the police car's MDT screen. Mr. Yun can't say whether anyone saw the return message on the screen in Sgt. Koon's vehicle.

Patrick Conmay was an LAPD Lieutenant watch commander of Foothill Station on the night of March 2 and morning of March 3. He reports a conversation he had with Sgt. Koon on the morning of March 3, between 1:30 A.M. and 2:00 A.M. Sgt. Koon told him there had been a felony vehicle stop, where the passengers had been taken into custody without incident but the driver had acted strangely.

Sgt. Koon had described the driver's actions as strange in that he did not comply with instructions, put his hand in and out of his pockets, walked around, got back in and then out of the car. Sgt. Koon did not mention that Mr. King danced around, waved at the helicopter and smiled.

Robert Troutt was watch commander at LAPD's Valley Traffic Division on March 3, 1991. Sergeant Troutt could not recall the name of the officer who called him on March 3, 1991. His testimony is offered against Officers Powell and Wind. The officer to whom Sgt. Troutt spoke said that the suspect (Rodney King) and the officers had been involved in an altercation. The suspect received injuries and had to be booked at the county jail ward, so the booking was done telephonically.

The crime charged was felony-evading. There was no mention of alcohol intoxication or drugs by the unknown officer who called in the report.

John Amott worked at the Valley Traffic Division of Van Nuys Station. The LAPD sergeant was day watch commander on March 3, 1991. His testimony relates to Officers Powell and Wind.

Two LAPD officers, whom he can't identify, brought in a report on Rodney King. Sgt. Amott had a conversation with one of them, who Mr. Stone stipulates is Officer Powell, who also authored the report.

The charge in the report was felony-evading. But there was also discussion of the suspect's intoxication and Sgt. Amott said that a blood or urine sample might have to be obtained, and possibly the blood sample had already been obtained at the hospital. But Sgt. Amott didn't tell the officers to get any such samples because these were not necessary elements for the felony-evading charge.

Ewing Kwock is an LAPD detective in the robbery/homicide division. He listened to and transcribed the two reel-to-reel tapes made of the transcriptions during the pursuit of Mr. King.

Addison Arce is also a detective in the LAPD robbery/homicide division. He reviewed the videotape of the beating and arrest. He testifies that in the video he saw Officer Briseno "appearing to impact Mr. King with his foot" and that the officer appears to be wearing a high top boot. He also testifies that several officers not charged with any crime had their boots on Mr. King's back in the same part of the neck and back as Officer Briseno's boots.

Detective Arce viewed Officer Powell holding a hand-held radio in his left hand speaking into the radio speaker. He testifies that he has viewed the videotape of the beating approximately fifty times.

There are no more prosecution witnesses.

Stipulations

At this point, both sides stipulated (agreed) that the following facts were not in dispute:

- Officer Powell wrote the arrest report and the booking recommendation.

- Officer Wind wrote use-of-force reports and the daily activities report for himself and Officer Powell.

- Sgt. Koon wrote the sergeant's daily report. Officer Solano (one of the officers who initially tried to subdue Mr. King) wrote the daily activities report for himself and Officer Briseno.

- The boots of Officer Wind, Briseno and Powell, and the PR 24 batons of Officer Powell and Wind, and the taser used by Sgt. Koon, are all the property of those parties.

- The CHP audiotape is a true and accurate copy.

- The blood sample of Rodney King, showing .19 percent ethanol at 12.55 A.M. is admitted, as is a urine sample of Mr. King's taken at 6:30 A.M., showing no trace of PCP or barbiturates or cocaine or amphetamines or methamphetamines.

THE DEFENSE PRESENTS ITS CASE

In our review of the case presented by the defense, our focus is on the defense experts. But first we want to very briefly summarize the rest of the defense evidence.

Sgt. Koon testified that Mr. King was muscular—"buffed out"—which led him to believe that Mr. King was probably an ex-convict. He believed that Mr. King was under the influence of PCP because he was super strong, because he had a one-track mind, and because he equated Mr. King's actions with "a monster." In particular, Mr. King, even though ordered to stay down, even though shot twice with a taser and groaning from the electrical shock from the taser, and even though hit with PR 24 batons, did not stay down.

Sgt. Koon testified that he was scared. He says he's accountable for the violent and brutal actions his officers took to subdue Mr. King. He didn't enjoy the actions of his officers, but he considered them a managed and controlled use-of-force.

Officer Powell also testified that he believed Rodney King was under the influence of PCP. Mr. King had a blank stare, slow stiff movements, was sweating, and didn't comply. Officer Powell says he, too, was scared, particularly because of Mr. King's great strength in pushing him and the other officers off.

Officer Powell testified that he never struck Mr. King in the jaw or in the face. He acted quickly when Mr. King ran straight at him, with his arms extending out, moving quickly. Officer Powell started to react, but checked his swing as he hit Mr. King. He saw Mr. King fall like a rag doll, landing on his face after the initial swing. Mr. King's head bounced up.

Officer Powell testified he was scared to death, that he feared for his life, that he feared that Mr. King would get his gun. He testified that he never talked about hitting "home runs" on Rodney King. He denied laughing about the beating. He denied that the term "gorillas in the mist" was a racial slur.

Officer Briseno told the jury that he also thought Mr. King was on PCP because of Mr. King's walk, his stare, his sweatiness, and his lack of reactions to the taser.

Officer Briseno testified that Officer Powell's blows were to the shoulders and above, and possibly to the head. He testified that the other officers were out of control and that his stomp to Mr. King's head was to prevent the other officers from continuing the beating.

Officer Wind did not testify.

The defense also called nine of the twenty-one officers who were present at the scene, including the one African-American officer. These officers all testified that they believed Mr. King was on PCP and out of control.

The defense called medical experts, who testified that the facial injuries to Mr. King were consistent with a person who had fallen, rather than one who has been struck with a baton.

We have purposely kept the defense testimony brief as it relates to these officers, because you may believe that there is, as the prosecutor asserted (and as several officers acknowledged) a Code of Silence when a police officer is accused of a crime. Or you may disbelieve the officers because of their actions the night of the beating, or because of their comments after the beating, or because you consider the testimony of the defendants "self-serving". But any lack of belief in the defense witnesses doesn't affect the prosecution's responsibility to prove the charges beyond a reasonable doubt.

It is noteworthy then, that the prosecution called no expert during its initial presentation to address the problem of how the defendants should have effected the arrest of Rodney King. The prosecution had the Singers testify that, in their opinion, the early part of the incident had resulted in Mr. King being struck in the head by Officer Powell with a baton. Officer Melanie Singer testified that neither that blow nor the subsequent four or five blows were appropriate or necessary or consistent with CHP training. But neither of the Singers were experts in use-of-force.

The prosecution evidently felt the tape spoke for itself. They didn't call a use-of-force expert—even though they had one, whom they called on rebuttal. (The prosecution had another expert, Sgt. Fred Nichols, who had testified at the grand jury proceeding that the defendants had used excessive force. He was excused from testifying by Judge Weisberg as a rebuttal witness.[33]) And they chose not to call Rodney King, who could have testified whether he was struck in the head, whether he was trying to escape, what the officers said. In the Federal trial, which resulted in convictions of Officer Powell and Sgt. Koon, the Federal prosecutors did call use-of-force experts and Mr. King as part of their Case-in-Chief.

The defense called two use-of-force experts, who had worked with LAPD and had definite opinions as to whether the defendant's actions were in accord with LAPD departmental policy.

Mr. Mounger called Sgt. Charles Duke, who had joined LAPD in 1970. Since 1974, he had continually trained police officers who worked for LAPD and for other agencies.

He had spoken at roll calls and other meetings regarding the escalation and de-escalation of force from 1982 up to the time of his testimony. He had taught at the FBI academy, Department of Energy, U.S. Marine Corps, San Diego Police Department, U.S. Army. He had training in hostage negotiations, counter-sniper, SWAT, chemical agents, PR 24 baton (twice) and supervisory schools. He had received postgraduate certificates from the State of California, from basic to supervisory. He had received approximately ninety commendations including the police medal for bravery.

Sgt. Duke had spent two years teaching full-time at the police academy, but for nineteen years he worked as a street policeman. During that time, he had reviewed thousands of uses-of-force. He had taken thirty to forty PCP suspects into custody.

The gist of Sgt. Duke's testimony was that the use-of-force he saw on the videotape was reasonable within the policies and procedures of the LAPD. He testified that as far as he could tell, Mr. King had not been struck in the head at the beginning of the incident because of the position of the baton wielded by Officer Powell, the lack of a head "snap back," and the motion of Officer Powell's hands coming down. Officers are instructed not to intentionally or deliberately hit the head, neck or spine with their PR 24 batons. In the video, he saw no such strikes.

Sgt. Duke testified that Mr. King acted as if he were a significant danger and as if he were high on PCP. That opinion was based on Mr. King's actions when he got out of the car, his lack of response to the baton blows and taser, his rigidity, and because of the incredible strength he exhibited.

According to Sgt. Duke, there were three other types of use-of-force which were better ways to have dealt with a suspect such as Mr. King. These were leg grabbers, nets, and upper-body control holds.

With leg grabbers, the suspect is diverted by officers in front. Leg grabbers, with claws that come around the legs and are locked, are then thrown around the suspect. The suspect no longer has a foundation so the suspect's movements are limited.

Nets, used in combination with leg grabbers, are thrown over the suspect, who becomes entangled in them. There is no longer a danger of being struck by flailing arms or of an officer losing a weapon to the suspect.

With the upper-body control, the carotid artery in the neck is pressured. The flow of blood to the brain is restricted and the suspect is rendered unconscious.

Unfortunately, none of these uses-of-force were available to the officers, either because of political (upper body control holds had been a hot issue because they allegedly caused the death of some suspects) or monetary reasons.

The tape is reviewed over and over with Sgt. Duke. Hypotheticals are presented to him, based on possible interpretations of what appears on the video. Sgt. Duke sticks to his evaluation—the police officers beat Mr. King because Mr. King was dangerous, was not under their control, had not signaled that he would comply with the officers' demands; and the officers had no other tools—except deadly force—to use than the PR 24 batons, kicks or stomps.

Sgt. Duke also testifies that he has reviewed a number of incidents in which excessive force was charged. He formally and officially opined that excessive force had been used in up to twenty-five occasions.

The above testimony is meant to establish Sgt. Duke's objectivity in this case and credibility as an expert witness—he is not simply a defender of the police on all occasions.

The second defense expert is retired LAPD Captain Robert Michael, a consultant on law-enforcement tactics and use-of-force. He began in the Costa Mesa (CA) Police Department in 1959, where he investigated uses-of-force. He was an instructor at Orange Coast College in police tactics, at the Orange County Police Officer Academy, and at the post-sergeant's school, during 1959-1966.

Capt. Michael left the Costa Mesa Police Department as a lieutenant, took a pay cut and joined LAPD as a recruit. He became an instructor at the police academy from 1969-1972. He was promoted to sergeant and came to review all uses-of-force. This review involved evaluation, follow-up investigation, and recommendations to the commander. He eventually became a lieutenant, and then captain. In that latter capacity he commanded a patrol and a detective division, and he reviewed uses-of-force. He was the police adjudicator of his units.

He completed all his Ph.D. requirements, except his dissertation. He taught at numerous colleges and police academies in California and Arizona, obtained advanced certificates in those states, and certifications to teach in Florida, and wrote a book called *Officer Survival Tactics* (self-published). He testified both for and against police officers in administrative hearings and California Courts on uses-of-force. However, he had never before testified in a criminal trial where an officer had been accused of using excessive force.

Capt. Michael had researched studies on "lag time" beginning in 1963. Lag time refers to the length of time between a suspect's actions and an officer's perception and reaction. He testified that, based on Mr. King's actions and reactions to the commands, the taser, and the swarm, Mr. King was a "credible threat" to the officers on the scene.

Capt. Michael reviewed the videotape one hundred times in its entirety prior to his testimony, and some specific sections up to 300 times. In his opinion, each time the officers applied force, it was reasonable and necessary. The tape is reviewed extensively with him. Capt. Michael says there were numerous escalations and de-escalations, and each was proper in the sense it was reasonable and necessary based on the specific circumstances with which the officers were confronted that night. There were ten distinct uses-of-force.

Capt. Michael described most of these escalations and de-escalations in detail before his testimony ended. The basic response was always the same—the officers' actions were in line with police procedures.

The testimony of Sgt. Duke and Captain Michael was long and drawn out. It was not presented to the jury in the abbreviated and summary version presented here.

The videotape was reviewed over and over, with the tape stopped, replayed, refocused. Each of Rodney King's movements was analyzed. Did his head snap back when Officer Powell first struck him in the area of the head at the beginning of the tape?

(These were the "head shots" which the Singers described.) When Mr. King's feet were in a certain position, was that because he was attempting to rise, or an involuntary response to the beating? Was he reaching for something that could have been a weapon when he put his hands behind him, or was he trying to comply with the officers' instructions?

Each movement of the officers was scrutinized. Was Officer Powell using his baton correctly or ineffectively? Was he continually beating Mr. King, or was he hitting him, then stepping back to reevaluate? Were the blows struck by Officer Wind and Officer Powell necessary at a certain point, or were these simply examples of the officers out of control? Did Officer Briseno stomp on Mr. King, or was he simply pushing him back to the ground? And when the stomp or thrust with the boot occurred, had Mr. King already signified that he was in compliance, as proned out as he was likely to get?

As these questions were asked and answered, as the tape was played and replayed, frame by frame, it all seems likely to have had an anesthetizing effect on the jury. How many times can you look at eighty-two seconds of tape before it begins to become dull? Does everything become depersonalized when you, the juror, can't hear the batons striking or the officers yelling, can't see the officers or Mr. King except from one perspective (the camera's focus), can't feel the adrenaline running through the officers or Mr. King, can't experience the fear that they may have felt? At a certain point, perhaps it is no longer Rodney King, victim, being beaten over and over by heavy-duty batons, but more of an intellectual exercise. And if this has happened, hasn't the defense won a significant battle?

THE PROSECUTION'S REBUTTAL

During its rebuttal, the prosecution presented Commander Michael Bostic, who the prosecution said was the Department's highest ranking use-of-force expert. This expert testified that the police officers had five opportunities to terminate the beating. He testified that the level of force was outside the policy of the LAPD, beginning about twenty seconds into the eighty-two second videotape. He testified that his opinion was based on viewing the full videotape only five times.

The prosecution also presented Dr. Norman Shorr, a surgeon who repaired bone fractures around Mr. King's right eye. Dr. Shorr testified that Rodney King's facial injury was "more likely" caused by a blunt object—such as a baton—than by a fall to the ground.

Again, one wonders, why this testimony was presented on rebuttal, rather than as part of the prosecution's Case-In-Chief.

Chapter 23

Closing Statements:
Argument Versus Substance

I t's April 20, 1992, and all the evidence is in—at least, all the evidence the jurors may legitimately consider in reaching their verdicts. But before the curtain falls, the last act in the Rodney King beating trial must be played out. The lawyers get to do their thing—they get to argue.

The judge reminds the jury that what they hear now is not evidence but the lawyers' "interpretation of how they view the evidence that you have seen."

As you look at the Closing Statements, be they by the prosecution or defense, in the Rodney King beating trial or the trial at your local court, keep in mind that these arguments seek to persuade by selection, by emphasis, by implication, by misdirection. The good trial attorney is like a magician, asking you to watch the ball, and not focus on the rest of the act. The good juror keeps that in mind when making a final assessment of the "reality"— the evidence.

The Prosecution Goes First

Mr. White reminds the jurors they are the "impartial judges of the facts." He asks them not to speculate on why Rodney Glenn King was not called, and to draw no inferences from the failure of Mr. King to testify.

But why wasn't he called? asks Mr. White. Mr. White suggests that Mr. King would not be reliable, due to his .19 blood alcohol reading; that he was "severely traumatized by this event"; that either side could have called him.

Mr. White contends that the videotape is the central piece of evidence. "It is the most objective piece of evidence you can have."

Would you, as a juror, have agreed with Mr. White? Do you think that this videotape—or any videotape, filmed from a certain angle, starting in the process of an incident rather than at its beginning—is the "most objective" evidence? Do you agree that Mr. King's testimony as to what happened would have been unreliable? Do you believe that it would have been as easy for the defense to call Mr. King, interview him, "prep" him, as it would have been for the prosecution?

Mr. White proceeds to integrate his sixteen charts with his oral argument and the video. He refers back to the elements of the crime. He says that a baton is a "deadly weapon." He says that Mr. King suffered "great bodily injury" as evidenced by his broken legs, his five facial fractures. He says the force used was "unreasonable" that it was unlawful unless it was in "self-defense or in defense of others or in effecting an arrest, overcoming resistance or preventing escape."

The prosecutor differentiates "general intent" crimes, in which the act in itself is to establish the crime, and "specific intent" crimes, in which the individual has a purpose in mind while committing the act. Assault by a deadly weapon (a baton, a shod foot) is a general intent crime, while assault with intent to do great bodily harm requires a specific intent.

Acknowledging that there was some "reasonable force", Mr. White goes on to state that it ended when Mr. King was not trying to escape, not trying to resist, not doing anything. At that point, there is an assault. Mr. White makes his case as follows:

"As soon as you look on that tape and say enough is enough, you've got this man down, he's not doing anything, he is not trying to escape, he is not trying to resist, when you reach that point on that tape where you say

enough is enough, that is when unreasonable force starts
and that is what you have to determine."

Mr. White goes back to the videotape, and analyzes the
officers individually. He says Officer Powell is "relentless in his
baton blows" that the videotape shows "unreasonable brutality".

The prosecutor also says on several occasions that the
video shows that Officer Powell hit Mr. King in the head and
that Officer Powell knew he hit him in the head. Mr. White also
says: "... everyone in the case agreed, from defense expert to
defense witnesses to prosecution witnesses, that a strike to Mr.
King's head and an intentional deliberate strike to his head by
Officer Powell at the beginning of the video was an excessive
use-of-force." Then, according to Mr. White, all further force is
unreasonable.

*Mr. White did not say if he was referring to Officer Powell only,
or whether further force by anyone after the first strike was unreasonable. We believe Mr. White intended his "further force" reference
to apply to any officer who struck Mr. King after the first strike.*

Later on, however, Mr. White acknowledges that "*if* [em-
phasis added] the first baton blow was a deliberate and intentional baton blow by Mr. Powell to the head of Mr. King" *then*
the force was unreasonable.

On several occasions Mr. White says: "...at some point you
have to look at that video, enough is enough, stop, go in there,
handcuff him, this is not right, but they continued to hit him."

Mr. White buttresses his "strike to the head" theory by
Officer Melanie Singer's testimony; by Officer Powell's statement that Mr. King suffered numerous head wounds; by the
nature of the facial wounds; by Officer Wind's tapping on his
baton when asked by Nurse Lawrence Davis what happened to
Mr. King's face; by Sgt. Koon's statement to Officer Powell not
to hit Mr. King in the head.

According to Mr. White, Officer Powell thought the beating
was funny, that he was laughing when he phoned for the
ambulance. He rejects Officer Powell's testimony that he was
not laughing or giggling.

Mr. White also focuses on Officer Powell's typing, "Oops" on his computer, and then typing "I haven't beaten anyone this bad in a long time." These, according to Mr. White, were admissions of unreasonable force, and proved Officer Powell's guilt. Finally, Mr. White claims that there was taunting in the hospital—Officer Powell saying "Rodney, we hit quite a few home runs out there tonight."

The use of the phrase "gorillas in the mist" shows the racism of Officer Powell, asserts Mr. White. He claims that Officer Powell's "lies"—in regard to whether he was a quarter of a mile away from Glenoaks and Van Nuys or a mile away—show not only that Officer Powell filed a false report, but that he can't be trusted. Mr. White acknowledges that "lies in the report, the false report, the taunting at the hospital, the MDT, the pre-offense statement, gorillas in the mist" are all circumstantial evidence, but that they show Officer Powell's state of mind.

Clearly, Mr. White sees Officer Powell's conduct as the most egregious. And while he repeatedly says the videotape is the best evidence, he is asking the jurors to "infer" from things that happened before and after the incident that Officer Powell did use unreasonable force and intended to do so.

If you read the transcript, more argument is actually spent by the prosecution detailing Officer Powell's lies, and his falsified report, than on the beating. But isn't the beating far more important than the supposed false reports?

While Mr. White starts with Officer Powell, and then goes on to the other defendants, throughout his argument he returns to Officer Powell. There is no chronological sequence of events for the jury to review, rather almost a series of vignettes.

Mr. White now turns to Sgt. Koon. Sgt. Koon did not strike any blows, but he aided and abetted the beating. Sgt. Koon was in charge. He ordered Officer Melanie Singer back, he ordered the swarm. He ordered the officers back when the swarm didn't work. He shot Rodney King with the taser twice. He tells Officer Powell either "Stop it, that's enough" or "Don't hit him in the head" (depending on whether you believe Officer Melanie Singer or Sgt. Koon).

Mr. White then spends a great deal of time detailing why Sgt. Koon is a liar, who also filed a false report. Mr. White finally returns to the beating itself. He says:

"Clearly Mr. King wasn't complying immediately, and I hate using that word, but he wasn't complying right away, but he was complying. He did as they told him to do."

Mr. White says Mr. King was complying but not complying because he put his hands where they could be seen, he put them on to his head, he got to his knees as instructed, he got down on the ground as instructed. That's how Mr. King complied.

But how does one comply and not comply at the same time?

Mr. White then speaks again about the lies, the false reports.

Regarding Officer Wind, Mr. White says that there is a point in time when everyone can agree that unreasonable force started and that "is real late in the video." At that point, there are unreasonable baton strikes and kicks by Officer Wind.

Mr. White argues that Officer Wind remained silent when Officer Powell taunted Mr. King at the hospital, and that silence was an *adoptive admission*. By his silence, Mr. Wind was agreeing with the baseball game comment. Officer Wind also silently affirmed he knew Mr. King was hit in the face when he patted his baton when Nurse Davis questioned what happened to Mr. King's face.

Last, but not least, according to Mr. White, there is Officer Briseno. Mr. White says: "I imagine that the force that you can get with a stomp to that area could cause just as much damage as a baton to that area." Mr. White states that at the time Mr. King was at his most compliant, Officer Briseno delivers this "forceful stomp." "A 140-pound man with supposedly his off leg can cause Mr. King's 250-pound body to fly like that, that is excessive force," says Mr. White.

Having finished with Officer Briseno, Mr. White returns to his argument that "the evidence is clear, considering Laurence

Powell's denials and his track record of truthfulness, this first strike, this first baton strike was to the head and it was intentional. And if it was intentional, it was unreasonable and everything that followed it was unreasonable."

Mr. White attacks the defense experts, arguing that Mr. King is not aggressive, he's just trying to get away from the baton blows, he's trying to comply. Sure, he's not perfectly prone, but what can you expect from a man the officers "think is under the influence of PCP."

Mr. White concludes by talking about seeing the movie, *Fievel, An American Tale* with his daughter. He reports that the cat says that he's not a cat, to the mouse the cat is pursuing. The cat says, "No, no, you can't trust your eyes." And the defendants are trying to tell you, who are you going to trust, them or your own eyes.

Although you haven't seen the eighty-two seconds that has been shown to the jurors, in whole or in part, at normal and varying speeds, nor the charts nor the stills, nor have you read the complete trial transcript nor heard it live, you can still ask whether the prosecution has made an effective presentation? Is there a coherent view of what happened? Does the prosecution case rise or fall on the videotape, or are there arguments which have convinced you that the defendants—all, some or one of them—are guilty of the charges against them beyond a reasonable doubt and to a moral certainty?

THE DEFENSE GOES NEXT

Mr. Stone for Officer Powell

Mr. Stone begins the Closing Statements on behalf of defendant Powell. But his argument really helps all the defendants.

It was duty, affirms Mr. Stone, that compelled Officer Powell—and the others—to pursue Mr. King's vehicle when the CHP called for help, and that duty required the officers to try to handcuff Mr. King. Duty required Officer Powell to stand his ground, rather than run back to his car when Mr. King fought off the effects of the taser and moved towards Officer Powell.

But duty, says Mr. Stone, did not require Officer Powell to end up on a gurney in an emergency room, or to end toes up on a slab in the morgue. According to a sign displayed at the police gymnasium, "there are no second place ribbons in a street fight." Officers do not get paid to lose street fights, to roll around in the dirt with the likes of Rodney Glenn King. That is not their duty. And if it were, "the thin blue line that separates the law-abiding from the not law-abiding will disintegrate."

When confronted with his choice as to what to do, Officer Powell did not have the opportunity to reflect, to peruse his alternatives, to discuss tactics with Sgt. Koon. "He didn't have an opportunity to run the scenario backwards and forward on a video screen in slow-motion, in real time and super slow-motion and to examine freeze frames. He did not have an opportunity to see blow-ups of what he was about to do before he did it." He couldn't stop and have a sidebar conference. He didn't have time to develop a plan. He only had time to do what he was trained to do.

So, says Mr. Stone, there is no middle ground, no compromise. Either Officer Powell is a responsible, faithful, courageous police officer, or a brutal thug who abused and beat another human being with no justification.

This is the lens that Mr. Stone asks the jury to look through.

He says that the intent of the officers was to take Mr. King into custody, not to administer punishment. He believes that all the officers acted in good faith.

It was Rodney King who controlled his own destiny. He could have avoided drinking, avoided getting in his car, avoided running from the CHP at speeds of 115 mph. It was Mr. King's choice to do these things, to run red lights, to drive eighty mph on city streets. It was Mr. King who chose to remain in the car when Mr. Allen and the other passenger, the sleeping Mr. Helms, exited the car without any problem. And neither Mr. Allen nor Mr. Helms— "both black people, African-Americans" —were beaten.

When the officers approached him to handcuff him, Mr. King chose to fight the officers off from his push-up position. He chose to fight off the effects of the taser, to run right over Officer Powell. And finally he chose to give up.

Having drawn the picture of the officers as the thin blue line, and Mr. King as the person who chose not to cooperate with these officers, Mr. Stone proceeds next to attack the prosecution theory.

There is no charge of racially based actions, as Mr. White had attempted to imply. This was simply a distraction for the jurors to think about because the prosecution doesn't have a strong case.

Mr. Stone then talks of "pockets of evidence" which he outlines in color in the chart he shows the jurors. Some of these pockets are relevant to the beating, some not. It is the use-of-force evidence that is Mr. Stone's focus during a lengthy review of all that transpired.

Mr. Stone starts with a review of what happened at the scene of Mr. King's stop. It is a felony high-risk crisis car stop. CHP, he says, made its first mistake when it ordered the suspects out on both sides, rather than from the same side of the car. This divided the officers' attention.

Although the other passengers proned out, and had no problems with the police, Mr. King was rocking back in and out of the car for a long time. And, if Officer Melanie Singer was correct (when she said she was going to cite the driver for not wearing a seat belt), it couldn't have been that Mr. King was having trouble getting his seat belt undone (as Mr. Allen had testified). This rocking back and forth, following a 7.8 mile high-speed chase with abrupt stops, was a danger signal to the officers. Had Mr. King stopped where he did deliberately, because it was dark—a good place to escape? Was he trying to get something from the car while he rocked back and forth?

Then, according to Mr. Stone, the officers' suspicion and anxiety were heightened because of Mr. King's bizarre behavior when he exited the car. He looked around, probably to size up the situation. He wouldn't put his hands up, or down, or on the car. He looked up at the helicopter, he waved and laughed and danced. And all this with guns pointing at him.

Officer Melanie Singer approached with her gun out. She said she wasn't afraid, that she thought she had the situation under control. But her husband, Officer Tim Singer, was scared—he thought that Rodney King's actions were like something out of a monster movie. In any case, Sgt. Koon took over. He ordered his officers in, using the swarm technique. This involves grabbing limbs, then smothering the suspect with the officers' body weight. But Mr. King rose up and threw the officers off.

At that point, Sgt. Koon used the taser. Mr. King was temporarily incapacitated, but regained his composure, and lunged at Sgt. Koon. Sgt. Koon fired the taser again.

Only at this point did the video begin. Mr. King is turning and moving towards Officer Powell. Mr. King, who is six-three, "somewhere between 230, 250 pounds, maybe six-four, has just been zapped with 50,000 volts of electricity from this taser, which momentarily felled him, and yet he is able to turn and move in the first few frames of that video in a period of less than two seconds from on the ground to a full charge toward or in the direction of Officer Powell."

Officer Powell swings. Mr. Stone characterizes this as a check swing (Officer Powell's testimony) or an incomplete or blocked swing (testimony of other witnesses). Mr. King falls, whether from the effect of the tasers or the swinging baton. His head bams and bounces up and down, after it hits the asphalt with considerable velocity. It is this fall, according to Mr. Stone, which caused the facial injuries. He argues briefly here, and more extensively later, that the expert medical evidence is consistent with this theory.

Mr. King is on his feet, he's coming up again, and Officer Powell knocks him back down with the baton. Officer Powell is ready to strike again. Officer Briseno moves forward to intercede. Mr. King rolls away, is getting to his feet. He's on both feet, Mr. Stone says, kind of leaning over on his right side as he starts to come up. Sgt. Koon says to hit him in the knees, the joints, the legs.

Officers are yelling at Mr. King to get down, stay down. The officers, both observers and participants, testified they thought he was attempting to get into the same position again, that is, trying to get up.

Mr. King is rolling around, and the officers are striking him. This is terrible, says Mr. Stone. It makes him sick, "just like it did the President of the United States." Mr. Stone added "because he doesn't understand, he's not looking at this through the perception of the officers."

Then comes a period when Mr. King is not moving, and Officer Powell is trying to get the handcuffs out of his back pocket, where he's put them. Officer Briseno "sees whatever he sees, does whatever he does."

Mr. King is then on his knees again. The power strokes resume, until the point Mr. King puts his hands behind his head and says "I give." Then Sgt. Koon says, "Okay, he gives, he gives, that's it," and there are no more strikes, hits, or kicks. The officers put two sets of handcuffs on Mr. King because they believe, according to Mr. Stone, that Mr. King is a duster, on PCP.

Let's stop and assess. Has Mr. Stone created a reasonable, a plausible picture? And if it's not reasonable or plausible, is it possible? Does it, in other words, raise a reasonable doubt?

Mr. Stone then says the video doesn't conclusively show whether the initial baton strike was to the head. Officer Powell testified that he did not strike Mr. King in the face.

Officer Melanie Singer testified it was a head shot, it was a full power stroke to the right side of Mr. King's head, splitting his head open from the ear to the chin. There were then four more full baseball-type power strokes to Mr. King's head.

Mr. Stone asks the jurors to handle the baton in the jury room and to ask themselves whether Officer Singer's testimony can be believed. Mr. King didn't lose consciousness, didn't suffer a skull fracture. And where's the medical evidence of these strikes? It isn't there, he says.

Officer Tim Singer testified the first two head blows were administered when Mr. King was standing. They were above the right eye. But he couldn't explain the lack of any injury or mark.

Officer Rolando Solano (Officer Briseno's partner on March 2-3, 1991) testified that there were two head blows before the video started. But no one else saw them. (*Officer Solano's testimony was not given during the prosecution's Case-in-Chief.*)

So none of the witnesses are consistent with each other. The video is taken from 175 feet away, it is two-dimensional and doesn't define spatial relationships. The video distorts eyewitnesses' testimony, their memory. Several witnesses have admitted as much. Mr. Stone then adds that many people, even the lawyers, didn't realize that this video, this dynamite piece of evidence—"how deceptive that wonderful piece of evidence really is."

Mr. Stone then reviews the law in regard to reasonable force. He talks about judging the "reasonableness" from the perspective of reasonable officers confronting the same or similar circumstances.

He says the suspect is in control and the reason for that is because the officer's escalation or de-escalation of force depends on what the suspect does.

Since use-of-force depends on what the suspect does, Mr. Stone asks the jury to consider the force used by Officer Powell—the baton strikes. He says it's ugly and awful to see and hear the baton in use, but officers are taught to inflict pain and to immobilize if they are going to use the baton.

It would have been objectively unreasonable for the officers to let Mr. King rise once they realized the taser hadn't worked. There would have been an increased threat of flight, of resistance and running.

After a lengthy discussion of the police reports, and whether Officer Powell's report was deceptive, Mr. Stone returns to the use-of-force. He argues that the video, the medical evidence, and the testimony as to the head strikes are conflicting. The reason Mr. King acted as he did is unclear.

Mr. Stone then recalls Mr. White's statement on closing that if the defense believed Mr. King had anything relevant to say, the defense would have called him. Mr. Stone argues that Rodney King could have cleared up these questions. It is not the responsibility of the defense to call anybody. It's the prosecution's burden to prove the defendant guilty.

After another extremely long discussion of the false reports, Mr. Stone points to inaccuracies or inconsistencies in the version of events as perceived by others. He declares that Mr. White misrepresented Officer Powell's testimony. "So Mr. White made an inaccurate statement. When my client makes [an] inaccurate statement, they call him a perjurer."

Mr. Stone concludes by discussing direct and circumstantial evidence and points out that if circumstantial evidence is susceptible to two reasonable interpretations, the jury must adopt the one which points to the defendant's innocence. He reminds the jury that the prosecution has the burden of proof of beyond a reasonable doubt, and the jurors must feel an abiding conviction to a moral certainty of the truth of the charge.

Finally, he thanks the jury for its patience for listening to a very long and sometimes tedious argument. His argument has taken considerably longer than did Mr. White's (which itself was three and one-half hours).

Mr. De Pasquale for Officer Wind

Although Officer Wind had other law enforcement experience, at the time of the incident he was a probationary trainee, the lowest on the LAPD totem pole. He had been on the Los Angeles streets for about ninety days. Mr. De Pasquale wants Officer Wind to be judged separately from the other defendants, as he is entitled to be.

The lawyer points out that it would have taken an enormous amount of liquor for someone of Mr. King's size to reach a .19 blood alcohol level, since Mr. King weighed around 250 pounds. And alcohol makes a person uninhibited, willing to take more risks.

Officer Wind and the other officers had to deal with this wild, drunken driver. They couldn't just walk away from the situation. They had the right to use reasonable force. And consider that a prosecution rebuttal witness, Annette Olivas (Officer Wind's instructor) testified that it was not good to let a suspect get into a push-up position, and even worse if the suspect is on his knees or on his feet.

Mr. De Pasquale tells the jurors that when Mr. King charges Officer Powell, and Mr. King goes down, Officer Wind is behind Officer Powell. And Commander Bostic "in his full-dress Class A uniform, thinks it would be nice to walk in and handcuff Mr. King." Officer Wind observes for seven seconds. (Mr. De Pasquale plays the video.) Officer Wind appears to start a swing, then checks it so as not to hit Mr. King in the head.

Sgt. Koon has directed his officers to hit Mr. King in the joints, the elbows, the wrist, knees and ankles because the other blows were having no effect. Officer Wind, after these directions, swings at Mr. King six times in seven seconds. Officer Wind's posture is cautious, withdrawn, quick feet, sliding. Mr. King moves upward. There are twelve more swings.

Mr. King is down. Officer Wind spends nineteen seconds watching. Then Officer Briseno makes his stepping movement. Officer Wind does not see what Officer Briseno is doing, only that there is a very strong forceful quick movement by Mr. King. There are five more swings by Officer Wind.

Officer Wind then tries kicking Mr. King. This is less painful to Mr. King than the blows. He pushes Mr. King six times with his leg to keep him down. Then he watches, only becoming involved when he has to become involved.

Mr. De Pasquale discusses the alleged adoptive admission of Mr. Wind when he remained silent in regard to the baseball game statement, the "hitting homeruns". What is Officer Wind supposed to do when somebody makes a dumb, tasteless comment? His silence shows nothing.

And while Nurse Davis said that Officer Wind picked up his night stick when a question arose as to what happened to Mr. King's face, according to the other nurse, Carol Edwards, the actual question was what Mr. King was hit with. In either case, Officer Wind didn't make any comment, didn't make any jokes, didn't laugh or grin.

Officer Wind's actions were not nice, and perhaps weren't the best choices in the world, but he didn't do anything gratuitously, didn't take any cheap shots. He performed his actions in the line of service which protects society. Under the standard of proof in criminal cases, Officer Wind is entitled to a not guilty verdict.

Mr. Barnett for Officer Briseno

Mr. Barnett talks about the jurors' duties, especially the duty to vote not guilty if there is a reasonable doubt as to the defendant's guilt. He reiterates the circumstantial evidence instruction to adopt a reasonable interpretation which points to the defendant's innocence.

Officer Briseno is not being charged with the specific intent crime of inflicting great bodily injury. He is not being charged with aiding and abetting. At the time Officer Briseno put his foot on Mr. King he believed Mr. King needed to be cuffed and taken into custody and that he needed to stop the beating of Mr. King by Officers Wind and Powell. And Officer

Briseno didn't want to use his hand to keep Mr. King down because he wanted to keep his own head out of the strike zone.

Prosecutor White called this an unnecessary stomp. But Officer Briseno didn't have the opportunity to sit around and clinically analyze what he should have done. He is the only officer who tried to stop the beating by attempting to restrain Officer Powell.

After his initial attempt to stop the beating, Officer Briseno didn't join in, he didn't do anything to punish Mr. King. When he finally stepped on Mr. King's neck, he did so with his off (weak) leg. Officer Briseno is 140 pounds, Mr. King 250 pounds. Officer Briseno's force was not only not excessive, it was insufficient to restrain Mr. King, for he was forced backwards off Mr. King's back.

Mr. White suggested that Officer Briseno should have done nothing or tied up with Mr. King, or thrown his body over Mr. King. But even as a Monday morning quarterback, does throwing his body over Mr. King seem reasonable? asks Mr. Barnett.

Mr. Barnett talks about Commander Bostic, the prosecution's use-of-force expert and his testimony. Having arrested four armed robbers that very night, one can assume Officer Briseno had more experience in that one evening than Commander Bostic had in the past decade.

Commander Bostic says he would have done things differently, but he doesn't say what Officer Briseno should have done, even with the luxury of reviewing the video numerous times, over a week to ten days. And Commander Bostic is the expert.

Consider the statement by Officer Briseno to Officer Solano before he knew there was a video, before he had a chance to make things up. This was right after the incident. He said that what the officers did was wrong, was all wrong.

And although the other officers tried to get Officer Briseno to backup their version, he wouldn't. When the other defendants had their experts testify that the hundreds of strikes and kicks by the other defendants were justified, but Officer Briseno's step was not (unless he believed Mr. King was going for a gun), Officer Briseno refused to go that route. This officer is honest throughout, declares Mr. Barnett.

Mr. Barnett then attacks the testimony of others who had been brought in to undermine Officer Briseno's testimony. Mr.

Barnett argues that these people lied, they misrepresented. Why would they do this? It's the bunker mentality, the thin blue line, the "us against them" mentality alluded to in Mr. Stone's argument.

Mr. Barnett continues. For almost three hours, Mr. White described why the jury should convict Officers Wind and Powell. In so doing, Mr. White was a most effective defense attorney for Officer Briseno. But Mr. White betrays a fundamental misunderstanding of the burden of proof. Where did Officer Briseno's foot go? What did he do? Was this force needed? Mr. White challenged the defense to answer questions for which the prosecution had no answer. That's not the defendant's burden, says Mr. Barnett.

The lawyer for defendant Briseno closes by telling his own version of *A True American Tale*, not the tale of Fievel but the tale of an officer who arrested four robbers that night, who labored under the false accusations of this indictment, an outcast in his own department, subject to lies and perjury for telling the truth, who took heroic action and tried to intervene to stop the beating. The reward for these acts is that Officer Briseno is vilified and victimized.

The prosecution had a tactical choice to make in regard to Officer Briseno. They chose to say he acted feloniously, that his **exculpatory** *statements were untrue. In so doing, they undermined the case he was making against Officer Powell and Wind, because why would anyone believe a liar and a felon? Might it have been better to offer him immunity from prosecution for his testimony against the other officers?*

Mr. Mounger for Sergeant Koon

Speaking for Sgt. Koon, Mr. Mounger says he wants to talk about "the truth". Sgt. Koon was there to effect an arrest. Nobody has said what the proper police procedure is when you are dealing with some big guy, six-three, 250 pounds at 1:00 in the morning, with a case of beer in his belly, and that big guy doesn't want to comply.

In his Opening Statement, Mr. White said that Mr. King was acting silly. But that's what a high school girl does at her senior prom, not something you do at 1:00 A.M. when several police officers are pointing guns at you.

Is Sgt. Koon guilty of the charges? He has to play the cards he is dealt, to use the men he has available, the tools the police department has given him. Here's this big man, this scary suspect—four officers couldn't control him. He resisted arrest because as a parolee, he was in violation of the law and didn't want to go to jail. If that wasn't the reason for his actions, says Mr. Mounger, the prosecution could have called Mr. King.

From the beginning when he assumed control, Sgt. Koon was trying to eliminate deadly force. Officer Melanie Singer, with a gun in her hand, could have caused deadly force if she had been allowed to proceed.

Sgt. Duke is an expert on use-of-force, with twenty-one years of experience, nineteen of them on the street. He has taught in several states and in Canada. Captain Michael has taught in California, is licensed in Arizona and Florida, has taught in forty states and testified in thirty.

The People's expert, Commander Bostic, says the officers should have gang-tackled Mr. King. But who is Commander Bostic? At the moment, he's the use-of-force chairman of LAPD, but next week he could have a different job. He tells you a police officer's safety is equal to a suspect's safety. But that's not correct, says Mr. Mounger. The beating is terrible, but what are the options? Even today, the LAPD doesn't have tranquilizer guns, nets, leg grabbers, velcro blankets. So what should Sgt. Koon have ordered his officers to do? Let Mr. King drive off?

Mr. Mounger agrees with Mr. White. None of this was necessary. All Mr. King had to do was to let himself be handcuffed.

Mr. White has said that at some point enough is enough. But how is that communicated to the officers?

After a discussion of the false report charges, Mr. Mounger returns to the charges that Sgt. Koon is an accessory. Sgt. Koon testified that he believed his officers were doing the only thing they could, based on the tools available to them. Mr. Mounger says:

> **"I'm not asking you to like it. I'm not asking you to say they're innocent. I'm asking you to say they are not guilty. I'm going to tell you that the People have not**

proven beyond a reasonable doubt that there was a reasonable way to do this."

Sgt. Koon tried to use the minimum amount of force to get Mr. King to comply. He was dealing with a man he believed was on PCP, a man Officer Tim Singer thought was in a monster movie. Sgt. Koon did what was reasonable and necessary under the circumstances.

The Prosecution Has the Final Word

Mr. White says that desperate men do desperate things, and so it was with Attorneys Mounger, De Pasquale and Stone. They embarrassed officers who are doing their jobs by hiding behind talk of a thin blue line. The defendants are not above the law, as their lawyers suggest.

Mr. White spends a good deal of time on Mr. Stone's "big lie," which deals with the time it takes to reach Glenoaks and Van Nuys.

As regards Officer Powell, Mr. White says that when things look bad, it's always someone else's fault. Officer Powell mocked, taunted and laughed at Mr. King. He said "Oops, I haven't beaten anyone this bad in a long time." There are not two reasonable interpretations for these actions, as Mr. Stone would have the jury believe. There is only one reasonable interpretation.

Even if you give Officer Powell the benefit of the doubt, what then? Maybe Mr. King shouldn't have moved toward Officer Powell. But does that give Officer Powell the right to jump on him, after he's fallen face first into the pavement, and start hitting Mr. King with his baton?

Mr. King doesn't have the duty to say, "I give." He only has to refrain from using any force or other means to resist arrest, and then the officers must stop using force. But Mr. King continued to be beaten after he had ceased to resist. You don't see "the old Charlie Duke/Robert Michael idea, the old bent leg, cocked leg, he's on the rise" in the video, says Mr. White.

The defendants treated Mr. King like an animal. Officer Powell was acting like a thug. Mr. King is trying to put his hands behind his back when he's hit, when Officer Briseno stomped on his neck.

Fifty-six blows in eighty-two seconds. They pounded him.

Mr. White says the reasonable method the officers should have used was the swarm technique. That's what Sgt. Koon should have ordered. But he didn't, and then he covered it up by saying that he did.

As to Officer Briseno, "he may not have had an evil heart" or "evil mind" but the force he used was "unreasonable." Mr. White then told the jury that they would have to judge Officer Briseno's action "under the reasonable person standard instruction the court is going to give you."

Then, at long last, closing arguments are over, and the lawyers are finished. It bears repeating: these Closing Statements are not evidence, just as the Opening Statements are not. The jurors now must decide. However, before they begin deliberations, they have to be told how a decision is made. They have to await the jury instructions.

CHAPTER 24

JURY INSTRUCTIONS:
THE LAW'S GUIDE TO DECIDE

"... the judge shall limit his or her responsibility to communicating, simply and concisely, the applicable law to the jury, leaving to counsel advocacy and argumentation."

So states the publication commonly called "CALJIC," the philosophical springboard for almost all jury instructions in criminal cases in California.

What is clear from the quoted statement is that the judge is expected to maintain an almost passive role in assisting jurors to understand the meaning of the instructions given to them. It is left up to the lawyers in the case to provide appropriate guidance to the jury. CALJIC instructions are written by lawyers for use by lawyers and judges. They are supposed to apply the following four benchmarks:

- An instruction should be an accurate statement of the law.

- An instruction should be brief and concise as practicable.

- An instruction should be understandable to the average juror.

- An instruction should be completely neutral, unslanted and free of argument.

Combining these four guidelines in each instruction is a tall order, considering the fact that normally jury instructions are grouped together in a single paragraph even though there may be two, five, ten or more distinct and separate points of law covered.

Jury instructions more or less follow the same pattern in states other than California. They are generally given to the jury at the end of the case after Closing Statements which is just before the jury goes into deliberations. In one sense, the instructions may be the freshest recollection in the jurors' minds as they enter the jury room. The problem is that the evidence in the case may be stale. And if correct verdicts are to be reached, jury instructions and a keen recollection of the evidence must go hand in hand.

Although the law permits jurors to receive the instructions in hard-copy form, many judges throughout the United States *do not* give the instructions to the jurors to peruse. Sometimes, jurors will request the instructions from the court and then, at the judge's discretion, they may get them. Sometimes, judges will provide instructions to the jurors before the end of the trial.

Judge Lance Ito in the *Simpson* case read numerous preliminary instructions to the jury on the first day they entered the courtroom to hear the case. He informed the jury:

> **"This is sort of my effort to give you a gauge or rule by which you should look at the evidence as it is presented to you."**

This was an unusual and commendable effort to provide some guidance to the jury *before* any evidence in the case was introduced. But, a moment later, Judge Ito told the jury:

> **"So I encourage you each to listen very carefully to my instructions on the law. However, you need not take any detailed notes as to their contents since they will be available to you in their exact written form in the jury room."**

Then, in his effort to provide some guidance to the jurors, Judge Ito proceeded to read them instructions for nearly twenty minutes. That's a long time to concentrate on hearing sentence after sentence after sentence of accurate, concise, understandable, unslanted and free-of-argument statements of the law. And even though Judge Ito knew the jury instructions in the case would not be given in final form to the jury until many months later, he still told the jurors not to take detailed notes.

Did the judge really expect jurors to retain, with any degree of accuracy, what he had read? If it were important to understand these instructions, why not give the jurors a hard copy to use in making notes, and keep with them throughout the trial?

In Chapter 4, you were introduced to the contents of jury instructions from examples taken from the Rodney King beating trial. As we indicated earlier, to make the instructions more meaningful and user-friendly, we separated them into their segments so you could review the components in a more relevant and meaningful context.

But what would you do as a juror, particularly a juror in the *Powell* trial? You are very tired, burned out, and want the case to end, yet you still want to perform your duty. So you try to be attentive. You expect the judge to give you those most important instructions which will bring everything together and make your job easier.

As Judge Weisberg starts reading the instructions, you listen very carefully. You have nothing to look at, so the only thing you can do is listen. The jury instructions which were actually given in *People v. Powell* are set out on the following pages. They are not broken down as they were earlier, since we want you to see what the judge read.

As you glance through the following thirteen pages, notice where you first think you would stop taking in whatever was being read to you, where you no longer feel interested, much less alert. Note any points where, even after rereading, you don't understand the judge. And mark the point where you think you would have stopped listening if you had been one of the *Powell* jurors.

JURY INSTRUCTIONS
PEOPLE V. POWELL ET AL[34]

As I indicated yesterday, I will now instruct the jury on the law, and as I indicated, I will be reading these instructions to you and they will be made available to you in their written form in the jury room. (Judge Weisberg then begins reading the jury instructions to the jury.)

Ladies and gentlemen of the jury, you have heard all the evidence and the arguments of the attorneys and now it is my duty to instruct you on the law that applies to this case. The law requires that I read the instructions to you and you will have these instructions in their written form in the jury room to refer to during deliberations.

You must base your decision on the facts and the law.

You have two duties to perform. First, you must determine the facts from the evidence received in the trial and not from any other source. A fact is something proved directly or circumstantially by the evidence or by stipulation. A stipulation is agreement between the attorneys regarding the facts.

Second, you must apply the law as I state it to you to the facts as you determine them and in this way arrive at your verdict and any finding you are instructed to include in your verdict.

You must accept and follow the law as I state it to you, whether or not you agree with the law. If anything concerning the law said by the attorneys in their arguments or at any other time during the trial conflicts with my instructions on the law, you must follow my instructions.

You must not be influenced by pity for a defendant or by prejudice against him. You must not be biased against the defendant because he has been arrested for this offense, charged with a crime or brought to trial. None of these circumstances is evidence of guilt and you must not infer or assume from any or all of them that he is more likely to be guilty than innocent.

You must not be influenced by mere sentiment, conjecture, sympathy, passion, prejudice, public opinion or public feeling. Both the

People and the defendant have a right to expect that you will conscientiously consider and weigh the evidence, apply the law and reach a just verdict regardless of the consequences.

If any rule, direction or idea is repeated or stated in different ways in these instructions, no emphasis is intended and you must not draw any inference because of its repetition. Do not single out any particular sentence or any individual point or instruction and ignore the others. Consider the instructions as a whole and each in light of all the others. The order in which the instructions are given has no significance as to their relative importance.

Statements made by the attorneys during the trial are not evidence, although if the attorneys have stipulated or agreed to a fact, you must regard that fact as conclusively proved as to the party or parties making the stipulation or entering into the stipulation. If an objection was sustained to a question, do not guess what the answer might have been, do not speculate as to the reason for the objection.

Do not assume to be true any insinuation suggested by a question asked a witness. A question is not evidence and may be considered only as it enables you to understand the answer. Do not consider for any purpose any offer of evidence that was rejected or any evidence that was stricken by the court. Treat it as though you had never heard of it.

As I indicated to you yesterday and at the beginning of the argument phase of the trial, the arguments of the attorneys are not evidence. If—and let me go further and talk to you a little bit about the argument of counsel.

If in argument any counsel made reference or seemed to make reference to the veracity or personal integrity of any other attorney, you are to disregard any such comment. Such comment should play no role in how you decide this case.

And as I've already told you, the comments of counsel are not evidence and you are the sole and exclusive judges of what the evidence is.

You must decide all the questions of fact in this case from the evidence received in this trial and not from any other source. You must not make any independent investigation of the facts or the law or consider or discuss facts as to which there is no evidence. This means, for example, that you must not on your own visit the scene, conduct experiments or consult reference works or persons for additional information. You must not discuss this case with any other person, except a fellow juror, and you must not discuss the case with a fellow juror until the case is submitted to you for your decision and only when all the jurors are present in the jury room.

The word "defendant" applies equally to each defendant unless you are expressly instructed otherwise.

Evidence consists of testimony of witnesses, writings, material objects or anything presented to the senses and offered to prove the existence or nonexistence of a fact. Evidence is either direct or circumstantial.

Direct evidence is evidence that directly proves a fact without the necessity of an inference. It is evidence which, by itself, if found to be true, establishes that fact.

Circumstantial evidence is evidence that, if found to be true, proves a fact from which an inference of the existence of another fact may be drawn. An inference is a deduction of fact that may logically and reasonably be drawn from another fact or group of facts established by the evidence.

It is not necessary that facts be proved by direct evidence. They may be proved also by circumstantial evidence or by a combination of direct evidence and circumstantial evidence. Both direct evidence and circumstantial evidence are acceptable as a means of proof. Neither is entitled to any greater weight than the other.

However, a finding of guilt as to any crime may not be based on circumstantial evidence unless the proved circumstances are not only, one, consistent with the theory that the defendant is guilty of the crime, but two, cannot be reconciled with any other rational conclusion.

Further, each fact which is essential to complete a set of circumstances necessary to establish the defendant's guilt must be proved beyond a reasonable doubt. In other words, before an inference essential to establish guilt may be found to have been proved beyond a reasonable doubt, each fact or circumstance upon which such inference necessarily rests must be proved beyond a reasonable doubt.

Also, if the circumstantial evidence as to any particular count is susceptible of two reasonable interpretations, one of which points to the defendant's guilt and the other to his innocence, you must adopt that interpretation which points to the defendant's innocence and reject that interpretation which points to his guilt.

If, on the other hand, one interpretation of such evidence appears to you to be reasonable and the other interpretation to be unreasonable, you must accept the reasonable interpretation and reject the unreasonable.

The specific intent with which an act is done may be shown by the circumstances surrounding the commission of the act, but you may not find the defendant guilty of the offense charged in counts III, IV and V unless the proved circumstances are not only, one, consistent with the theory that the defendant had the required specific intent or mental state, but two, cannot be reconciled with any other rational conclusion.

Also, if the evidence as to any such specific intent or mental state is susceptible of two reasonable interpretations, one of which points to the existence of the specific intent or mental state, and the other to the absence of the specific intent or mental state, you must adopt that interpretation which points to the absence of the specific intent or mental state.

If, on the other hand, one interpretation of the evidence as to such specific intent or mental state appears to you to be reasonable and the other interpretation to be unreasonable, you must accept the reasonable interpretation and reject the unreasonable.

If you find that before this trial a defendant made a willfully false or deliberately misleading statement concerning the crimes for which he is now being tried, you may consider such statement as a circumstance tending to prove a consciousness of guilt. However, such conduct is not sufficient by itself to prove guilt and its weight and significance, if any, are matters for your determination.

Evidence has been admitted against one or more of the defendants and not admitted against the others. At the time this evidence was admitted you were admonished that it could not be considered by you against the other defendants. Do not consider such evidence against the other defendants.

Certain evidence was admitted for a limited purpose. At the time this evidence was admitted you were admonished that it could not be considered by you for any purpose other than the limited purpose for which it was admitted. Do not consider such evidence for any purpose except the limited purpose for which it was admitted.

You have seen a lot of exhibits during the course of the trial used in examination of various witnesses. Not all of the exhibits that were referred to during the trial have been received in evidence. The exhibits that have been received in evidence will be provided to you, along with a list of those exhibits. Don't speculate or be concerned as to why some exhibits have not been received. You are to utilize the exhibits that have been received in evidence.

Some of the exhibits that were received were received only as to a particular defendant or defendants and were so limited at the time the exhibits were received into evidence. The list of exhibits that will be provided to you includes the limitations, if any, that apply to each exhibit.

You are instructed that testimony and/or exhibits that have been received only as to a particular defendant or defendants may be considered by you only in the case of that defendant or defendants and must not be discussed or considered by you in the case of any other defendant.

And as I say, the exhibit list has on it reference to those limitations on the physical exhibits, so when you look at the list, you will be able to identify which exhibits have been received for a limited purpose as to certain defendants and not as to others and you are to follow those limitations in your deliberations as well.

Neither side is required to call as witnesses all persons who may have been present at any of the events disclosed by the evidence or who may appear to have some knowledge of these events or to produce all objects or documents mentioned or suggested by the evidence.

Evidence that on some former occasion a witness made a statement or statements that were inconsistent or consistent with his or her testimony in this trial may be considered by you not only for the purpose of testing the credibility of the witness, but also as evidence of the truth of the facts as stated by the witness on such former occasion.

If you disbelieve a witness's testimony that he or she no longer remembers a certain event, such testimony is inconsistent with a prior statement or statements by him or her describing that event.

Every person who testifies under oath is a witness. You are the sole judges of the believability of a witness and the weight to be given the testimony of each witness. In determining the believability of a witness you may consider anything that has a tendency in reason to prove or disprove the truthfulness of the testimony of the witness, including but not limited to any of the following:

The extent of the opportunity or the ability of the witness to see or hear or otherwise become aware of any matter about which the witness has testified; the ability of the witness to remember or to communicate any matter about which the witness has testified; the character and quality of that testimony; the demeanor and manner of the witness while testifying; the existence or nonexistence of a bias, interest or other motive; evidence of the existence or nonexistence of any fact testified to by the witness; the attitude of the witness towards this action or towards the giving of testimony; a statement previously made by the witness that is consistent or inconsistent with the testimony of the witness; an admission by the witness of untruthfulness; the witness's prior conviction of a felony.

Discrepancies in a witness's testimony, or between his or her testimony and that of others, if there were any, do not necessarily mean that the witness should be discredited. Failure of recollection is a common experience and innocent misrecollection is not uncommon.

It is a fact also that two persons witnessing an incident or a transaction often will see or hear it differently. Whether a discrepancy pertains to a fact of importance or only to a trivial detail should be considered in weighing its significance.

A witness who is willfully false in one material part of his or her testimony is to be distrusted in others. You may reject the whole testimony of a witness who willfully has testified falsely as to a material point unless from all the evidence you believe the probability of truth favors his or her testimony in other particulars.

You are not bound to decide an issue of fact in accordance with the testimony of a number of witnesses which does not convince you as against the testimony of a lesser number or other evidence which appeals to your mind with more convincing force.

You may not disregard the testimony of the greater number of witnesses merely from caprice, whim or prejudice or from a desire to favor one side against the other. You must not decide an issue by the simple process of counting the number of witnesses who have testified on the opposing sides. The final test is not in the relative number of witnesses, but in the convincing force of the evidence.

The fact that a witness has been convicted of a felony, if such be a fact, may be considered by you only for the purpose of determining the believability of that witness. The fact of such a conviction does not necessarily destroy or impair the witness's believability. It is one of the circumstances that you may take into consideration in weighing the testimony of such a witness.

You should give the testimony of a single witness whatever weight you think it deserves; however, testimony by one witness, which you believe concerning any fact, is sufficient for the proof of that fact. You should carefully review all the evidence upon which the proof of such fact depends.

Motive is not an element of the crime charged and need not be shown; however, you may consider motive or lack of motive as a circumstance in this case. Presence of motive may tend to establish guilt. Absence of motive may tend to establish innocence. You will therefore give its presence or absence, as the case may be, the weight to which you find it to be entitled.

A defendant in a criminal trial has a constitutional right not to be compelled to testify. You must not draw any inference from the fact that a defendant does not testify. Further, you must neither discuss this matter nor permit it to enter into your deliberations in any way. In deciding whether or not to testify the defendant may choose to rely on the state of the evidence and upon the failure, if any, of the people to prove beyond a reasonable doubt every essential element of the charge against him. No lack of testimony on a defendant's part will make up for a failure of proof by the people so as to support a finding against him on any such material or essential element.

Let me read that last one again since I misread it.

In deciding whether or not to testify the defendant may choose to rely on the state of the evidence and upon the failure, if any, of the people prove beyond a reasonable doubt every essential element of the charge against him. No lack of testimony on the defendant's part will make up for a failure of proof by the people so as to support a finding against him on any such essential element.

An admission is a statement made by a defendant, other than at his trial, which does not by itself acknowledge his guilt of the crime for which such defendant is on trial but which statement tends to prove his guilt when considered with the rest of the evidence.

You are the exclusive judges as to whether the defendant made an admission, and if so, whether such statement is true in whole or in part.

If you should find that the defendant did not make the statement, you must reject it. If you find that it is true in whole or in part, you may consider that part which you find to be true.

Evidence of an oral admission of a defendant should be viewed with caution. If you should find from the evidence that there was an occasion when a defendant, under circumstances which reasonably afforded him an opportunity to reply, failed to make a denial in the face of an accusation expressed directly to him or in his presence charging him with the crime for which such defendant now is on trial or tending to connect him with its commission and that he heard the accusation and understood its nature, then the circumstance of his silence on that occasion may be considered against him as indicating an admission that the accusation thus made was true.

Evidence of such an accusatory statement is not received for the purpose of proving its truth, but only as it supplies meaning to the silence of the accused in the face of it.

Unless you find that a defendant's silence at the time indicated an admission that the accusatory statement was true, you must entirely disregard the statement.

Evidence has been received from which you may find that a statement of motive was made by a defendant before the offense with which he is charged was committed. It is for you to determine whether such a statement was made by a defendant and whether or not such statement constitutes a statement of motive.

No person may be convicted of a criminal offense unless there is some proof of each element of the crime independent of any admission made by him outside the trial.

The identity of the person who is alleged to have committed a crime is not an element of the crime. Such identity may be established by an admission.

A person is qualified to testify as an expert if he has special knowledge, skill, experience, training or education sufficient to qualify him as an expert on the subject to which his testimony relates. A duly qualified expert may give an opinion on questions in controversy at a trial. To assist you in deciding such questions you may consider the opinion, with the reasons given for it, if any, by the expert who gives the opinion. You may also consider the qualifications and credibility of the expert.

You are not bound to accept an expert opinion as conclusive, but should give to it the weight to which you find it to be entitled. You may disregard any such opinion if you find it to be unreasonable.

In this case expert witnesses have testified about two types of facts: facts to which they have special qualifications and experience which allow them to testify as expert witnesses and facts on which they have no special expertise.

In particular, in rendering an opinion as to the use-of-force in this case, one or more expert witnesses expressed an opinion on what physical acts are shown on exhibit 2, the so-called Holliday videotape. Such experts have no more skill than a lay person in viewing the videotape and determining what it shows in this regard. To the extent that you find that the videotape is important to you in your deliberations and decision in this case, you are the sole judges of what physical acts are shown on the tape.

Expert witnesses merely express their opinions of what physical acts are shown on the videotape. These opinions were the assumption which formed the basis for an answer to a hypothetical question. The expert witnesses were assuming that the tape showed a particular action or application of force for the purpose of expressing their opinion as to whether such force was reasonable or unreasonable, appropriate or excessive under the circumstances of the hypothetical question.

If you find that the videotape shows something other than which a particular expert witness assumed to be true for a hypothetical question, you may consider that difference in determining what weight, if any, to give the expert opinion expressed in answering that question.

In determining the weight to be given an opinion expressed by any witness who did not testify as an expert witness, you should consider his or her credibility, the extent of his or her opportunity to perceive the matters upon which his opinion is based, and the reasons, if any, for giving that opinion. You are not required to accept such an opinion but should give it the weight, if any, to which you find it to be entitled.

In examining an expert witness, counsel may propound to him or her a type of question known in the law as a hypothetical question. By such a question the witness is asked to assume to be true a set of facts and to give an opinion based on that assumption.

In permitting such a question the court does not rule and does not necessarily find that all the assumed facts have been proved. It only determines that those assumed facts are within the probable or possible range of the evidence. It is for you, the jury, to find from all the evidence whether or not the facts assumed in a hypothetical question have been proved.

If you should find that any assumption in such a question has not been proved, you are to determine the effect of that failure of proof on the value and weight of the expert opinion based on the assumed facts.

In resolving any conflict that may exist in the testimony of expert witnesses, you should weigh the opinion of one expert against that of another. In doing this you should consider the relative qualifications and credibility of the expert witnesses, as well as the reasons for each opinion and the facts and other matters upon which it was based.

A defendant in a criminal action is presumed to be innocent until the contrary is proved, and in case of a reasonable doubt whether his guilt is satisfactorily shown, he is entitled to a verdict of not guilty.

This presumption places upon the people the burden of proving him guilty beyond a reasonable doubt.

Reasonable doubt is defined as follows:

It is not a mere possible doubt, because everything relating to human affairs and depending on moral evidence is open to some possible or imaginary doubt. It is that state of the case which, after the entire comparison and consideration of all the evidence, leaves the minds of the jurors in that condition that they cannot say they feel an abiding conviction to a moral certainty of the truth of the charge.

The persons concerned in the commission of a crime who are regarded by law as principals in the crime thus committed and equally guilty thereof include, one, those who directly and actively commit the act constituting the crime, and two, those who aid and abet the commission of the crime.

A person aids and abets the commission of a crime when he or she, one, with knowledge of the unlawful purpose of the perpetrator, and two, with the intent or purpose of committing, encouraging or facilitating the commission of the crime by act or advice, aids, promotes, encourages, or instigates the commission of the crime.

Mere presence at the scene of a crime, which does not itself assist the commission of the crime, does not constitute or amount to aiding and abetting. Mere knowledge that a crime is being committed and the failure to prevent it does not amount to aiding and abetting.

In the crime charged in Count I, namely assault by force likely to produce great bodily injury and with a deadly weapon, and in the crime charged in Count II, namely officer unnecessarily assaulting or beating any persons, there must exist a union or joint operation of act or conduct and general criminal intent.

To constitute general criminal intent it is not necessary that there should exist an intent to violate the law. When a person intentionally does that which the law declares to be a crime, he is acting with general criminal intent even though he may not know that his act or conduct is unlawful.

In each of the crimes charged in Counts III, IV and V, namely filing a false police report and accessory after the fact, there must exist a union or joint operation of act or conduct and a certain specific intent in the mind of the perpetrator.

Unless such specific intent exists, the crime to which it relates is not committed. The specific intent required is included in the definitions of these charged crimes.

In the special allegations of the intentional infliction of great bodily injury in Count I and Count II, charged against the defendants Laurence Powell and Timothy Wind, there must exist a union or joint operation of act or conduct and a certain specific intent in the mind of the perpetrator. Unless such specific intent exists, the allegation to which it relates is not committed. The specific intent required is included in the definition of the special allegations charged.

In each of the crimes charged in Counts III and IV, namely filing a false police report, there must exist a certain mental state in the mind of the perpetrator. Unless such mental state exists, the crime to which it relates is not committed.

In the crime of filing a false police report the necessary mental state is knowledge that the statement was false.

Well, I'm about halfway through. If anybody needs a break at any time, just let me know and we'll take a break.

At this point, we will stop. Enough is enough. If you want to continue reading the second half of the instructions, you can find the rest in Appendix D beginning with (JI-125) at page 330.

Finally, the agony is over. Even if you were a lawyer, who understood everything the judge was talking about, you would probably reach a saturation point where your mind could absorb nothing more. So if you didn't have that background, or weren't trained to concentrate for long periods of time on phrases like "cloaked with authority", would you remember what was just read?

Once again, we have to wonder why the critical instructions are given now, at the end of the trial, *after* jurors have already heard the testimony, made judgments about it, and probably formed opinions based on the evidence. Regrettably, most jurors learn of the law that is to be applied to the case on which they sat just as the *Powell* jurors did. If they understand most of what the judge says, they would be remarkable indeed.

In Part IV of this book, you saw that jury instructions could be extremely informative and helpful if presented at the right time in the right way. At present, they are more often an obstacle than an aid to understanding.

As we have indicated, the overwhelming number of jury instructions given in California are used in their CALJIC form, word for word, although there may be gender changes made to reflect the sex of the defendant. Sometimes it is necessary for the lawyers to provide "customized" instructions. These crafted instructions are given to the judge who decides whether they can be used when the standard instructions are considered inadequate.

In most trials, the lawyers submit the jury instructions they want the judge to use prior to the trial. This is not difficult because the lawyers know what evidence they have and what arguments they will make.

It is interesting to note that there are jury instructions which tell the jurors how to deal with the jury instructions! Judge Weisberg informed jurors:

> If any rule, direction or idea is repeated or stated in different ways in these instructions, no emphasis is intended and you must not draw any inference because of its repetition.   (JI-19)

> Do not single out any particular sentence or any individual point or instruction and ignore the others.   (JI-20)

> Consider the instructions as a whole and each in light of all the others.   (JI-21)

> The order in which the instructions are given has no significance as to their relative importance.   (JI-22)

> The purpose of the court's instructions is to provide you with the applicable law so that you may arrive at a just and lawful verdict.   (JI-173)

Whether some instructions apply will depend upon what you find to be the facts. (JI-174)

Disregard any instruction which applies to facts determined by you not to exist. (JI-175)

Do not conclude that because an instruction has been given that I'm expressing an opinion as to the facts. (JI-176)

As I have indicated, the instructions I'm now giving to you will be made available in written form during your deliberations. Since they're part of the official record, they must not be defaced in any way. (JI-182)

You will find that the instructions may be typed, printed or handwritten. Portions may have been added or deleted. You must disregard any deleted part of an instruction and not speculate as to what it was or as to the reasons for its deletion. You are not to be concerned with the reasons for any modifications. Every part of the text of an instruction, whether typed, printed or handwritten, is of equal importance. You are to be governed only by the instruction in its final wording. (JI-183)

Until now we have focused on the ways to evaluate credibility and to weigh evidence. We have tried to make understandable each element of a charge, so that you can decide what is relevant to your determination and what is mere sound and fury, signifying nothing. We have explained the burden of proof, which the prosecution must meet in regard to each element of the crime. We have talked about inferences (which are reasonable, and not guesses) and when inferences can't be drawn (speculation, or the reason a privilege is claimed, such as that against self-incrimination).

If you compared the jury instructions we included above with those in Appendix C, you saw how many more were given to the jury. These other instructions refer to definitions, special situations that were present at this particular trial, explanations of what the juror should use specifically to determine whether crimes had been committed in this case.

There are instructions defining an "admission" and when silence can act as an admission and when it couldn't (Wind's failure to say something regarding Powell's taunting of Mr. King), when a police officer's use-of-force is appropriate, definitions for words contained in the charges such as "likely to produce serious bodily injury", "willful", etc. These instructions deal with the charges and how they are proved.

There are instructions for all of the different crimes, from arson to rape to kidnapping. While most of the instructions set forth in this book are given in most criminal cases, the instructions referring to specific crimes will only be included if that crime is at issue in the trial.

There were many instructions given to the *Powell* jury, but we want to highlight those few which we consider of particular significance in terms of Counts I and II. We want you to focus on these instructions as you decide the *Powell* case.

First, let's keep in mind what the prosecution must prove:

The people have the burden to prove that the force used was not lawful and without lawful necessity. If you have a reasonable doubt that the use-of-force was unlawful and without lawful necessity, you must find the defendant not guilty. (JI-146)

The reasonableness of a particular use-of- force must be judged from the perspective of a reasonable officer under the same or similar circumstances. (JI-147)

The test of reasonableness is not capable of precise definition or mechanical application. It is—its proper application requires careful attention to the facts and circumstances of each particular case, including the severity of the crime at issue, whether the suspect poses an immediate threat to the safety of the officers or others and whether he is actively resisting or attempting to evade arrest by flight. The question is whether the totality of the circumstances justifies a particular sort of force. (JI-148)

During a lawful arrest an officer may also take necessary measures to determine whether the person is in
fact carrying a weapon. (JI-149)

With the charges in mind, let's review instructions which
help determine whether the police defendants committed an
important and necessary element of the crime, namely, whether
their conduct was unlawful.

An arrest is made by an actual restraint of the person
arrested or by his submission to the custody of an
officer. (JI-137)

In making an arrest the officer may subject the person
being arrested to such restraint as is reasonable for
the arrest and detention. (JI-138)

A peace officer who is making an arrest may use
reasonable force to make such arrest or to prevent
escape or to overcome resistance. (JI-139)

The officer need not retreat or desist from his efforts
by reason of the resistance or threatened resistance of
the person being arrested. (JI-140)

Where a peace officer is making an arrest, the person
being arrested—and the person being arrested has
knowledge, or by the exercise of reasonable care,
should have knowledge that he is being arrested by a
peace officer and such peace officer is making an
arrest, it is the duty of the person to refrain from
using force or any other means to resist such arrest
unless unreasonable or excessive force is being used to
make the arrest. (JI-141)

However, a peace officer is not permitted to use unreasonable or excessive force in making an otherwise lawful
arrest. If an officer does use unreasonable or excessive
force in making or attempting to make an arrest, the
person being arrested may use reasonable force to protect himself against such excessive force. (JI-142)

It is lawful for a peace officer to use force in the arrest if a reasonable peace officer in the same or similar circumstances would believe that such force is necessary to make the arrest or to prevent escape or to overcome resistance. In doing so, such peace officer may use that force and means that a reasonable peace officer, in the same or similar circumstances, would believe to be necessary to make such arrest or to prevent escape or to overcome resistance. (JI-143)

The right of a peace officer to use reasonable force exists only so long as it would appear to a reasonable peace officer, in the same or similar circumstances, that that force is necessary to make such arrest or to prevent escape or to overcome resistance. (JI-144)

When that force would no longer appear to a reasonable peace officer, in the same or similar circumstances, to be necessary, the right to use reasonable force no longer exists and the use of such force is not reasonable. The use-of-force that is not reasonable is unlawful and without lawful necessity. (JI-145)

There are additional jury instructions which may need to be considered since issues may intertwine. Other instructions also may have to be referred to because of the need to understand the meaning of some of the terms. But the instructions we've set out here, while far from simple, straightforward and clear, are the ones of paramount importance to you.

Jury instructions are the most important tool given to jurors by the court. They are an effort to balance all concerns and give the juror objective and understandable assistance in reaching a verdict. They have a great deal of potential, if used in a constructive way at the appropriate time.

Chapter 25

JURY DELIBERATIONS:
A VISIT TO HELL?

Y ou've seen the video over and over, at regular speed, slow-motion, freeze-framed, enlarged. You have also seen the batons, the boots, the taser, heard the witnesses, learned about LAPD training from the experts and what the experts believe is an appropriate use-of-force. You've reviewed the medical evidence as to Mr. King's injuries and heard the experts testify as to what they believe caused these injuries.

And you have heard the lawyers, all six of them, from Opening Statements, through their questioning and objecting at the trial, to their Closing Statements.

Now all you have to do is apply those "accurate", "brief and concise", "understandable", and "completely neutral, unslanted, and free of argument" jury instructions to decide the case.

You, the jury, must agree on a verdict, if on nothing else. But you are all individuals with one vote each. In order to reach agreement, you each need to be prepared to articulate a position and also to explain why that is your position. And each of you must be open to listening to the other jurors, some of whom you may neither like nor respect.

Over the course of a lengthy trial, it is inevitable that jurors learn about each other before they reach the jury room. Sometimes friendships develop. At other trials, as in the *O.J. Simpson* trial, jurors grow to dislike each other.

The court, of course, has given instructions as to how jurors should act in the jury room:

> Do not hesitate to change an opinion if you are convinced it is wrong; however, do not decide any question in a particular way because the majority of the jurors, or any of them, favor such a decision. (JI-178)

> Do not decide any issue in this case by chance, such as by the drawing of lots or by any other chance determination. (JI-179)

> The attitude and conduct of jurors at all times are very important. It is rarely helpful for a juror at the beginning of deliberations to express an emphatic opinion on the case or to announce a determination to stand for a certain verdict. When one does that at the outset, a sense of pride may be aroused and one may hesitate to change a position even if shown it is wrong. Remember that you are not partisans or advocates in this matter, you are impartial judges of the facts. (JI-180)

> In your deliberations do not discuss or consider the subject of penalty or punishment. That subject must not in any way affect your verdict. (JI-181)

It would be great if jurors could count on this kind of rationality and civility. Often it does occur. But as the first trials of the Menendez brothers (for the killing of their parents) illustrated, mini-wars may develop. In Erik Menendez's first trial, which ended in a hung jury, the six men and six women jurors reached a state of total hostility. In other instances, racial prejudice may be perceived as the cause of dissension. Or it may simply be different personalities rubbing one another the wrong way.

Sometimes a juror has been excused because the other jurors have complained that the individual is unable or unwilling to participate in the discussions.

Even if jurors are basically nice, friendly, rational people, difficulties may arise. Let's face it: the instructions are confusing. People may not see the same thing (e.g., the baton blows) in the same way. One person may have a gut feeling that a witness was reliable, while others may not. Some may remember testimony one way, while others remember it differently. (This causes major problems in those courts where the judge won't let the jurors read the transcript.) Some jurors may use their life experiences to decide that a particular cop who testified was credible, while others may use their life experiences to conclude that cops are trained to lie. Arguments may arise as to what reasonable doubt is and whether the prosecution has met its burden of proof. One person may believe the defendant is guilty but that the evidence isn't sufficient to convict. Others may believe the evidence is sufficient, or if not sufficient, that the person should be convicted anyway as the defendant obviously is a danger to society.

We each bring our own way of dealing with friction into the jury room. To suffer the least amount of stress during your stay, each juror must make it a personal priority to treat everyone with courtesy, consideration *and* patience.

In addition, a juror who can quietly spell out the reasons for coming to a certain conclusion, using the information contained in the jury instructions to help explain that conclusion, is much more likely to have the other jurors listening carefully than if the juror's attitude (spoken or unspoken) is: "I'm right and you're wrong."

The imaginary "Juror's Table" we discussed in Chapter 19 provides a workable model for jury deliberations. It requires the jury to identify each count the defendant is charged with committing. The individual elements that must be proven are then identified and discussed one by one. If a defendant is charged with more than one crime, the above process would be repeated for each crime.

Another problem may arise if jurors have a different view of the law, and what powers are given to jurors. According to Judge Weisberg:

> ... you must apply the law as I state it to you to the facts as you determine them and in this way arrive at your verdict and any finding you are instructed to include in your verdict. (JI-6)

You must accept and follow the law as I state it to you, whether or not you agree with the law. (JI-7)

If anything concerning the law said by the attorneys in their arguments or at any other time during the trial conflicts with my instructions on the law, you must follow my instructions. (JI-8)

Jurors are also told what the parties expect from them:

Both the people and the defendant have a right to expect that you will conscientiously consider and weigh the evidence, apply the law and reach a just verdict regardless of the consequences. (JI-18)

There is a substantial minority position—the jury nullification approach referred to briefly in Chapter 10—that advocates telling jurors they have the right to disregard the instructions the judge gives them as to the state of the law and decide the case on the basis of their individual ideas of fairness and justice.

While many adherents of jury nullification acknowledge certain past limitations of the practice—such as the unwillingness of Southern white juries to convict Caucasians of killing African-Americans or Jews—they believe that juries should be allowed to act as they wish. A brief rundown on their arguments and our response follows.

1.   Laws are often unfair or unjust.

We don't disagree with that statement. But we question the advisability of leaving laws to idiosyncratic evaluation, where an individual's personal feeling about justice and fairness determines whether an acquittal or conviction should result. Doesn't this potentially imply a denial of responsibility for any of our actions? Aren't the laws based upon what the majority has decided? Do we really want a system where there is no equal justice for all?

2.   Jurors who are determined to nullify will do so.

We can't prevent juries from rendering a crude justice but we don't have to encourage vigilante rule.

3.   Juries are the conscience of the community.

Who appointed them? Not those who wrote the U.S. Constitution. In fact, many analysts would say that juries are a peculiar minority of the community consisting of the under- or unemployed, tending to be people with little education, who don't read the newspapers or watch or listen to the news. They are young, elderly, and they are disproportionately white.

4.   Juries don't understand the law/fact distinction anyway.

That may be true. All the more reason for them to read a book like this!

5.   In the two states which instruct about jury nullification, Indiana and Maryland, there has not been a substantial use of it.

First, we don't know the validity of the studies which have analyzed jury nullification.

Second, and more important, do we want to support a process that voids duly enacted laws which are subject to judicial scrutiny because there are only some instances where nullification is applied? This could lead to a few murderers on the streets because the jurors didn't like the laws or liked the defendants; a few innocent people thrown in jail because a jury doesn't like long-hairs or Jews or gang members.

Finally, should our jury system really depend on how popular the accused is or how unattractive the accuser? Do we really want our juries to reflect popular prejudice, rather than to be impartial judges? Is the media so accurate in their reports that we can rely on them to make us aware of the facts? If the criminal jury system isn't entirely successful, do we abandon the process or try to improve it?

We stand with those who founded our country, when they decided that our nation's justice should be based on laws, not men. If we were on trial, we would rather be judged by an impartial jury than by the conscience of our communities.

If a person who believes in jury nullification is on your jury, there may not be much you can do. A hung jury may result. Rationality can rarely overcome prejudice or stubbornness.

Too many of these people think they, and they alone, have the true answers. Facts, logic and reason are irrelevant to those who "know" they are "right."

* * * * * * *

Up to now, we've looked at the deliberations in terms of the problems they present. Sometimes, they go smoothly. The *O.J. Simpson* jury was finished in a matter of hours. Whether they "deliberated" is questionable, but certainly there was none of the backbiting or bickering that had manifested itself during the trial. In *People v. Powell*, deliberations lasted far longer. There appeared, at least to outsiders, to be some give-and-take, some discussion of a complex set of facts and some confusing law.

The point is that as a juror you have to stand the heat, because you can't get out of the kitchen. You enter the jury room with the hope that rational dialogue will occur, but you must be prepared for a battle that may shock you.

Chapter 26

And Your Decision Is?

The evidence is in. The last argument has been made. The instructions have been read. Now it's time to decide whether the four officers have been proven guilty, beyond a reasonable doubt, of the crime charged.

Let's review the facts and the law without sentiment, passion, or prejudice. Let's not be influenced by public opinion or public feeling, as Judge Weisberg said. Let's look at the evidence. Did the prosecution prove its case?

> In Count I, the officers were charged with assault with a deadly weapon, baton or shod feet.

> In Count II, they were charged with excessive force under color of authority.

It is undisputed that Rodney King had been drinking; that he was driving over 100 mph; that he didn't respond to the lights and sirens from the pursuing CHP car, nor to the loudspeaker admonitions to stop, nor to the request of one of the passengers to pull over. He drove along city streets at over sixty mph and ran several red lights. He stopped the car only when there was no place to go.

After the stop, as all the witnesses agreed, Mr. King did not get out of the car right away. When he did get out, he failed to follow CHP Officer Melanie Singer's commands. According to her, he danced, doing a pitter-patter. He waved at the helicopter. He grabbed his right buttock and shook it at her. But he didn't prone out. He kept his arms in a push-up position, and his legs bent with his toes in the air.

Ms. Singer approached him with her gun drawn. According to her, her action was consistent with her training. According to the defense experts, and to her husband, Officer Tim Singer, this was incorrect police procedure.

The testimony is that Sgt. Koon had been trained to avoid drawing a gun in such a situation. Therefore, when he saw a violation of correct police procedure, he believed it was reasonable for him to take over the situation.

Melanie Singer testified that approximately six officers approached Mr. King, trying to grab portions of his clothes. But Mr. King swung his arms wildly, hitting one officer. In her report, filed shortly after the incident, she reported Mr. King was swinging and kicking at the officers.

Sgt. Koon testified that he had initiated a swarm, in which a group of officers would force the suspect to the ground so he could be handcuffed. According to him and Officer Powell and Melanie Singer, Mr. King threw the officers off.

All the witnesses agree that Mr. King was not successfully handcuffed, despite the efforts of the officers.

Ms. Singer testified that Sgt. Koon told Mr. King to stop resisting or he would use a taser. When Mr. King didn't get on the ground as instructed, Sgt. Koon shot him with the taser. Mr. King screamed, grabbed his side, but didn't fall. The suspect continued flailing his arms and Sgt. Koon shot him again in the chest with the taser.

There is a dispute as to whether the taser worked. Ms. Singer said she didn't hear a clicking sound; Sgt. Koon says he did. One of the Emergency Room nurses testified that the taser hadn't worked, as the cartridges hadn't embedded themselves in Mr. King's skin. Ms. Singer testified they were embedded in Mr. King's skin.

The only witness who could testify as to whether Sgt. Koon believed the taser worked was Sgt. Koon. He testified that he believed it worked. The only person who could testify as to whether he received an electrical shock was Rodney King. Mr. King wasn't called as a witness.

Mr. King staggered "almost like a monster," according to Ms. Singer, after the second taser hit him. It appeared that his body weight was carrying him in a certain direction, toward her. He fell four or five feet away from her.

Mr. Singer testified that Rodney King staggered towards him.

Both Singers testified that Officer Powell struck Mr. King in the face five or six times, and acknowledged that their testimony, in other areas, was sometimes inconsistent with what was shown on the video. Mr. Singer attributed this to excitement, to tunnel vision. Ms. Singer said the initial baton blow was a power swing, hitting Mr. King across the top of the cheekbone, and splitting his face from the top of the ear to the chin. Ms. Singer indicated that photos taken after the incident showed no such injury. She also said that she had spoken with Rodney King approximately five minutes after this head shot, and he seemed perfectly coherent.

Mr. Singer described Rodney King's approach towards him as akin to a scene from a monster movie. And "after the monster gets shot, he just keeps coming." He testified that he was scared because neither the two taser shots nor the baton strikes to the head stopped Mr. King's advance.

Officer Powell denied striking Mr. King in the face.

During the prosecution's Case-in-Chief, there was no testimony from an expert that a baton could have caused the facial injuries. There was defense expert testimony that the fall could have caused those injuries. On rebuttal, the prosecution did introduce an expert who testified that the facial injuries could have been caused by a blunt instrument, such as a baton.

During the prosecution's Case-in-Chief, there was no expert testimony that Officer Powell's baton struck Mr. King in the face. The two defense experts, Sgt. Duke and Capt. Michael, testified that, based on their knowledge as applied to their review of the video, Mr. King was not struck in the face.

Both these defense experts also said that the use-of-force applied by the police officers was appropriate, given Mr. King's actions and reactions to the officers' instructions and beating.

Testimony showed that the experts had not always found officers' use-of-force appropriate, but that in this case they did.

Evidence was presented to show that other uses-of-force (verbal commands, swarm, taser, leg grabbers, nets, upper body control holds) would have been preferable, but that they were tried to no avail or were not available.

Rodney King was not called to testify why he was acting the way he did, whether he was trying to get up and attack the officers or to get away from the officers because of the beating, the tasers. Rodney King did not testify as to what the officers told him to do, what names (if any) they called him. And Rodney King did not say he was struck in the face.

Let's pause here to consider the evidence, using as tools the jury instructions and the definitions of legal terms, and apply the beyond a reasonable doubt standard.

What would a reasonable police officer have concluded about Rodney King's behavior? Has the defense proved that Rodney King was struck in the face with Officer Powell's baton? We can't show you the video, but we have watched it at normal speed, and as slow as frame by frame, and we can't say whether Mr. King was hit in the face based on our viewing.

The next part of the prosecution case is based primarily on the videotape. No LAPD police officer is called as a witness, even though many were present at the scene, and Rodney King isn't called to give firsthand testimony as to the incidents shown on the tape.

Commander Bostic was the witness for the prosecution who testified about the propriety of the beating. He was put on only after the defense experts, to rebut what they said. His credentials were that he was the use-of-force chairman of LAPD. He testified that Mr. King should have been gang-tackled and that there were a number of points when the beating could have been stopped. Mr. King should have been taken into custody at one of those points. Commander Bostic was attacked by Mr. Mounger for his lack of publication, lack of training experience, lack of teaching and licensing credentials. Next week, said Mr. Mounger, Commander Bostic could have a different job. According to Mr. Mounger, Commander Bostic incorrectly equated a suspect's safety with an officer's safety.

Mr. Barnett also questioned Commander Bostic's experience. He argued that Officer Briseno had more experience on the night of the arrest than Commander Bostic had in the past ten years. The lawyer viewed the expert testimony skeptically because Commander Bostic's only suggestion was that Officer Briseno should have done nothing, tied up with Mr. King, or thrown his 140-pound body over Mr. King.

Prosecutor White's argument was that the videotape tells all. Officer Powell is guilty because he hit Mr. King in the head and he continued to hit him after he was on the ground. Powell is a thug, who used phrases like "gorillas in the mist" and typed "I haven't beaten anyone this bad in a long time."; he taunted Mr. King at the hospital; he lied in his police reports. Jurors should infer from this that Officer Powell willfully, unreasonably and unlawfully beat Mr. King.

Officer Wind is guilty because he kicked and beat Mr. King as shown late in the video. Mr. King was doing nothing to justify the beating. Officer Wind patted his baton at the hospital, from which jurors could infer that Mr. King was hit in the face. He didn't say anything when Officer Powell taunted Mr. King, which jurors could infer is an adoptive admission that Officer Wind agreed with Officer Powell.

Officer Briseno is guilty because, when Mr. King was at his "most compliant". Officer Briseno delivered such a forceful stomp that it caused Mr. King's 250-pound body to go flying.

Sgt. Koon is guilty because he was in charge and didn't control his officers. He filed false reports. He is a liar.

There is one other arrow in the prosecutor's quiver. It involves the direct testimony of Officer Briseno (a witness not called by the prosecution, since he was one of the codefendants) that the beating was wrong and, specifically, that Officer Powell had to be restrained.

In their testimony, defendants Koon and Powell denied they had done anything wrong, given the situation which presented itself. There was Mr. King's superhuman strength, their belief he was on PCP, their inability to determine whether he had a concealed weapon. They used the tools that were available.

The defense experts, who viewed the video, said the officers had acted correctly in terms of LAPD practice and procedures. They de-escalated the force they applied when Mr. King seemed more compliant, and they stopped hitting and kicking him when he gave up.

In Counts I and II it seems clear that the prosecution has to introduce pieces of evidence to establish:

- the batons and boots were deadly weapons;

- they were used in such a way as to produce great bodily injury;

- the defendants were police officers;

- they acted under color of authority;

- Rodney King was beaten by the officers, except by Sgt. Koon.

In addition to the above, the crucial points to examine are whether an assault occurred and whether the police officers' actions were unlawful or without lawful necessity (see JI-129, 138-145); and whether, in relation to Officers Wind and Powell, there was a specific intent to inflict great bodily injury.

Ask yourself whether the prosecution proved, beyond a reasonable doubt, all, some or none, of the following. Remember, if you would like to infer, and the circumstantial evidence is subject to two interpretations, you are obligated to reject the one conclusion that points to a defendant's guilt and adopt that which points to innocence.

- Laurence Powell struck Rodney King in the face with the baton.

- The officers acted unreasonably at some point because: Rodney King was not trying to escape or was no longer resisting and a reasonable police officer would have so concluded.

- Officer Briseno's stomp was not for the purpose of protecting or defending Rodney King from attack. Sgt. Koon aided and abetted the unlawful beating.

- Officers Powell and Wind not only unlawfully inflicted great bodily injury but specifically intended to do so.

The task of the jurors was to render verdicts based on the evidence. Were their decisions unreasonable? If so, can you explain why? If not, can you support those decisions?

On the critical issues of a police officer's use of reasonable force and unlawful police conduct, let's return to some of the points mentioned in Chapter 24:

- Rodney King, when he jumped up, ran towards Officer Powell. Was this charge an attack on Officer Powell or an attempt by Mr. King to escape? Did Officer Powell have the right to defend himself at that point in time?

- The taser appeared to work, as Mr. King convulsed and grimaced, but he was not stopped. Would a reasonable officer have been frightened?

- Mr. King appeared to have superhuman strength, an indication of PCP. According to the Singers, Mr. King reminded them of a monster who, according to Mr. Singer, just keeps coming. Did the officers reasonably conclude that Mr. King was on PCP and therefore a threat to their safety?

- There is no distinct and identifiable point in the video where the parties agree that Rodney King submits. Is there evidence that he was ever in a prone position during the time of the beating?

- Much of the medical evidence does not substantiate the testimony that Mr. King was struck in the head by Officer Powell's baton or that, as Melanie Singer testifies, Mr. King's face was split from ear to chin. Even if you believe the video shows Mr.

King was struck in the face, can you make such a finding beyond a reasonable doubt, if the finding is inconsistent with the medical evidence?

- What impact does the defense experts' testimony have on the unlawfulness of the officers' conduct? Does that testimony raise a reasonable doubt as to the lawfulness of the officer's behavior?

- In view of Officer Briseno's attempt to stop Officer Powell from striking Mr. King, can you say beyond a reasonable doubt that his later stomp of Mr. King was unlawful and unnecessary?

- Can you conclude anything from Officer Wind's failure to testify?

If you believe that the video shows an unlawful attack, can you maintain your belief in view of the evidence actually presented in this case? Remember, there is no disagreement that what the video shows is abhorrent. The issue is not whether it is unpleasant to watch or whether we wish it had not happened, the issue is whether the assault upon Mr. King that night in March 1991 was unlawful after considering all of the evidence in the case.

Let's return to the juror's table metaphor. You have pieces of evidence left on the table which have been sorted into boxes which represent the essential elements that have to be established in order to find guilt. Examining the evidence *still on the table,* remaining in each box, are you very sure that the proven facts establish that the defendants, as officers, used deadly weapons while acting under color of authority?

Do you have a piece or pieces of evidence which you are very sure establish that the police officers' actions were unlawful and unnecessary? Are there "very sure" pieces of evidence which show that Officer Powell and Wind specifically intended to inflict great bodily injury?

And your decision is ...

PART VI

MAKING JUSTICE WORK

Chapter 27

OUR BLUEPRINT:
A MULTI-PRONGED APPROACH

We've covered a lot. First, we showed how trials in general work, or don't work. We tried to shed some light on the roles of the parties, with particular emphasis on your role as a juror. Then we showed you the evidence in a specific trial, the *People v. Powell* case.

At this point, we'd like to make our closing arguments for the changes we envision. Some of these changes would take very little to implement. Laws could simply be enforced, techniques in use could be improved, and money could be allocated. You, as jurors, could begin to decide cases using the recommendations we make. Judges could help by simplifying and more thoroughly explaining the process.

We hope that we've shown you where some of the faults lie in the current criminal-justice system. We hope that we've also shown you things that actually work in the criminal justice field and which have been inaccurately portrayed by the media.

Now we would like to recap both our suggestions for immediate change and to suggest some long-term solutions.

SUGGESTIONS FOR IMMEDIATE CHANGE

Jury Service

One positive thing that *People v. Simpson* accomplished was that it demonstrated the tremendous hardship of sitting on a sequestered jury. While most people will never be in a similar

situation, all of the problems related to jury service were presented in their most extreme fashion. These included wasted time,
loss of income, nasty lawyers, problems with other jurors, emotional stress and diminished contact with friends and family.

To correct some of the problems which involve jury service,
laws must be enforced which require jurors to serve and jurors
must be encouraged to serve. With "three-strikes", and with the
other changes which increase prosecutions and lengthen sentences, there needs to be a greater pool of jurors.[35] Furthermore, these jurors must reflect a cross section of the public. If
the rich or well-educated can obtain deferments and if the poor
or unemployed aren't part of the jury pool,[36] and if anyone can
ignore a jury summons with impunity,[37] only a small part of the
public will serve.

It's easy to be critical of bad jury verdicts when neither you
nor your pals are the ones making those ridiculous judgments.
However, when your spouse, your boss, your child, or your
doctor are sitting on juries, rendering those ludicrous verdicts,
it's harder to say that jurors are idiots. It's easy to attack jurors
as too old or too young, too black or too white, too male or too
female, when only a small fraction of citizens serve. It's much
harder to attack juries if all members of the community serve.

A carrot and stick approach is necessary. The carrot is
better pay (currently $5 per day for jurors in California and
similar pittances in many other states), shorter service times,
less waiting around at the courthouse, and shorter trials. The
stick is the imposition of fines or, in flagrant cases, incarceration for those who ignore the jury summons.

These changes will require new and expanded ways of drawing up jury lists, authorizing money for better pay for jurors and
stricter enforcement of laws which require jury service.

Judges can start immediately to make jury service less
onerous by protecting jurors during voir dire. The juror is not
on trial. So there must be a limit to the intrusiveness of the
questions, the length and nature of the questionnaires, the
numbers of questions permitted during oral examination. In the
past, the American jury system has survived without such
invasion of privacy. England currently survives without it. The

United States in the 1990s can provide fair trials without letting lawyers stick their noses into every aspect of a juror's life.

Freedom of Speech v. Fair and Speedy Trial

The media wants it all. They want all the information and they want to share the saleable, titillating information with the world. The lawyers also want it all. They want to give their spin to the public before the other side does. Lawyers are like politicians. They use every opportunity to make their point before a camera. The *O.J. Simpson* trial showed lawyers and the media at their worst.

Our plan is to restrict the media, without abridging the First Amendment guarantee of a free press.

Consider televised trials. Televising a trial can change the nature of the trial itself. It makes it more difficult to ensure a fair retrial. But, on balance, televising some trials is worthwhile, as long as there are strict limits imposed. The public has a right to know how the system is actually working. A trial can be a highly informative and important learning vehicle.

A televised trial should show the lawyers, the judge and those witnesses the judge believes can be shown on TV without jeopardizing their safety or without unnecessarily invading their privacy. Jurors, generally, should not be viewed.

At the first inkling of improper conduct on the part of the lawyers or if the media does not follow the specific rules laid down by the judge, the cameras should be removed from the courtroom and not allowed to return. No second chances.

For sensational trials, the judge should generally keep the cameras out of the courtroom. If the judge has any concern that cameras will jeopardize the fairness of the trial, the cameras should not be allowed. We can then see if the media wants to televise trials in order to inform the public how trials work, or merely wants to provide TV coverage of high-profile cases in order to ensure high ratings.

Media-circus trials cause problems because they mislead the public. Commentators make day-to-day or minute-to-minute analyses. These are often based on facts and information the jurors don't have. TV also misleads by implying that jurors are making up their minds as to the guilt or nonguilt of an individual every time a new witness testifies. Jurors are explicitly told not to do that and most jurors don't.

Under the First Amendment, let the commentators comment, the newspapers summarize or quote, the magazines do their "in-depth" analyses. That is part of American tradition. But the Republic survived 200 years without cameras in the courtroom and Americans were not denied freedom of the press then, and placing reasonable restrictions on cameras won't deny freedom of the press now. So while the camera may not improve the justice system, it can shed new light on the justice system by allowing viewers to see the actual tedious, slow-moving process as the trial unfolds. All this can take place, in most states, under procedures now in effect.

As for lawyers, the first step is to limit lawyers' statements *outside* the courtroom. The California Supreme Court has already taken that first step. As of October 1, 1995, lawyers (representing clients in both civil and criminal cases) are restricted as to what they may say about pending cases. It is a violation of ethics to discuss with the media anything that "will have a substantial likelihood of materially prejudicing" the outcome of the case. There is an exception when the information released "is necessary to mitigate adverse publicity generated by the other side."[38]

Remember that lawyers are "officers of the court". As such, they have a legal duty to abide by and uphold the law. They also are licensed by their Bar Associations. They certainly can vigorously defend their clients, but is it unreasonable for them to have limits imposed as to what they can say outside the courtroom when those comments are designed solely to circumvent the administration of justice by prejudicing a case?

Lawyers' freedom of speech can also be restricted during the trial. In the *O.J. Simpson* case, viewers saw Judge Ito impose monetary sanctions against some of the lawyers for inappropriate conduct in the court. The press reported how angry the Judge became, and the amounts of the sanctions. But the press and the media commentators did not point out that in California, it is only those sanctions of $1,000 or more which require automatic referral to the State Bar for investigation. Judge Ito did not sanction any lawyer during that trial for $1,000 or more. And if you're making thousands or millions, a $750 fine is hardly a deterrence. A slap on the wrist doesn't tell lawyers that the court is serious about speech in the courtroom which jeopardizes a fair trial.

We think that if lawyers engage in inappropriate behavior the judge should fine them a substantial amount of money, at least an amount sufficient to require a referral to the State Bar for an investigation.

Preparing Jurors

Our proposal is to require prospective jurors to sit through a videotape regarding their responsibilities as jurors when the jury pools have first been assembled.

Videotapes are currently shown in some jurisdictions, but the video we envision is different—simpler, yet more direct and challenging. It is neither a glorified presentation nor an innocuous civics lesson. It is hard-hitting, provocative and memorable so its message will be retained throughout the trial.

The videotape is designed to encourage ordinary people to take the first crucial steps towards becoming objective by examining their own impartiality or lack of it. The videotape will involve jurors immediately so they view themselves as judges of the facts rather than mere spectators. They are compelled to confront the idea that they must *not* substitute what they think happened (based on their emotions, beliefs or life experiences) but must only consider the evidence introduced at the trial. The authors are currently preparing such a video.

It is no reflection on jurors that they don't generally understand the judicial process. It is the rare judge who can clarify legalisms for ordinary people. To make the process easier to understand, our videotape will explain how a trial works and why jurors are needed.

The videotape will help jurors learn how to determine whether the evidence establishes that a defendant should be found guilty of committing a particular crime. They will see dramatizations, demonstrating ways to understand the charges and apply the evidence. They will learn how to make factual determinations as to whether the essential elements of the crime have been proved, so they can then make the ultimate decision as to the defendant's guilt.

The purpose of viewing the videotape is to make jurors appreciate just how important they are. Its goal is to clarify the way jurors are expected to function in a setting where they are not simply everyday Americans, but Americans who are impartial fact-finders. It will empower jurors by giving them the tools they need to fulfill their role in the system.

Limiting Argument by Attorneys

As all of us who watched the *O.J. Simpson* criminal trial saw and heard, lawyers are often prone to make statements without any evidentiary support in the case. While some judges properly restrict argument in Opening Statements, we think all judges should take a much more active role in limiting lawyers' arguments altogether in Opening Statements and during their introduction of evidence before the jury. Lawyers should use argument only in Closing Statements, and then only where there is some evidence which has been presented to support the argument. For example, if there's no evidence of a conspiracy, attorneys (as in the *O.J. Simpson* criminal case) should have been precluded from suggesting that a conspiracy existed even if opposing counsel doesn't object. Judges must step in, and instruct the lawyer to stop.

Limiting Hypothetical Questions by Experts

When a hypothetical question is given to an expert, the judge makes the threshold determination that the facts assumed for the hypothetical "are within the probable or possible range of the evidence." If the assumed evidence has not been introduced at the time the hypothetical question is asked, the judge should order the question and answer stricken. The judge should make this ruling even in the absence of an objection. The judge will have to do more work, but that's better than confusing the jurors with irrelevant hypotheticals that are erroneously considered by them.

In some states, this suggestion would require judges to take a more active role in the proceedings.

Focusing Jurors on the Charges

As we have emphasized throughout, it is essential to know how to focus on what is important and what is not, in order to be a good fact-finder. Jurors have not gone to school to become fact-finders, so we believe the system has the obligation to assist jurors in *immediately* identifying the critical facts, the individual elements of the crime that must be proved.

At the beginning of the trial, jurors must ask:

"What are the facts I need to decide in order to do my job?"

Although we have already set out the charges in the Rodney King beating trial that were read to the jury at the very beginning of the trial, they are again set out on the next pages so that you can contrast them with our recommendations.

We want simple, straightforward and comprehensible charges, instead of ones that contain legal mumbo jumbo. As we see it, the instructions in the Rodney King beating trial could have been reduced to what is set out on the following pages. Opposite the actual charges in the Rodney King beating trial is our rewriting of the charges in plain English:

JURORS ARE PRESENTLY TOLD THIS

COUNT I.

"The said Laurence M. Powell, Timothy B. Wind, Theodore J. Briseno and Stacey C. Koon are accused by the Grand Jury of the County of Los Angeles, State of California, by this indictment, of the crime of assault by force likely to produce great bodily injury and with a deadly weapon, in violation of Penal Code § 245 (A)(1), a felony committed prior to the finding of this indictment, and as follows:

"On or about March 3rd, 1991, in the County of Los Angeles, State of California, the said defendants, Laurence M. Powell, Timothy E. Wind, Theodore J. Briseno and Stacey C. Koon, did willfully and unlawfully commit an assault upon Rodney Glenn King with a deadly weapon, to wit, a baton and shod feet, and by means of force likely to produce great bodily injury.

"It is further alleged that in the commission of the above offense the said defendants, Laurence M. Powell and Timothy E. Wind, with the intent to inflict such injury, personally inflicted great bodily injury upon Rodney Glenn King, not an accomplice to the above offense, within the meaning of Penal Code § 12022.7 and also causing the above offense to be a serious felony within the meaning of Penal Code § 1192.7(C)(8).

"It is also further alleged that in the commission of the above offense the said defendants, Laurence M. Powell, and Timothy E. Wind, did willfully inflict great bodily injury or torture in the perpetration of the crime, within the meaning of Penal Code § 1203(E)(3).

WE PROPOSE JURORS BE TOLD THIS

COUNT I.

The defendants are Los Angeles Police Officers Laurence Powell, Timothy Wind, Theodore Briseno and Sgt. Stacey Koon.

The grand jury has determined that the defendants should be charged with the following crimes:

They are accused of the crime of assault by force likely to produce great injury to the body of Rodney Glenn King.

Specifically, on March 3rd, 1991, all four defendants willfully and unlawfully assaulted Mr. King with a deadly weapon. The deadly weapons were batons and the officers' boots. The assault was likely to produce great bodily injury.

In committing this charged crime, defendants Powell and Wind intended to, did inflict, and willfully inflicted great bodily injury on Mr. King.

JURORS ARE PRESENTLY TOLD THIS

COUNT II.

"For a further and separate cause of action, being a different offense of the same class of crimes and offenses as the charges set forth in aforestated count hereof, the said Laurence M. Powell, Timothy E. Wind, Theodore J. Briseno and Stacey C. Koon, are accused by the Grand Jury of the County of Los Angeles, State of California, by this indictment, of the crime of officer unnecessary assaulting or beating any person, a violation of Penal Code Section 149, a felony, committed prior to the finding of this indictment and as follows:

"On or about March 3rd, 1991, in the County of Los Angeles, State of California, the said defendants, Laurence M. Powell, Timothy E. Wind, Theodore J. Briseno and Stacey C. Koon, did willfully, unlawfully under color of authority, and without lawful necessity, assault and beat a human being, to wit, Rodney Glenn King, the said defendants being then and there public officers, to wit, Los Angeles Police Officers.

"It is further alleged that in the commission of the above offense the said defendants, Laurence M. Powell and Timothy E. Wind, with the intent to inflict such injury, personally inflicted great bodily injury upon Rodney Glenn King, not an accomplice to the above offense, within the meaning of Penal Code Section 12022.7 and also causing the above offense to be a serious felony within the meaning of Penal Code Section 1192.7 (C)(8)

"It is also further alleged that in the commission of the above offense the said defendants, Laurence M. Powell and Timothy E. Wind did willfully inflict great bodily injury or torture in the perpetration of the crime, within the meaning of Penal Code Section 1203(E)(3)."

WE PROPOSE JURORS BE TOLD THIS

COUNT II.

Additionally, all four defendants are accused of unnecessarily assaulting or beating Mr. King, while acting as police officers.

Specifically, on March 3rd, 1991, all four defendants willfully, unlawfully under color of authority, and without lawful necessity, assaulted and beat Rodney Glenn King.

In committing this crime, defendants Powell and Wind intended to, did inflict, and willfully inflicted great bodily injury upon Mr. King.

As such changes become accepted, we would like to break them down even further into their component parts. For example, Count I could be further restructured as follows:

COUNT I

<u>The defendants are</u>:

> Los Angeles Police Officers
> Laurence Powell,
> Timothy Wind,
> Theodore Briseno, and
> Sgt. Stacey Koon.

<u>They are charged with</u>:

> Willfully
> (that is, deliberately
> or intentionally)
>
> and Unlawfully
>
> Assaulting (hitting)
>
> Rodney King
>
> With a deadly weapon
> (that is, batons and the
> boots of the defendants).
>
> This assault was likely
> to produce great injury
> to the body of Mr. King.

**<u>Powell and Wind additionally
are charged with</u>:**

> Willfully inflicting great injury
> to the body of Mr. King.

Jurors, like cameras, must be in focus in order to get a clear picture. We believe that reducing the number of words and phrases and eliminating reference to Penal Code Sections make it easier for jurors to understand the crucial elements of the charges. Phrases with obscure meanings such as, "serious felony", "aforestated count hereof", and "prior to the finding of this indictment" are unnecessarily confusing. And jurors don't have to know specific Penal Code Sections to decide the case.

When you compare what the jurors in *People v. Powell* heard with what we propose they should have heard, it seems obvious that the jury would have been more focused if it had heard the charges worded the way we suggest.

To maximize understanding, we propose that jurors be told, *at the same time the charges are read to them,* the definitions of any words in the charges which have special legal meanings. In terms of the Counts I and II that were read to the jury, some of the words defined for the jury would be: "willfully", "likely to produce great bodily injury", and "unlawfully under color of authority".

In some jurisdictions, our recommendations will require statutory or judicial amendments so that substitutions can be made for the actual statutory language and reference to the Code sections can be eliminated. The time for change is now.

SOME LONG-TERM SOLUTIONS

There are also important structural changes to make which will undoubtedly take longer to implement because these changes are more radical, or more controversial, or because a number of laws or policies will have to be changed, or because some people have a vested interest in retaining the status quo.

An End to Peremptory Challenges and Jury Consultants

It is our opinion that peremptory challenges should be *totally* eliminated. Jurors shouldn't be excluded simply because they are educated, or uneducated, or members of a particular group, or of a particular age. If compromise is necessary, the number of challenges should be radically reduced to no more than five on a trial where the potential penalty is life imprisonment or death, to no more than three for other felony charges, and to one in a misdemeanor case.

Most Americans want justice to be meted out on a level playing field. Most Americans believe persons charged with crimes should have their guilt or nonguilt determined by a jury of their peers.

Peremptory challenges are an attempt to slant the playing field and to ensure that jurors do not represent the community but only that part of the community which is predisposed to convict, or to acquit, depending on which side uses the peremptory challenge. Once challenges are limited to those which are for cause, the composition of the jury will far better reflect the make-up of the community.

Lawyers won't like this change, because many think they can spot hostile or favorable jurors. Perhaps the most significant impact will be on jury consultants. They won't be needed or at the very least their significance will be drastically reduced. Their job is to obtain a favorable jury through the astute use of peremptories. To accomplish that goal, they may conduct demographic studies, check out the jurors' zip codes, evaluate the particular neighborhood in which a juror lives, review jurors' credit references, education, and associates. They then use this data to "scientifically" and systematically remove selected jurors through the use of peremptories.

We want to eliminate these consultants because:

1.   They undermine our confidence in the criminal-jury system by making the jury selection process appear unfair, and in some cases be unfair.

2.   They intrude into the lives of people who are simply fulfilling their civic duty.

3.   They institutionalize a system of unequal justice making it far more difficult for the People to prosecute wealthy defendants successfully.

4.   They make it far more likely that the side with money, either the prosecution or the defense, rather than the side with justice, will prevail.

Elimination of Unanimous Verdicts

As part of our proposal to eliminate peremptory challenges, we favor changing the requirement for a unanimous jury verdict in all but death penalty cases where we would retain it because of the finality of the consequences of a conviction. Currently, unanimous verdicts are required in all states other than Louisiana and Oregon. Some states are considering verdicts based on ten of twelve jurors.

We've told you why we think peremptories are bad, but at least they screened out some people who were biased but whose biases couldn't be established. Under our system, these people would now be allowed to serve.

We've studied the pros and cons of nonunanimous juries. In our view a conviction or acquittal can occur when eleven members of the panel agree.

We don't like the 10-2 verdict, because that means you've convinced fewer than ninety percent of the jurors. With an 11-1 requirement, one side will have to convince over ninety percent of the jurors of the correctness of its position. So if, as a number of TV commentators have suggested, the beyond a reasonable doubt standard means at least ninety percent certainty, a conviction would be based on more than ninety percent of the jurors having satisfied themselves that they were certain that guilt had been proved beyond a reasonable doubt.

We do not abandon unanimity lightly. We believe that in large part it has worked well and that, in some cases, it has prevented miscarriages of justice. But we believe that with peremptories eliminated, there is too great a chance that prejudice on the part of one individual will prevent a conviction or an acquittal.

Jury Instructions and Structuring the Case

Jury instructions are helpful and important. However, they have been accorded little significance because of when they are given to the jury, how they are given, and how clarification of them is handled (or not handled).

If the consequences were not so serious, the way courts currently deal with jury instructions would be a subject of amusement. Imagine taking a course in school about life in the 20th century. You have no idea, until the end of the semester, what aspect of language, art, military history, politics you are supposed to understand. Pretty silly, isn't it? No rules, no agenda, no structure until the course is over. Then you are told that the final exam questions all involve Prohibition and its repeal. You must review your notes on the actual subject because you've taken lots of irrelevant notes on Picasso, the Second World War, and the breakup of the USSR.

Giving jury instructions at the close of the trial is akin to what we've just discussed, because you're given an enormous amount of information and don't know how to evaluate the evidence while it's being presented, or which material is relevant to the questions you must answer.

But jury instructions, properly and promptly given, can make the law understandable and have tremendous potential for empowering jurors and for streamlining our current system.

Jury instructions are frequently submitted to the court prior to the start of the trial. It's clear, then, that the lawyers know the direction they are planning to go, the strategy of the case, and what instructions they want the court to use. We would require the lawyers to identify, prior to the start of every trial, the jury instructions they want to see given in the case. As part of the suggestions for immediate change, we advocate general instructions applicable to every case be given to jurors even before the trial begins. These would be given in the videotape discussed earlier and would include such topics as the burden of proof instruction and the evaluation of evidence.

The lawyers would be asked to map out the order of presentation in the case, the areas to be examined, identifying what evidence, and what witnesses they will present and in what sequence. The lawyers would give this information to the judge. Since the defense presents its case after the prosecution, and may modify its manner of presentation based on the People's case, the judge would give the jury a chart in outline form, indicating the direction the prosecution will take. This chart would be presented to the jury by the judge prior to Opening Statements, after its review by the defense.

There is a problem when witnesses cannot appear in the expected order. When that occurs, the chart would be revised.

Specific jury instructions would be given and read to jurors immediately before the particular testimony or evidence is introduced, but the instructions would not be constantly repeated. For example, if several experts will testify, jurors would receive written and oral instructions before the first expert takes the witness stand to testify.

The instructions would relate to the testimony or other evidence which was actually presented. Thus, jurors would have immediate access to the rules which govern their evaluation of the evidence in the particular situation. It is far more effective to tell the jurors how to make these judgments when they have just listened to the witnesses, rather than to inform them at the end of the trial, long after the witnesses have testified.

The burden on the attorneys and on the judge may increase, while the jurors' job will be simplified. That's as it should be, since the judge and lawyers are paid well and take the job voluntarily, while poorly paid jurors serve involuntarily.

Our approach gives information to the juror in an improved and timely manner. The juror will be able to listen to a few instructions each day, and comprehend these instructions far more easily than listening to seemingly endless minutes of spoken words at the end of the trial.

We propose that jury instructions be given in the format we have used in this book. In addition, we propose that they be grouped together by subject. Thus, jurors would not only hear and read the instruction but simultaneously know how it fits into the case.

Some critics may argue that jurors will err by becoming prematurely attached to positions. We don't agree. We think jurors will be willing and able to discard some evidence when more persuasive evidence is introduced. And jurors who will form opinions prematurely under our system do so now under the current procedures. Under our proposal, they will at least form those opinions from a position of knowledge, rather than ignorance.

At the end of the trial, the judge would review the instructions, but the jurors would already have been exposed to them.

During the implementation phase of the process we've described, there may be some difficulties and some judge time will have to be spent resolving problems that might arise. Again, change takes time. But eventually we expect that all the changes we are proposing will become *routine*.

Providing contemporaneous explanations will have a dramatic effect on improving a juror's interest and knowledge of the case *as it progresses*. The jurors, the lawyers and the judge in the case will all be more focused. We are replacing juror bewilderment with knowledge and understanding.

Focusing Jurors on the Disputed Facts

In order to simplify the jurors' task, and to make that task less onerous by shortening trials and maximizing judicial efficiencies, we propose that in appropriate instances, attorneys must agree that certain facts are not in dispute. These stipulations would be made before the trial starts. The judge would summarize these stipulations and give each juror a copy of them.

In the *Powell* case, a great deal of time was spent laying the foundation so that relevant evidence could be submitted. The jury was only permitted to hear the messages by the police on the different communication systems after witnesses had testified as to how the system worked, and that it was working on March 2 and 3, 1991. The jury didn't need to hear about the workings of the system from A to Z when the defense only disputed one or two aspects of its operation and did not dispute its accuracy. So it could have been a stipulated fact, rather than a tedious, multi-hour presentation.

Lawyers who fail or refuse to enter into stipulations, when the facts are not in dispute, must be warned. If the problem continues, they must be sanctioned.

Once judges and lawyers became comfortable with this stipulation process, the jury's focus could be further narrowed. They would be able to concentrate on the disputed facts which are germane to the verdict.

For instance, in the *Powell* case, we have presented our version of Count I. Ideally, jurors would be told that it had been stipulated that Defendants Powell and Wind struck Mr. King with their batons and that the batons entered as exhibits were the actual batons used or highly similar to those used.

It would be stipulated that Defendant Briseno used his left shoe to force Rodney King to the ground.

It would be stipulated that Defendant Koon was the officer in charge and that he twice fired a taser at Rodney King.

The jury would be told it had to decide the following in relation to all four defendants:

- Was the assault willful?

- Was the assault unlawful?

- Was it likely to produce great bodily injury?

The jury would be told it had to decide the following in relation to defendants Powell and Wind:

- Did they intend to inflict great bodily injury on Mr. King?

- Did they do so?

- Did they willfully do so?

Once the jurors know what questions they have to answer, they can put the items of evidence into the appropriate boxes on the Juror's Table, which we described in Chapter 19. If an item of evidence can't be put into any of the boxes because it doesn't relate to a question the jury has to answer or the juror doesn't understand its meaning, jurors don't have to consider that item of evidence and it can be tossed off the table and not be considered any further. The item is irrelevant to the charges.

Trials will be shorter, so it will be easier for jurors to remember what they saw and heard. And they will be concentrating on the crucial facts, rather than on every fact.

In summary, these are our proposals:

- Expand jury lists to include a more representative body of jurors in the community.

- Eliminate or drastically reduce the use of peremptory challenges.

- If peremptory challenges are significantly reduced, *then* make a final verdict dependent on a 11-1 vote in non-capital cases.

- Eliminate jury consultants in criminal trials.

- Make jury service less costly to jurors, less time-consuming and less easy to avoid.

- Allow television of trials, but only on a very limited basis, with strict controls imposed by judges if their orders are accidentally or intentionally violated.

- Limit out-of-court statements by prosecutors and defense attorneys.

- Show a videotape that tells jurors, up-front, what trials are about and how they can become impartial jurors.

- Require general instructions to be given at the beginning of the case, and specific instructions, as needed, throughout the trial.

- Simplify jury instructions.

- Make the charges simple and understandable, at the beginning of the trial and again at the end.

- Maximize the use of stipulations to achieve more focused juries and help shorten trials.

- Limit hypothetical questions.

- Limit lawyers' argument.

- Require judges to take a more active role throughout the trial.

We recognize that lawyers and judges will have to learn new approaches, change old habits and perhaps refine the way they have done business for many years. However, instead of viewing these changes with trepidation, we hope they will be considered a new opportunity for revitalization. After all, no one is satisfied with our current system—so why not fix it by applying "rules" of consistency, logic and common sense.

But none of these changes will make a difference unless impartial jurors are sitting in the jury box and impartial judges are sitting on the benches.

Chapter 28

Our Final Word

Wₑ don't know how soon, or whether, our recommendations to improve the criminal-justice system will be accepted. But you, as a juror, can begin to change the system today. The key is to strive at all times to be impartial. You will need to know who you are, what unsuspected biases you have. And you'll need to understand the way others will try to manipulate you.

Here are a few pointers on how to avoid being manipulated:

Don't Trust the Media

Newspapers, magazines, radio, TV—none of these are interested in justice, how the system works, if it works, or why it works. They are interested in ratings and selling their products. There is nothing wrong in watching Court TV, or listening to "expert" commentators, or reading "analyses" of the jurors, lawyers or judges. But truth is often revealed slowly, painstakingly, and in a boring way. And the media can't afford that kind of truth. It doesn't sell.

Don't Trust the Lawyers.

Simply, lawyers are under no obligation to tell the truth. They may obfuscate or prevaricate because of what they believe to be ethical reasons (to get their clients off or to convict someone they truly believe is guilty). They may distort the truth or mischaracterize the evidence because that helps make them famous or controversial, or because they like winning, or because it will help them make more money, or because they will get on talk shows. Keep in mind, they are not all seekers of the truth.

Don't Trust the Witnesses.

Witnesses have myriads of reasons to lie. They may mislead out of self-interest, out of hatred, to protect a family member or friend or member of their group (police officer, gang member, man, woman, Christian, Muslim, Caucasian, African-American). They may lie because they are liars. Or they may testify inaccurately simply because they don't really know what they saw or heard or did.

Don't Rely On the Judge To Help You.

Some judges like power. So some judges will try to keep you in the dark, because that makes them more powerful. Some judges simply cannot talk to ordinary people. You won't understand what they mean, and they can't or won't explain it to you. Some judges will let great quantities of irrelevant information in, either because they don't know better, or because they're afraid of making decisions or of being reversed on appeal. Sidebar conferences will be endless, and hours or days will go by when no evidence comes in.

Don't Trust the Other Jurors.

They may have an axe to grind. They may have some personal experiences which makes them eager to acquit or convict. They may just like the lawyer or the defendant or cops. Or they may want to get the trial over. Listen to them and be willing to adjust your opinion if they make sense. But they have been subject to the same attempts to mislead, misinform, and mischaracterize that you have.

And Don't Trust Yourself.

Most of us believe we're fair. But all of us have prejudices, whether or not we're aware of them. We may be more inclined to believe a good-looking person than one who is unattractive. We may have had bad experiences with Caucasians and Hispanics, and good ones with African-Americans, which may color the way we view the representatives of these groups when they testify. We may believe men are cold and calculating, women intuitive and emotional.

It really doesn't matter what we believe, as long as these beliefs don't affect our ability to judge impartially when we're sitting on a jury. So each time we're ready to believe or disbelieve a witness, to make a factual finding, let's step back and ask ourselves:

Was our determination based on objective evidence?

Did one side or the other really "Prove it!"?

CONCLUSION

We ask you to take an extremely skeptical approach when we suggest that you trust no one. There are some great and good judges, lawyers, witnesses, reporters, jurors. But each must earn your trust and respect.

If you adopt this approach, you're well on the road to becoming an impartial juror. Strive to do what is right, even though the task is a lonely one, and the rewards few. The American justice system will be better because of your efforts. You will be able to say: "I did my job. I was as good and fair a juror as I could be. I made a difference."

IMPARTIALITY PRETEST:
YOUR CHANCE TO TEST YOUR IMPARTIALITY

Pretend you are an observer in the courtroom. Based on the information provided immediately above, would you agree or disagree with the underlined statement?

The defense counsel is arrogant and theatrical and is obviously trying to get you to concentrate on his act, rather than on the facts. You personally can't stand that type of person.

   1.   <u>The defense has a weak case.</u>

The defendant is an extremely attractive woman, conservatively dressed, and without make-up.

   2.   <u>One who looks like that couldn't have abused her children.</u>

The victim, a retarded young woman, is ugly. The handsome college president who allegedly sexually abused her, is good looking and successful. She's neither. He could do far better with women without harassing this particular person.

   3.   <u>The charges are probably false.</u>

The defendant appears contemptuous of the whole trial process. He doesn't listen to the witnesses, to the judge, even to his own lawyer.

   4.   <u>The defendant is probably guilty.</u>

The defendant screams out "You liar" at a witness who just testified that the defendant fired the deadly shot. She's just trying to convince you of her innocence. Her lawyer probably told her to act that way.

5.   <u>She is probably guilty.</u>

The defendant screams out "You liar" at a witness who just testified that the defendant fired the deadly shot. That must be a spontaneous reaction since he couldn't have known what the witness would say.

6.   <u>He's probably innocent.</u>

The defendant appears calm and answers every question in a straightforward manner without blinking. She makes direct eye contact with the attorney asking the questions. She appears very truthful although there is other evidence which contradict the claimant's testimony.

7.   <u>Based on her demeanor, she is telling the truth.</u>

The defendant bursts into tears as the gruesome murder is described in court. He is obviously remorseful for the terrible crime he committed.

8.   <u>The defendant is guilty.</u>

The defendant shows no emotion whatsoever as the grisly details of the slashing murders are presented.

9.   <u>Only a cold blooded killer could remain unmoved. He's guilty.</u>

10.   <u>The defendant's demeanor doesn't indicate he's guilty or not guilty.</u>

Neither the judge nor defense counsel say anything when the district attorney boldly proclaims to the jury "Why else would he have been arrested if he weren't guilty.".

11.   <u>The lack of any reaction means the defendant is not guilty, because the prosecutor is improperly trying to influence the jury with his argument.</u>

12.   <u>But the evidence could still prove the defendant's guilt.</u>

Your community is comprised of law-abiding and church-going residents who always are nicely dressed and polite to one another. The defendant is a long-haired young man whose clothes stink, is foul-mouthed, and an atheist.

13. <u>The defendant may or may not be guilty.</u>

14. <u>But his testimony should be discredited because he doesn't respect society or believe in the Bible.</u>

The defendant is a policeman accused of using excessive force. He works in the worst part of town. The residents of that neighborhood are always screaming "police brutality".

15. <u>The policeman is entitled to a presumption of innocence.</u>

16. <u>"Where there's smoke, there's fire", so the cop is probably guilty.</u>

Two years ago when you were a college student, you were beaten by the police after a routine traffic stop. You hate the police and do not trust them. The defendant is a policewoman accused of committing a similar crime against another college student.

17. <u>The policewoman is probably guilty.</u>

18. <u>But since she's a woman, it will be much harder for the prosecution to prove its case because it's highly unlikely a woman would engage in such conduct</u>

End of Quiz

APPLYING THE
"JUROR'S TABLE"
TO A MURDER CASE

Let's consider a case where the charge is first-degree murder. The prosecution must prove that Accused (A) is guilty of first-degree murder because he killed Victim (V). To prove this, the prosecution must prove the following three facts, if it is to prevail in court:

V is dead;

A killed V;

and

A premeditated the killing.

These are the boxes that are on the Juror's Table, and the boxes which need to be filled in order to establish guilt.

In most murder cases, it's easy to establish that the victim is dead. There is direct evidence: the body is there. In some cases, though, only the remains of certain parts of the body are found or the alleged victim's body cannot be found. Then the prosecution will have to use circumstantial evidence to establish the identity of the victim.

If the prosecution presents no facts to prove that V is dead, A should be acquitted. If some facts are presented, but the jurors are not very sure of those facts, an acquittal should result.

In our scenario, the prosecution has found only certain body parts—the skull, an arm and leg. Forensic evidence is introduced in order to establish from the dental records that the head is that of V, and that the DNA shows the arm and leg are consistent with V, or with a person of V's heritage. You put these pieces of evidence in one of the boxes on the Juror's Table.

The experts testify that there is a one percent chance that the dental records are inaccurate, and a one percent chance the DNA records are inaccurate. But notice how the statistics show different things: the dental records are specifically tied to the victim, while the DNA evidence only shows that the DNA is consistent with V's DNA.

The defense convincingly proves to you that the DNA evidence was handled sloppily, and that the expert is a racist. You throw out the DNA evidence by removing it from the box, and tossing it off the Juror's Table. It's gone. You believe the dental evidence.

Is there reasonable doubt as to whether the victim is dead?

Your answer should be NO. V is dead.

Initially two facts could theoretically, singly or together, establish V's death. You've discarded the DNA fact, and are left with the dental evidence, which is enough, because it is ninety-nine percent certain that the head belonged to V.

So, since there is reasonable doubt as to the DNA evidence, you have thrown it out. But what remains is still sufficient. Is there still some doubt? Sure, one in 100. If you were to refuse to find a fact based on a ninety-nine out of 100 possibility, very few criminals would ever be convicted.

Now let's suppose the opposite occurred, and it is the dental records which have been sloppily handled by the racist expert. You take that evidence out of the box, and toss it off the table. Your task is now more difficult. You will have to evaluate the entire body of evidence. How did the expert link the DNA to V? Is there other circumstantial evidence available? Are there reports of V's abandoned car being found near the place where the body parts were discovered? Can the death be shown to have occurred at approximately the same time V was reported missing, or no longer seen by friends or family?

You may need this other circumstantial evidence to satisfy yourself that the remains are specifically V's, not just the remains of a person similar to V. If the evidence is insufficient, an acquittal should result because one of the three crucial facts has not been established. There is no convincing evidence left in the box.

Let's change the facts, but not the charge. To establish that A killed V the prosecution calls six witnesses. Four witnesses testify that they saw A kill V. Two witnesses testify that A admitted killing V.

You believe two of the eyewitnesses, and the two witnesses who testify as to the confession.

You disbelieve the other two eyewitnesses. One is a notorious liar, the other has made racist comments in the past. Both are police officers. As to those two eyewitnesses to the crime, there is certainly reasonable doubt in your mind whether it was A who killed V. So you totally discount their testimony, disregarding it as if it had never been offered as proof. You discard those pieces of evidence. They are no longer on the Table.

Again, this does not mean that there is reasonable doubt as to the essential fact that A killed V. You've thrown out the trash—the liar's and the racist's testimony. If the evidence that is left is sufficient to convict, it doesn't matter that the witnesses who are disbelieved are lying, racist cops. You are not considering their testimony because you consider their testimony not trustworthy.

Is there still some doubt that A killed V? Sure, eyewitnesses can be wrong. Confessions are sometimes made when the person making the confession didn't commit the crime. But doubt is not the same as reasonable doubt.

The facts that V was killed, and A killed V, are established by direct evidence (the eyewitnesses). If you believe the eyewitnesses, nothing more is needed to establish the fact that A killed V.

The confession is circumstantial evidence because the witnesses are not reporting what they saw but what they were told. If you believe the witnesses were reporting accurately and that A was telling the truth, then the facts of the killing and that A committed the killing, are established. Because there are still unproven facts, you must continue your analysis.

The last element necessary to establish first-degree murder is the premeditation aspect. That must be established by circumstantial evidence. Again, premeditation must be established beyond a reasonable doubt. There must be facts presented such as A lying in wait to shoot V, or A reloading a gun and returning to kill V, before a valid and convincing inference can be drawn. If this element cannot be established, A must be found not guilty of first-degree murder. A could still be found guilty of second-degree murder or manslaughter, because in those charges premeditation need not be established.

In the above scenario, we hypothesized that there were actual and reliable percentages as to DNA and dental evidence.

In the real world of the courtroom, percentages are presented and challenged, and you have to determine which percentage is correct. Is the DNA analysis really ninety-nine percent reliable as the prosecution expert asserts or ninety-two percent reliable as the defense says? Jurors have to make that decision based on the expert's presentation. They will also have to determine whether to believe or disbelieve witnesses. That is why a decision is often so difficult even for those who understand what reasonable doubt means.

ADDITIONAL COUNTS
PEOPLE V. POWELL ET AL

COUNT III

"For a further and separate cause of action, being a different offense of the same class of crimes and offenses as the charges set forth in aforestated counts hereof, the said Laurence M. Powell is accused by the Grand Jury of the County of Los Angeles, State of California, by this indictment, of the crime of submission of false police report by peace officer, in violation of Penal Code § 118.1, a felony, committed prior to the finding of this indictment and as follows:

"On or about March 3rd, 1991, in the County of Los Angeles, State of California, the said defendant, Laurence M. Powell, did willfully and unlawfully, while employed as a peace officer for the Los Angeles Police Department, file a report with the agency which employs him regarding the commission of a crime, and an investigation of a crime, and knowingly and intentionally made statements in the report which he knew to be false, whether or not such statements were certified or otherwise expressly reported as true.

COUNT IV

"For a further and separate cause of action, being a different offense of the same class of crimes and offenses as the charges set forth in aforestated counts hereof, the said Stacey C. Koon, is accused by the Grand Jury of the County of Los Angeles, State of California, by this indictment, of the crime of submission of false police report by peace officer, in violation of Penal Code § 118.1, a felony, committed prior to the finding of this indictment and as follows:

"On or about March 3rd, 1991, in the County of Los Angeles, State of California, the said defendant, Stacey C. Koon, did willfully and unlawfully, while employed as a peace officer for the Los Angeles Police Department, file a report with the agency which employs him regarding the commission of a crime, and an investigation of a crime, and knowingly and intentionally made statements in the report which he knew to be false, whether or not such statements were certified or otherwise expressly reported as true.

COUNT V

"For a further and separate cause of action, being a different offense of the same class of crimes and offenses as the charges set forth in aforestated counts hereof, the said Stacey C. Koon, is accused by the Grand Jury of the County of Los Angeles, State of California, by this indictment, of the crime of accessory after the fact, in violation of Penal Code § 32, a felony, committed prior to the finding of this indictment and as follows:

"On or about March 3rd, 1991, in the County of Los Angeles, State of California, the said defendant, Stacey C. Koon, did willfully and unlawfully, having knowledge that the crimes of assault with a deadly weapon and assault under color of authority, felonies in violations of § 245(A)(1) and 149 of the Penal Code of the State of California, had been committed by Laurence M. Powell, who did harbor, conceal and aid said Laurence M. Powell with the intent that he might avoid and escape from arrest, trial conviction and punishment for said felony."[39]

Jury Instructions:
People v. Powell et al

Ladies and gentlemen of the jury, you have heard all the evidence and the arguments of the attorneys and now it is my duty to instruct you on the law that applies to this case.

The law requires that I read the instructions to you and you will have these instructions in their written form in the jury room to refer to during deliberations.*

JI-1   **You must base your decision on the facts and the law.**

JI-2   **You have two duties to perform.**

JI-3   **First, you must determine the facts from the evidence received in the trial and not from any other source.**

JI-4   **A fact is something proved directly or circumstantially by the evidence or by stipulation.**

JI-5   **A stipulation is agreement between the attorneys regarding the facts.**

JI-6   **Second, you must apply the law as I state it to you to the facts as you determine them and in this way arrive at your verdict and any finding you are instructed to include in your verdict.**

JI-7   **You must accept and follow the law as I state it to you, whether or not you agree with the law.**

* Jury instructions in bold are cited in the text.

JI-8   If anything concerning the law said by the attorneys in their arguments or at any other time during the trial conflicts with my instructions on the law, you must follow my instructions.

JI-9   You must not be influenced by pity for a defendant or by prejudice against him.

JI-10   You must not be biased against the defendant because he has been arrested for this offense, charged with a crime or brought to trial. None of these circumstances is evidence of guilt and you must not infer or assume from any or all of them that he is more likely to be guilty than innocent.

JI-11   You must not be influenced by mere sentiment,

JI-12   conjecture,

JI-13   sympathy,

JI-14   passion,

JI-15   prejudice,

JI-16   public opinion

JI-17   or public feeling.

JI-18   Both the people and the defendant have a right to expect that you will conscientiously consider and weigh the evidence, apply the law and reach a just verdict regardless of the consequences.

JI-19   If any rule, direction or idea is repeated or stated in different ways in these instructions, no emphasis is intended and you must not draw any inference because of its repetition.

JI-20   Do not single out any particular sentence or any individual point or instruction and ignore the others.

JI-21   Consider the instructions as a whole and each in light of all the others.

JI-22   The order in which the instructions are given has no significance as to their relative importance.

JI-23   Statements made by the attorneys during the trial are not evidence, although if the attorneys have stipulated or agreed to a fact, you must regard that fact as a conclusively proved as to the party or parties making the stipulation or entering into the stipulation.

JI-24   If an objection was sustained to a question, do not guess what the answer might have been.

JI-25   Do not speculate as to the reason for the objection.

JI-26   Do not assume to be true any insinuation suggested by a question asked a witness. A question is not evidence and may be considered only as it enable you to understand the answer.

JI-27   Do not consider for any purpose any offer of evidence that was rejected or any evidence that was stricken by the court. Treat it as though you had never heard of it.

As I indicated to you yesterday and at the beginning of the argument phase of the trial,

JI-28   the arguments of the attorneys are not evidence.

If — and let me go further and talk to you a little bit about the argument of counsel.

JI-29   If in argument any counsel made reference or seemed to make reference to the veracity or personal integrity of any other attorney, you are to disregard any such comment. Such comment should play no role in how you decide this case.

And as I've already told you,

JI-30   the comments of counsel are not evidence and you are the sole and exclusive judges of what the evidence is.

JI-31   You must decide all the questions of fact in this case from the evidence received in this trial and not from any other source.

JI-32   You must not make any independent investigation of the facts or the law or consider or discuss facts as to which there is no evidence.

JI-33   This means, for example, that you must not on your own visit the scene, conduct experiments or consult reference works or persons for additional information.

JI-34   You must not discuss this case with any other person, except a fellow juror, and you must not discuss the case with a fellow juror until the case is submitted to you for your decision and only when all the jurors are present in the jury room.

JI-35   The word "defendant" applies equally to each defendant unless you are expressly instructed otherwise.

JI-36   Evidence consists of testimony of witnesses, writings, material objects or anything presented to the senses and offered to prove the existence or nonexistence of a fact.

JI-37   Evidence is either direct or circumstantial.

JI-38   Direct evidence is evidence that directly proves a fact without the necessity of an inference. It is evidence which, by itself, if found to be true, establishes that fact.

JI-39   Circumstantial evidence is evidence that, if found to be true, proves a fact from which an inference of the existence of another fact may be drawn.

JI-40   An inference is a deduction of fact that may logically and reasonably be drawn from another fact or group of facts established by the evidence.

JI-41   It is not necessary that facts be proved by direct evidence. They may be proved also by circumstantial evidence or by a combination of direct evidence and circumstantial evidence.

JI-42   Both direct evidence and circumstantial evidence are acceptable as a means of proof. Neither is entitled to any greater weight than the other.

JI-43   However, a finding of guilt as to any crime may not be based on circumstantial evidence unless the proved circumstances are not only, one, consistent with the theory that the defendant is guilty of the crime, but two, cannot be reconciled with any other rational conclusion.

JI-44   Further, each fact which is essential to complete a set of circumstances necessary to establish the defendant's guilt must be proved beyond a reasonable doubt. In other words, before an inference essential to establish guilt may be found to have been proved beyond a reasonable doubt, each fact or circumstance upon which such inference necessarily rests must be proved beyond a reasonable doubt.

JI-45   Also, if the circumstantial evidence as to any particular count is susceptible of two reasonable interpretations, one of which points to the defendant's guilt and the other to his innocence, you must adopt that interpretation which points to the defendant's innocence and reject that interpretation which points to this guilt.

JI-46   If, on the other hand, one interpretation of such evidence appears to you to be reasonable and the other interpretation to be unreasonable, you must accept the reasonable interpretation and reject the unreasonable.

JI-47   The specific intent with which an act is done may be shown by the circumstances surrounding the commission of the act, but you may not find the defendant guilty of the offense charged in counts III, IV and V unless the proved circumstances are not only, one, consistent with the theory that the defendant had the required specific intent or mental state, but two, cannot be reconciled with any other rational conclusion.

JI-48   Also, if the evidence as to any such specific intent or mental state is susceptible of two reasonable interpretations, one of which points to the existence of the specific intent or mental state, and the other to the absence of the specific intent or mental state, you must adopt that interpretation which points to the absence of the specific intent or mental state.

JI-49   If, on the other hand, one interpretation of the evidence as to such specific intent or mental state appears to you to be reasonable and the other interpretation to be unreasonable, you must accept the reasonable interpretation and reject the unreasonable.

JI-50   If you find that before this trial a defendant made a willfully false or deliberately misleading statement concerning the crimes for which he is now being tried, you may consider such statement as a circumstance tending to prove a consciousness of guilt. However, such conduct is not sufficient by itself to prove guilt and its weight and significance, if any, are matters for your determination.

JI-51   Evidence has been admitted against one or more of the defendants and not admitted against the others. At the time this evidence was admitted you were admonished that it could not be considered by you against the other defendants. Do not consider such evidence against the other defendants.

JI-52   Certain evidence was admitted for a limited purpose. At the time this evidence was admitted you were admonished that it could not be considered by you for any purpose other than the limited purpose for which it was admitted. Do not consider such evidence for any purpose except the limited purpose for which it was admitted.

JI-53   You have seen a lot of exhibits during the course of the trial used in examination of various witnesses. Not all of the exhibits that were referred to during the trial have been received in evidence. The exhibits that have been received in evidence will be provided to you, along with a list of those exhibits.

JI-54   Don't speculate or be concerned as to why some exhibits have not been received. You are to utilize the exhibits that have been received in evidence.

JI-55 Some of the exhibits that were received were received only as to a particular defendant or defendants and were so limited at the time the exhibits were received into evidence. The list of exhibits that will be provided to you includes the limitations, if any, that apply to each exhibit.

JI-56 You are instructed that testimony and/or exhibits that have been received only as to a particular defendant or defendants may be considered by you only in the case of that defendant or defendants and must not be discussed or considered by you in the case of any other defendant.

And as I say, the exhibit list has on it reference to those limitations on the physical exhibits, so when you look at the list, you will be able to identify which exhibits have been received for a limited purpose as to certain defendants and not as to others and you are to follow those limitations in your deliberations as well.

JI-57 Neither side is required to call as witnesses all persons who may have been present at any of the events disclosed by the evidence or who may appear to have some knowledge of these events or to produce all objects or document mentioned or suggested by the evidence.

JI-58 Evidence that on some former occasion a witness made a statement or statements that were inconsistent or consistent with his or her testimony in this trial may be considered by you not only for the purpose of testing the credibility of the witness, but also as evidence of the truth of the facts as stated by the witness on such former occasion.

JI-59 If you disbelieve a witness's testimony that he or she no longer remembers a certain event, such testimony is inconsistent with a prior statement or statements by him or her describing that event.

JI-60 **Every person who testifies under oath is a witness. You are the sole judges of the believability of a witness and the weight to be given the testimony of each witness.**

JI-61 **In determining the believability of a witness you may consider anything that has a tendency in reason to prove or disprove the truthfulness of the testimony of the witness, including but not limited to any of the following:**

JI-62 **The extent of the opportunity or the ability of the witness to see or hear or otherwise become aware of any matter about which the witness has testified;**

JI-63 **The ability of the witness to remember or to communicate any matter about which the witness has testified;**

JI-64   The character and quality of that testimony;

JI-65   The demeanor and manner of the witness while testifying;

JI-66   The existence or nonexistence of a bias, interest or other motive;

JI-67   Evidence of the existence or nonexistence of any fact testified to by the witness;

JI-68   The attitude of the witness towards this action or towards the giving of testimony;

JI-69   A statement previously made by the witness that is consistent or inconsistent with the testimony of the witness;

JI-70   An admission by the witness of untruthfulness;

JI-71   The witness's prior conviction of a felony.

JI-72   Discrepancies in a witness's testimony, or between his or her testimony and that of others, if there were any, do not necessarily mean that the witness should be discredited.

JI-73   Failure of recollection is a common experience and innocent misrecollection is not uncommon.

JI-74   It is a fact also that two persons witnessing an incident or a transaction often will see or hear it differently. Whether a discrepancy pertains to a fact of importance or only to a trivial detail should be considered in weighing its significance.

JI-75   A witness who is willfully false in one material part of his or her testimony is to be distrusted in others.

JI-76   You may reject the whole testimony of a witness who willfully has testified falsely as to a material point unless form all the evidence you believe the probability of truth favors his or her testimony in other particulars.

JI-77   You are not bound to decide an issue of fact in accordance with the testimony of a number of witnesses which does not convince you as against the testimony of a lesser number or other evidence which appeals to your mind with more convincing force.

JI-78   You may not disregard the testimony of the greater number of witnesses merely from caprice, whim or prejudice or from a desire to favor one side against the other.

JI-79   You must not decide an issue by the simple process of counting the number of witnesses who have testified on the opposing sides. The final test is not in the relative number of witnesses, but in the convincing force of the evidence.

JI-80   **The fact that a witness has been convicted of a felony, if such be a fact, may be considered by you only for the purpose of determining the believability of that witness.**

JI-81   **The fact of such a conviction does not necessarily destroy or impair the witness's believability.**

JI-82   **It is one of the circumstances that you may take into consideration in weighing the testimony of such a witness.**

JI-83   **You should give the testimony of a single witness whatever weight you think it deserves; however, testimony by one witness, which you believe concerning any fact, is sufficient for the proof of that fact. You should carefully review all the evidence upon which the proof of such fact depends.**

JI-84   Motive is not an element of the crime charged and need not be shown; however, you may consider motive or lack of motive as a circumstance in this case. Presence of motive may tend to establish guilt. Absence of motive may tend to establish innocence. You will therefore give its presence or absence, as the case may be, the weight to which you find it to be entitled.

JI-85   A defendant in a criminal trial has a constitutional right not to be compelled to testify. You must not draw any inference from the fact that a defendant does not testify. Further, you must neither discuss this matter nor permit it to enter into your deliberations in any way.

(In deciding whether or not to testify the defendant may choose to rely on the state of the evidence and upon the failure, if any, of the people to prove beyond a reasonable doubt every essential element of the charge against him. No lack of testimony on a defendant's part will make up for a failure of proof by the people so as to support a finding against him on any such material or essential element. Let me read that last one again since I misread it.)

JI-86   In deciding whether or not to testify the defendant may choose to rely on the state of the evidence and upon the failure, if any, of the people prove beyond a reasonable doubt every essential element of the charge against him. No lack of testimony on the defendant's part will make up for a failure of proof by the people so as to support a finding against him on any such essential element.

JI-87   An admission is as statement made by a defendant, other than at his trial, which does not by itself acknowledge his guilt of the crime for which such defendant is on trial but which statement tends to prove his guilt when considered with the rest of the evidence.

JI-88   You are the exclusive judges as to whether the defendant made an admission, and if so, whether such statement is true in whole or in part.

JI-89   If you should find that the defendant did not make the statement, you must reject it. If you find that it is true in whole or in part, you may consider that part which you find to be true.

JI-90   Evidence of an oral admission of a defendant should be viewed with caution. If you should find from the evidence that there was an occasion when a defendant, under circumstances which reasonably afforded him an opportunity to reply, failed to make a denial in the face of an accusation expressed directly to him or in his presence charging him with the crime for which such defendant now is on trial or tending to connect him with its commission and that he heard the accusation and understood its nature, then the circumstance of his silence on that occasion may be considered against him as indicating an admission that the accusation thus made was true.

JI-91   Evidence of such an accusatory statement is not received for the purpose of proving its truth, but only as it supplies meaning to the silence of the accused in the face of it.

JI-92   Unless you find that a defendant's silence at the time indicated an admission that the accusatory statement was true, you must entirely disregard the statement.

JI-93   Evidence has been received from which you may find that a statement of motive was made by a defendant before the offense with which he is charged was committed. It is for you to determine whether such a statement was made by a defendant and whether or not such statement constitutes a statement of motive.

JI-94   No person may be convicted of a criminal offense unless there is some proof of each element of the crime independent of any admission made by him outside the trial.

JI-95   The identity of the person who is alleged to have committed a crime is not an element of the crime. Such identity may be established by an admission.

JI-96   **A person is qualified to testify as an expert if he has special knowledge, skill, experience, training or education sufficient to qualify him as an expert on the subject to which his testimony relates.**

JI-97   A duly qualified expert may give an opinion on questions in controversy at a trial. To assist you in deciding such questions you may
consider the opinion, with the reasons given for it, if any, by the
expert who gives the opinion.

JI-98   You may also consider the qualifications and credibility of the expert.

JI-99   You are not bound to accept an expert opinion as conclusive, but
should give to it the weight to which you find it to be entitled. You
may disregard any such opinion if you find it to be unreasonable.

JI-100   In this case expert witnesses have testified about two types of facts:
facts to which they have special qualifications and experience which
allow them to testify as expert witnesses and facts on which they
have no special expertise.

JI-101   In particular, in rendering an opinion as to the use-of-force in this
case, one or more expert witnesses expressed an opinion on what
physical acts are shown on exhibit 2, the so-called Holliday videotape. Such experts have no more skill than a lay person in viewing
the videotape and determining what it shows in this regard. To the
extent that you find that the videotape is important to you in your
deliberations and decision in this case, you are the sole judges of
what physical acts are shown on the tape.

JI-102   Expert witnesses merely express their opinions of what physical
acts are shown on the videotape. These opinions were the assumption which formed the basis for an answer to a hypothetical question. The expert witnesses were assuming that the tape showed a
particular action or application of force for the purpose of expressing their opinion as to whether such force was reasonable or unreasonable, appropriate or excessive under the circumstances of the
hypothetical question.

JI-103   If you find that the videotape shows something other than which a
particular expert witness assumed to be true for a hypothetical question, you may consider that difference in determining what weight, if
any, to give the expert opinion expressed in answering that question.

JI-104   In determining the weight to be given an opinion expressed by any
witness who did not testify as an expert witness, you should consider his or her credibility, the extent of his or her opportunity to
perceive the matters upon which his opinion is based, and the reasons, if any, for giving that opinion. You are not required to accept
such an opinion but should give it the weight, if any, to which you
find it to be entitled.

JI-105   In examining an expert witness counsel may propound to him or
her a type of question known in the law as a hypothetical question.

By such a question the witness is asked to assume to be true a set of facts and to give an opinion based on that assumption.

JI-106 In permitting such a question the court does not rule and does not necessarily find that all the assumed facts have been proved. It only determines that those assumed facts are within the probable or possible range of the evidence.

JI-107 It is for you, the jury, to find from all the evidence whether or not the facts assumed in a hypothetical question have been proved.

JI-108 If you should find that any assumption in such a question has not been proved, you are to determine the effect of that failure of proof on the value and weight of the expert opinion based on the assumed facts.

JI-109 In resolving any conflict that may exist in the testimony of expert witnesses, you should weigh the opinion of one expert against that of another. In doing this you should consider the relative qualifications and credibility of the expert witnesses, as well as the reasons for each opinion and the facts and other matters upon which it was based.

JI-110 A defendant in a criminal action is presumed to be innocent until the contrary is proved, and in case of a reasonable doubt whether his guilt is satisfactorily shown, he is entitled to a verdict of not guilty.

JI-111 This presumption places upon the people the burden of proving him guilty beyond a reasonable doubt.

JI-112 Reasonable doubt is defined as follows:

It is not a mere possible doubt, because everything relating to human affairs and depending on moral evidence is open to some possible or imaginary doubt. It is that state of the case which, after the entire comparison and consideration of all the evidence, leaves the minds of the jurors in that condition that they cannot say they feel an abiding conviction to a moral certainty of the truth of the charge.

JI-113 The persons concerned in the commission of a crime who are regarded by law as principals in the crime thus committed and equally guilty thereof include, one, those who directly and actively commit the act constituting the crime, and two, those who aid and abet the commission of the crime.

JI-114 A person aids and abets the commission of a crime when he or she, one, with knowledge of the unlawful purpose of the perpetrator, and two, with the intent or purpose of committing, encouraging or facilitating the commission of the crime by act or advice, aids, promotes, encourages, or instigates the commission of the crime.

JI-115   Mere presence at the scene of a crime, which does not itself assist the commission of the crime, does not constitute or amount to aiding and abetting. Mere knowledge that a crime is being committed and the failure to prevent it does not amount to aiding and abetting.

JI-116   In the crime charged in Count I, namely assault by force likely to produce great bodily injury and with a deadly weapon, and in the crime charged in Count II, namely officer unnecessarily assaulting or beating any persons, there must exist a union or joint operation of act or conduct and general criminal intent.

JI-117   To constitute general criminal intent it is not necessary that there should exist an intent to violate the law.

JI-118   When a person intentionally does that which the law declares to be a crime, he is acting with general criminal intent even though he may not know that his act or conduct is unlawful.

JI-119   In each of the crimes charged in Counts III, IV and V, namely filing a false police report and accessory after the fact, there must exist a union or joint operation of act or conduct and a certain specific intent in the mind of the perpetrator.

JI-120   Unless such specific intent exists, the crime to which it relates is not committed. The specific intent required is included in the definitions of these charged crimes.

JI-121   In the special allegations of the intentional infliction of great bodily injury in Count I and Count II, charged against the defendants Laurence Powell and Timothy Wind, there must exist a union or joint operation of act or conduct and a certain specific intent in the mind of the perpetrator.

JI-122   Unless such specific intent exists, the allegation to which it relates is not committed. The specific intent required is included in the definition of the special allegations charged.

JI-123   In each of the crimes charged in Counts III and IV, namely filing a false police report, there must exist a certain mental state in the mind of the perpetrator. Unless such mental state exists, the crime to which it relates is not committed.

JI-124   In the crime of filing a false police report the necessary mental state is knowledge that the statement was false.

Well, I'm about halfway through. If anybody needs a break at any time, just let me know and we'll take a break.

JI-125   The defendants are accused in Count I of the information of having violated § 245 (A)(1) of the Penal Code, a crime. Every person who commits assault upon the person of another with a deadly weapon or instrument or by means of force likely to produce great bodily injury is guilty of the crime of violation of 245 (A)(1) of the Penal Code.

JI-126   In order to prove such crime, each of the following elements must be proved:
One, a person was assaulted; and
Two, the assault was committed with a deadly weapon or instrument or by means of force likely to produce great bodily injury.

JI-127   A deadly weapon is any object, instrument or weapon which is used in such a manner as to be capable of producing and likely to produce death or great bodily injury.

JI-128   Great bodily injury refers to significant or substantial bodily injury or damage. It does not refer to trivial or insignificant injury or moderate harm. Actual bodily injury is not a necessary element of the crime. If such bodily injury is inflicted, its nature and extent are to be considered in connection with all the evidence in determining whether the means used and the manner in which it was used were such that they were likely to produce great bodily injury.

JI-129   As used in these instructions, assault is an unlawful attempt, coupled with a present ability, to apply physical force upon the person of another. In order to constitute assault, each of the following elements must be proved:
One, an unlawful attempt was made to apply physical force upon the person of another;
Two, at the time of such attempt the person who made the attempt had the present ability to apply such physical force; and
Three, the person making the attempt had a general criminal intent which in this case means that such person intended to commit an act that the direct natural consequences of which, if successfully completed, would be the application of physical force upon the person of another.

JI-130   An attempt to apply physical force is not unlawful when done in lawful defense of another.

JI-131   The people have the burden to prove that the attempt to apply physical force by defendant Briseno was not in defense of another. If you have a reasonable doubt whether the attempt by Briseno was not in lawful defense of another, you must find the defendant Briseno not guilty.

JI-132 It is lawful for a person who, as a reasonable person, has grounds for believing and does believe that bodily injury is about to be inflicted upon Rodney King, to protect that individual from attack. In doing so he may use all force and means, which such person believes to be reasonably necessary, and which would appear to a reasonable person, in the same or similar circumstances, to be necessary to prevent the injury which appears to be imminent.

JI-133 A necessary element of assault is that the person committing the assault have the present ability to commit a violent injury upon the person of another. This means that at the time of the attempt one must have had — must have the physical means to accomplish such an injury in the manner in which it is attempted. If there is no such ability, this element — if there is such ability, rather, this element exists even if the attempt to commit the injury fails for some other reason.

JI-134 **Each defendant is accused in Count II of the indictment of having violated § 149 of the Penal Code. Every public officer who, under color of authority, without lawful necessity, assaults or beats any person, is guilty of a violation of § 149 of the Penal Code.**

JI-135 **In order to prove such a crime, each of the following elements must be proved:**
One, the defendant was a police officer;
Two, a person was assaulted or beaten by a police officer;
Three, the assault or beating was committed under color of authority and without lawful necessity.

JI-136 A police officer is a public officer. An officer is acting under color of authority when he is performing an act that is made possible only because he is cloaked with the authority of law or when he is acting under pretense of law.
When an officer is performing any duty as a police officer, he is acting under color of authority.

JI-137 **An arrest is made by an actual restraint of the person arrested or by his submission to the custody of an officer.**

JI-138 **In making an arrest the officer may subject the person being arrested to such restraint as is reasonable for the arrest and detention.**

JI-139 **A peace officer who is making an arrest may use reasonable force to make such arrest or to prevent escape or to overcome resistance.**

JI-140 **The officer need not retreat or desist from his efforts by reason of the resistance or threatened resistance of the person being arrested.**

JI-141 **Where a peace officer is making an arrest, the person being arrested — and the person being arrested has knowledge, or by the exercise** of reasonable care, should have knowledge that he is being arrested by a peace officer and such peace officer is making an arrest, it is the duty of the person to refrain from using force or any other means to resist such arrest unless unreasonable or excessive force is being used to make the arrest.

JI-142 However, a peace officer is not permitted to use unreasonable or excessive force in making an otherwise lawful arrest. If an officer does use unreasonable or excessive force in making or attempting to make an arrest, the person being arrested may use reasonable force to protect himself against such excessive force.

As I have stated, a peace officer who is making a lawful arrest may use reasonable force to make such arrest or to prevent escape or to overcome resistance.

JI-143 It is lawful for a peace officer to use force in the arrest if a reasonable peace officer is the same or similar circumstances would believe that such force is necessary to make the arrest or to prevent escape or to overcome resistance. In doing so, such peace officer may use that force and means that a reasonable peace officer, in the same or similar circumstances, would believe to be necessary to make such arrest or to prevent escape or to overcome resistance.

JI-144 The right of a peace officer to use reasonable force exists only so long as it would appear to a reasonable peace officer, in the same or similar circumstances, that that force is necessary to make such arrest or to prevent escape or to overcome resistance.

JI-145 When that force would no longer appear to a reasonable peace officer, in the same or similar circumstances, to be necessary, the right to use reasonable force no longer exists and the use of such force is not reasonable. The use-of-force that is not reasonable is unlawful and without lawful necessity.

JI-146 The people have the burden to prove that the force used was not lawful and without lawful necessity. If you have a reasonable doubt that the use-of-force was unlawful and without lawful necessity, you must find the defendant not guilty.

JI-147 The reasonableness of a particular use-of-force must be judged from the perspective of a reasonable officer under the same or similar circumstances.

JI-148 The test of reasonableness is not capable of precise definition or mechanical application. It is—its proper application requires careful attention to the facts and circumstances of each particular case, including the severity of the crime at issue, whether the suspect poses an immediate threat to the safety of the officers or others and whether he is actively resisting or attempting to evade arrest by flight. The question is whether the totality of the circumstances justifies a particular sort of force.

JI-149   **During a lawful arrest an officer may also take necessary measures to determine whether the person is in fact carrying a weapon.**

(The court took a five minute recess. Judge Weisberg then continues reading.)

JI-150   Defendant Laurence Powell is charged in Count III with the crime of filing a false police report by a peace officer...

Defendant Stacey C. Koon is charged in Count IV with the crime of filing a false police report by a peace officer...

JI-151   The defendant Stacey C. Koon is accused in count V of the information of having committed the crime of being an accessory to a felony, in violation of § 32 of the Penal Code...

Every person who, after a felony has been committed, harbors, conceals or aids a principal in such a felony with the specific intent that such principal may avoid or escape from arrest, trial, conviction or punishment, having knowledge that said principal was — has committed such felony or has been charged with such felony or convicted thereof, is guilty of the crime of accessory to a felony in violation of Penal Code § 32.

JI-152   In order to prove such crime, each of the following elements must be proved:
One, a felony of assault with a deadly weapon and assault under color of authority was committed;
Two, the defendant harbored, concealed or aided a principal in that felony with the specific intent that such principal avoid or escape arrest, trial, conviction or punishment;
Three , the defendant did so with the knowledge that the principal committed the felony.

(Numerous instructions are given that apply to these charges. They are not included in our review of the charges.)

There has been reference in the testimony to felony evading.

JI-153   The law provides that any person who, while operating a motor vehicle and with the intent to evade, willfully flees or otherwise at-

tempts to elude a pursuing peace officer's motor vehicle, commits
that offense if,

A, the peace officer's motor vehicle is exhibiting at least one lighted
red lamp visible from the front and the person either sees or reasonably should have seen the lamp;

B, the peace officer's motor vehicle is sounding a siren as may be
reasonably necessary;

C, the peace officer's motor vehicle is distinctively marked;

D, the peace officer's motor vehicle is operated by a peace officer
who is wearing a distinctive uniform; and

E, the pursued vehicle is driven in a willful and wanton disregard
for the safety of persons or property.

There has also been reference in testimony to reckless driving.

JI-154   The law provides a person who drives any vehicle upon a highway
in a willful or wanton disregard for the safety of persons or property commits that offense.

JI-155   **You must decide separately whether each of the defendants is guilty or
not guilty. If you cannot agree upon a verdict as to all of the defendants, but you do agree upon a verdict as to any one or more of them,
you must render a verdict as to the one or more as to whom you agree.**

JI-156   **Each of the defendants is entitled to the individual judgment of
each of the jurors.**

JI-157   The defendant Briseno is entitled to be judged wholly apart from
the other defendants in this case because the people have accused
him of a separate and distinct act from the acts charged against the
other defendants.

JI-158   The instructions I have given to you relating to aiding and abetting
do not apply to the Defendant Briseno. He is not charged with aiding and abetting the other defendants and is being tried solely on
the basis of the single act which the people contend constitutes the
crime with which he is charged.

JI-159   The defendants Laurence Powell, Timothy Wind and Stacey Koon
are accused of having committed the crime of assault by force likely
to produce great bodily injury and with a deadly weapon in Count I
and with the crime of officer unnecessarily assaulting or beating
any person in Count II.

JI-160   The prosecution has introduced evidence tending to prove that there
is more than one act upon which a conviction on either /or both of
these Counts may be based.

JI-161   The defendant may be found guilty if the proof shows beyond a reasonable doubt that he committed any one or more of such acts; however, in order to return a verdict of guilty to Count I or II, all jurors must agree that he committed the same act or acts.

It is not necessary that the particular act agreed upon be stated in your verdict.

JI-162   Each count charges a distinct crime. You must decide each count separately. The defendant may be found guilty or not guilty of the crimes charged. Your finding as to each count must be stated in a separate verdict.

JI-163   The defendant Koon is accused in Count I of having committed the crime of assault by force likely to produce great bodily injury and with a deadly weapon and in Count II with the crime of officer unnecessarily assaulting or beating any person.

JI-164   The defendant Koon is charged in Count V of having committed the crime of accessory after the fact.

JI-165   The charges in Counts I and II are each made in the alternative to that charged in Count V and in effect allege that the defendant committed an act or acts which constitute either / or both of the crimes charged in Counts I and II or the crime of accessory after the fact.

JI-166   If you find that the defendant Koon committed an act or acts constituting one of the charged crimes, you then must determine which of such acts or crimes, rather, so charged was thereby committed.

JI-167   In order to find the defendant Koon guilty, you must all agree as to the particular crime committed, and if you find the defendant Koon guilty in either Count I or Count II or both, you must find him not guilty in Count V. If you find the defendant guilty in Count V, then you must find him not guilty in Counts I and II.

JI-168   It is alleged in Counts I and II that in the commission of the crimes therein described the defendants Laurence M. Powell and Timothy E. Wind, with the specific intent to inflict such injury, personally inflicted great bodily injury on Rodney Glenn King.

JI-169   If you find either defendant guilty in either count, you must determine whether or not such defendant, with the specific intent to inflict such injury, did personally inflict great bodily injury on Rodney Glenn King in the commission of the crimes charged in those counts.

JI-170   Great bodily injury, as used in this instruction, means a significant or substantial physical injury. Minor or moderate injuries of a temporary nature do not constitute greatly (sic) bodily injury and are not sufficient.

JI-171   The people have the burden of proving the truth of this allegation. If you have a reasonable doubt that it is true, you must find it to be not true. You will include a special finding on that question in your verdict using a form that will be supplied for that purpose.

JI-172   **I have not intended by anything I have said or done, or by any question that I may have asked or by any ruling I may have made, to intimate or suggest what you should find to be the facts or that I believe or disbelieve any witness. If anything I have done or said has seemed to so indicate, you will disregard it and form your own conclusions.**

JI-173   **The purposes of the court's instructions is to provide you with the applicable law so that you may arrive at a just and lawful verdict.**

JI-174   **Whether some instructions apply will depend upon what you find to be the facts.**

JI-175   **Disregard any instruction which applies to facts determined by you not to exist.**

JI-176   **Do not conclude that because an instruction has been given that I'm expressing an opinion as to the facts.**

JI-177   The people and the defendant are entitled to the individual opinion of each juror. Each of you must decide and consider the evidence for the purpose of reaching a verdict if you can do so. Each of you must decide the case for yourself but should do so only after discussing the evidence and instructions with the other jurors.

JI-178   **Do not hesitate to change an opinion if you are convinced it is wrong; however, do not decide any question in a particular way because the majority of the jurors, or any of them, favor such a decision.**

JI-179   **Do not decide any issue in this case by chance, such as by the drawing of lots or by any other chance determination.**

JI-180   **The attitude and conduct of jurors at all times are very important. It is rarely helpful for a juror at the beginning of deliberations to express an emphatic opinion on the case or to announce a determination to stand for a certain verdict. When one does that at the outset, a sense of pride may be aroused and one may hesitate to change a position even if shown it is wrong. Remember that you are not partisans or advocates in this matter, you are impartial judges of the facts.**

JI-181   In your deliberations do not discuss or consider the subject of penalty or punishment. That subject must not in any way affect your verdict.

JI-182   As I have indicated, the instructions I'm now giving to you will be made available in written form during your deliberations. Since they're part of the official record, they must not be defaced in any way.

JI-183   You will find that the instructions may be typed, printed or handwritten. Portions may have been added or deleted. You must disregard any deleted part of an instruction and not speculate as to what it was or as to the reasons for its deletion. You are not to be concerned with the reasons for any modifications. Every part of the text of an instruction, whether typed, printed or handwritten, is of equal importance. You are to be governed only by the instruction in its final wording.

JI-184   Do not disclose to anyone outside the jury, that means outside the twelve jurors deliberating, not even to me or any member of my staff, either orally or in writing, how you are divided numerically in your balloting as to any issue until I specifically direct you to do otherwise.

JI-185   You've been given notebooks. Some of you have taken notes during the trial; some have not. Notes are only an aid to memory and should not take precedence over independent recollection. A juror who has not taken notes should rely on his or her independent recollection of the evidence and not be influenced by the fact that other jurors have taken notes. Notes are for the note taker's own personal use in refreshing his or her recollection of the evidence.

JI-186   Finally, should any discrepancy exist between a juror's recollection of the evidence and his or her notes, he or she may request that the reporter read back the relevant proceedings and the trial transcript will prevail over the notes.

Let me just discuss with you briefly reading of testimony or rereading of testimony. You have seen, during the course of the trial, that the lawyers have transcripts, little books of testimony that they have been provided with on a daily basis by the court reporter.

The jury doesn't get that. You don't get transcripts like that. When you want testimony read back, if you do, during the course of the trial, you will prepare a note or your foreperson will prepare a note and give it to the bailiff and it will get to me requesting the testimony be read back.

It might be that you will want the entire testimony of a particular witness, you might want part of a testimony of a witness, you might want a certain issue that the witness discussed read back or you might want a particular portion of a day's testimony. Whatever is you want, we'll find it in the testimony, in the transcript, and it will be read back to you by the court reporter.

As I said, we won't give you the transcripts themselves, but orally the reporter will read back to you what it was that the questions were and the answers that were given to the questions during the proceedings that you have requested.

And depending upon how the parties want to deal with it, sometimes the reading of testimony occurs here in open court in the courtroom, sometimes it is done up in the jury room when the court reporter goes up and reads it, it depends on how we want to deal with it.

And when you make such a request, if you do, then we'll discuss it — I will discuss it with the lawyers and determine how the particular proceeding will be conducted as far as reading back of testimony.

As far as communicating with the court during the deliberations, you will be given notes or note pad or sheets that you are to utilize in requests, making requests of the court, and that is the procedure by which you will communicate with me if you have any requests for things such as reread or clarifications of legal rules, anything else.

The way to do it is to put it in writing and give it to the bailiff and then he will give it to me..

All right. [Judge Weisberg resumes reading the instructions.]

JI-187   In this case there are just two possible verdicts as to each count as to each defendant; guilty and not guilty.

JI-188   These verdict forms are going to be provided to you, and obviously only one possible verdict may be returned by you as to any particular count as to any particular defendant.

And if you have all agreed upon one verdict as to a particular count of any particular defendant, the corresponding verdict form is the only verdict form to be signed as to that count and that defendant and the other forms are to be left unsigned.

In a moment I'm going to give you the final instruction, and then what I will do is have the bailiff sworn in. The bailiff not only — because the jury will be sequestered, we'll have more than one bailiff sworn in to take custody of the jury during the time of your deliberations, and let me just give you a little more information about the conduct of the jury during deliberations.

As I've already indicated, the only time the jury can discuss this case, the only time you can discuss this case is when the twelve jurors who are all present in the jury room, in this building, in the jury room, and that is the only time you can discuss this case with anyone until the case is completed.

And that means during breaks and recesses, during the evening, at night, early morning before you come into the courthouse, even if all twelve jurors happen to be present in the same place, same time, you could not discuss the case and you must not discuss it.

You can only discuss it when you come here into the jury room and that is the only time you can discuss it, in the jury room when all twelve jurors are present. If there is not all twelve, you can't discuss it. If somebody left the room for some reason, you couldn't discuss it. You have to wait until all twelve jurors are there and you can discuss it and participate in your deliberations.

That also means that during breaks, if — I'm sure there will be, you must not discuss this matter, not only discuss it among yourselves, the twelve jurors, but the alternate jurors will be present during meals and things of that sort, too, and you obviously can't discuss it with them at all, since they are not going to be part of the twelve jurors deliberating, and you cannot discuss it with the bailiffs or anyone else.

You can only discuss this matter when all twelve jurors are present in the jury room during deliberations.

Now, I'm repeating it, but it is very important, it is a very important principle, but that is the only place and the only time when deliberations and discussions can occur. is when the twelve jurors are in the deliberation room, so —

And to the alternate jurors, you will be, during the day, during deliberations, kept apart from the other jurors, but at meals and other times you will have contact with them when deliberations are not occurring, and you are not to discuss the case with them or among yourselves at any time, because as I indicated yesterday, one of the twelve jurors who are deliberating might become unable to continue and we'll have to select an alternate juror to replace that juror, and we would, No. 1, do it by lot, as I did before, and secondly, when we do that, we have to be assured that you haven't discussed tis (sic) case among yourselves or with anyone else.

So I know there will be a temptation to do that, but please don't discuss this case with anyone, including among yourselves, or obviously as I've said, and I can't emphasize it enough, during any time you have contact with the other jurors, don't discuss the case with then at all.

What I'm going to do at this point is give you the final instruction and I'm going to send you the final instruction and I'm going to send you all up to the jury room. I know it is one o'clock and everyone is hungry. What I'm going to do is send you upstairs and ask that you select your foreperson and then after you do that, take your break and have lunch, and this break or any other breaks, the rules apply. Don't discuss this case at all during those breaks.

JI-188 You shall now retire and select one of your number to act as foreman or foreperson. He or she will preside over your deliberations.

In order to reach verdicts, all twelve jurors must agree to the decision and any — to any findings you have been instructed to include in your verdict.

As soon as all of you have agreed upon a verdict so that when polled each may state truthfully that the verdicts express his or her vote, have them dated and signed by your foreperson and then return with them to this courtroom. Return any unsigned verdict forms as well.

Notes

1   In November 1996 California voters rejected a proposition on the ballot to build the prisons necessary to incarcerate lawbreakers. It's somewhat ironic that the increased prison population was caused largely because of those same voters' enchantment with harsher penalties.

2   Los Angeles Times, January 16, 1992, page A-1

3   First Amendment of the U. S. Constitution:

> Congress shall make no law respecting an establishment of religion, or prohibiting the free exercise thereof; or abridging the freedom of speech, or of the press, or the right of the people peaceably to assemble, and to petition the government for a redress of grievances.

4   Sixth Amendment of the U.S. Constitution:

> In all criminal prosecutions, the accused shall enjoy the right to a speedy and public trial, by an impartial jury of the state and district wherein the crime shall have been committed, which district shall have been previously ascertained by law, and to be informed of the nature and cause of the accusation; to be confronted with the witnesses against him; to have compulsory process for obtaining witnesses in his favor, and to have the assistance of counsel for his defense.

5   Jury instructions represent accurate and concise statements of the law (in California). Most are found in California Jury Instructions Criminal (CALJIC). The instructions which are quoted beginning in

this chapter, Part III and much more extensively in Part IV, are designated *in this book* by JI followed by a number), such as (JI-1). Jury instructions are not identified to jurors in this manner. Normally, the jury instructions are grouped together in a single paragraph even though there are two, five, ten or more distinct and separate points of law. We have taken these single paragraphs and divided them into the respective points. For example, (JI-2), (JI-3), (JI-6) and (JI-9) through (JI-18) are contained in CALJIC Jury Instruction 1.00 entitled "Respective Duties of Judge and Jury."

Each instruction's number reflects the order in which it was read to the jury at the end of the trial.

Jury instructions are discussed in detail in Chapter 24. The first half of the instructions given in the Rodney King beating trial are set out in that chapter in paragraph format. All of the instructions excluding those dealing solely with Counts III and IV, are also set out in Appendix C using the numbering system discussed above.

[6]   California Evidence Code Section 140

[7]   Fourth Amendment to the U.S. Constitution:

> The right of the people to be secure in their persons, houses, papers and effects, against unreasonable searches and seizures, shall not be violated, and no warrants shall issue, but upon probable cause, supported by oath or affirmation, and particularly describing the place to be searched, and the persons or things to be seized.

[8]   Fifth Amendment to the U.S. Constitution:

> No person shall be held to answer for a capital, or otherwise infamous crime, unless on a presentment or indictment of a grand jury, except in cases arising in the land or naval forces, or in the militia, when in actual service in time of war or public danger; nor shall any person be subject for the same offense to be twice put in jeopardy of life or limb; nor shall be compelled in any criminal case to be a witness against himself, nor be deprived of life, liberty, or property, without due process of law; nor shall private property be taken for public use without just compensation.

[9]   California Evidence Code Section 1370 now provides an exception to the hearsay rule when there is a report which purports to describe a threat or injury to the person who is now unavailable to be called as a witness; the report was made at or near the time of the event, and was made under trustworthy circumstances; and the report was in writing, recorded, or made to a law enforcement official.

10   California Penal Code Section 686

11   California Penal Code Section 893 provides that the grand jury (in California) consists of United States citizens who are: (1) 18 years or older; (2) residents of the state and of the county or city and county for one year before being selected and returned; (3) in possession of natural faculties, ordinary intelligence, sound judgment, and fair character; and (4) possessed of sufficient knowledge of the English language. A grand juror cannot be serving as a trial juror, or have been discharged as a grand juror in the past year, or been convicted of malfeasance in office or any felony or high crime, or be serving as an elected public officer.

Grand jurors must be selected in a "manner which does not systematically exclude, or substantially underrepresent, the members of any identifiable group in the community." A "class" includes racial, ethnic and sexual groups, but not necessarily the young, the poor, the undereducated and blue collar workers. *People v. Newton* (1970) 8 Cal. App. 3d 359, 388

12   *Hawkins v. Superior Court* (1978) 22 Cal. 3d 584.

13   California Penal Code Section 995

14   *People v. Encerti* (1982) 130 Cal.App.3d 791

15   *People v. Slaughter* (1984) 35 Cal.3d 629

16   California Jury Instructions Criminal (See Note [5])

17   Webster's Ninth New Collegiate Dictionary (1991)

18   *Batson v. Kentucky* (1986) 106 S.Ct. 1712

19   *J.E.B. v. Alabama* (1994) 114 S.Ct. 1419

20   Los Angeles Times, February 6, 1993, page B-1

21   California Code of Civil Procedure Section 222.5

22   The questions used in the text and set out below are reported in California Criminal Law, Procedure and Practice, 1986 Edition prepared by the California Continuing Education of the Bar:

        Have you or anyone close to you ever been the victim of a crime such as the one charged in this case?

Is there something you have not told us that might affect you while you are deliberating in this case? Can you tell me what that is? Would you be willing to talk to me without the other jurors present or to the judge in chambers?

Have you ever been arrested? Has a member of your family or a close friend ever been arrested?

23   California Evidence Code Section 210

24   Leading questions may be asked by the lawyer who initially called a witness if that witness is found by the court to be a hostile witness to that lawyer's side. Kato Kaelin was considered a hostile witness to the prosecution which had called him in the *O.J. Simpson* case.

25   See Appendix C for following additional jury instructions in which jurors are asked to weigh the evidence:

(JI-50)	(JI-60)	(JI-74)
(JI-82)	(JI-83)	(JI-84)
(JI-99)	(JI-103)	(JI-104)
(JI-108)	(JI-109)	

26   The criteria are taken from CALJIC (5th Edition) instruction 2.92 entitled "Factors to Consider In Proving Identity by Eye Witness Testimony".

27   California Evidence Code Section 780

28   *People v. Simpson*, Vol. 73, pages 11543-4.

29   In the July 1995 Supplement (5th Edition) to CALJIC, language relating to "moral evidence" or to a "moral certainty" is no longer required to be a part of the reasonable doubt jury instruction. As noted in CALJIC, this action was taken based on the decision of *People v. Freeman* (1994) 8 Cal. 4th 450. There, the California Supreme Court suggested that the terms "moral evidence" and "moral certainty" added nothing to the jury's understanding of reasonable doubt.

30   This is the preponderance of the evidence standard ("burden of proof") which exists in civil trial.

31   *People v. Powell* (Vol. 44, pages 5246-50)

32   In the *Powell* case, as in almost all cases with multiple defendants (for example, the trial of the Menendez brothers) each felony defen-

dant will choose, or have assigned, a lawyer to represent the interest of the individual defendant.

[33] Sgt. Nichols claimed that, as a consequence of his damaging testimony against the officers before the grand jury, he had been ostracized, demoted, was now suffering severe stress and was being badgered by both sides. Judge Weisberg excused him from testifying on the legal ground that he had seen confidential statements from three of the defendants that they were forced (coerced) to give to Internal Affairs as part of the Department's investigation of the King incident. Los Angeles Times, April 15, 1992, page B-3

[34] The following are the instructions read to the jurors on the morning of April 23, 1992 by Judge Weisberg. They are found in Volume 78, beginning at page 14064.

[35] In Sacramento [California], where the number of criminal trials has doubled in the last three years, the number of potential jurors not responding to eligibility questionnaires has tripled." (Sacramento Bee, January 29, 1996, page 1)

[36] New York State amended Section 506 of its Judiciary Law effective July 20, 1994 to insure a more diverse pool of potential jurors. Such section reads:

> The commissioner of jurors shall cause the names of prospective jurors to be selected at random from the voter registration lists, and from such other available lists of the residents of the county as the chief administrator of the courts shall specify, such as lists of utility subscribers, licensed operators of motor vehicles, registered owners of motor vehicles, state and local taxpayers, *persons applying for or receiving aid to dependent children, medical assistance or home relief, persons receiving state unemployment benefits* and persons who have volunteered to serve as jurors by filing with the commissioner their names and place of residence.

[37] Los Angeles County implemented a program that could fine people who refuse to appear for jury service up to $1,500. In June 1996, eighteen people who failed to appear for a hearing on the issue of their failure to report for jury service were, in fact, fined $1,500. It remains to be seen how effective this approach will be. Los Angeles Daily Journal, June 26, 1996, page 3

[38] Rule of Professional Conduct 5-120 approved by the California Supreme Court and effective October 1, 1995 states in part:

"A member who is participating or has participated in the investigation or litigation of a matter shall not make an extra-judicial statement that a reasonable person would expect to be disseminated by means of pubic communication if the member knows or reasonably should know that it will have a substantial likelihood of materially prejudicing an adjudicative proceeding in the matter."

[39]   *People v. Powell* (Vol. 44, pages 5250-54)

A Glossary for Jurors*

ACCESSORY AFTER THE FACT a person who knows that another individual has committed a "felony" yet still aids or assists the lawbreaker in escaping capture or punishment

ACQUITTAL a judicial determination that the individual charged with a crime is not guilty of that crime

ADOPTIVE ADMISSION actions—whether by silence or through statements—which show agreement with the statements or actions of another person

ALLEGATION a contention that a certain set of facts is true, often made in a pleading or a criminal "charge"

ARRAIGNMENT the reading of the criminal "charges" to the accused, at the time the accused enters a guilty, not guilty, or nolo contendere ("no contest) plea

BATTERY intentional and wrongful physical contact without the person's consent, generally causing injury, or an offensive touching

BATTERED-SPOUSE SYNDROME a defense to a criminal charge based on the contention that the otherwise criminal acts of the accused should be partially or totally excused because of spousal violence, whether by physical, psychological, or verbal abuse

BEYOND A REASONABLE DOUBT the amount of evidence necessary to convict the defendant; a very high standard applied only in criminal cases

* If word or phrase is in quotes, it has been defined in this Glossary.

BURDEN OF PROOF responsibility of a party in a civil or criminal action to present enough evidence to establish its case—in criminal law, the prosecution's responsibility to prove the defendant's guilt "beyond a reasonable doubt"

CASE-IN-CHIEF the part of the criminal trial in which the party with the initial "burden of proof", the prosecution, presents the evidence deemed necessary to meet its "burden of proof", after which presentation the prosecution rests its case

CHANGE OF VENUE a change in the location of the trial site

CHARGE (1) a formal statement of the specific crime which the defendant has allegedly committed; (2) jury instructions and final address to the jury by the judge before the jury begins its deliberations

CIRCUMSTANTIAL EVIDENCE evidence presented which establishes certain facts, from which the finder of fact is asked to "infer" that certain other facts logically and reasonably must also exist

CONTEMPT OF COURT a determination by a judge that an individual has failed to follow the judge's instructions, and therefore is subject to fine or imprisonment

COUNT a specific part of the "indictment" designating a distinct criminal offense, different from any of the other counts

CROSS-EXAMINATION the questioning of one side's witness by the opposing party which occurs after "direct examination"

DEPOSITION the testimony of a witness, not in the courtroom (often in a lawyer's office) but under oath, and transcribed

DIMINISHED CAPACITY a defense based on the claim that due to intoxication, drug use, trauma, or mental disability or disease, the defendant could not have formed the specific intent necessary for a guilty finding as to the charged crime

DIRECT EXAMINATION the questioning of a witness by the party which called the witness

DISCOVERY the right of the defense—and sometimes the prosecution—to obtain access to evidence, or names of witnesses, the other party plans to present at an early stage of the trial, so that the party can effectively prepare its case

DNA deoxyribonucleic acid, an analysis which results in the classification of an individual's genetic information, used in criminal cases to establish that a certain individual is highly likely or highly unlikely to be the perpetrator of the crime

DOUBLE JEOPARDY Constitutional (5th and 14th Amendments) guarantee that after conviction or acquittal, there cannot be a second prosecution-for the same offense, and that there cannot be multiple punishments for the same offense

EVIDENCE "testimony", documents, objects, things which can be sensed— not "allegations" or argument

EXCLUSIONARY RULE Constitutional guarantee (4th and 14th Amendments) that evidence obtained in violation of the 4th Amendment's search and seizure protections cannot be introduced as "evidence" in the trial of the defendant

EXCULPATORY tending to clear, or actually clearing a person from alleged fault or guilt

FELONY a more serious crime than a "misdemeanor", often limited to those crimes which are punishable by death, or by imprisonment for one year or more

"FOR CAUSE" a determination by a judge that a juror cannot perform his or her duties and therefore should not be allowed to serve on the particular jury

FORENSIC scientific examiners of legal "evidence"

FORUM SHOP the attempt by a party to have the case tried in a location which the party feels to be more favorable

GRAND JURY at common law, a jury of twelve to twenty-three, whose duties include determining whether probable cause exists that a crime has been committed and whether an "indictment" should be returned against a particular individual. Called a "grand" jury because there are as many or more members than in a typical twelve person jury.

HEARSAY a statement, other than one made by the witness while testifying in court or at hearing, offered as evidence to prove the truth of the matter which is being asserted

> Example: A witness testifies that Tom told her that "Jim is a liar."
> If the attorney wants to establish that Jim is a liar, the testimony is hearsay. If the attorney wants to establish that Tom said "Jim is a liar", the testimony is not hearsay because it is not being used to prove that Jim is, in fact, a liar.

HUNG JURY a jury which cannot agree that the defendant is guilty or not guilty of the crime; a deadlocked jury

HYPOTHETICAL QUESTION a question posed to an expert based on the assumption that a certain set of possible facts is true

INADMISSIBLE a decision by the judge that the jury cannot hear or see certain evidence

INDICTMENT a charge or accusation which must be proved at trial; an accusation, or true bill presented in writing by a "grand jury" to the court, charging that a person has committed a specific crime or crimes

INFERENCE a reasoning process, by which a fact or proposition sought to be proved, is deduced as a logical and reasonable consequence from other facts or propositions already proved

INVOLUNTARY MANSLAUGHTER killing a person accidentally or without design while committing a nonfelonious but unlawful act, or while committing a lawful act without proper caution or required skill

IRRESISTIBLE IMPULSE a type of insanity defense to a "charge," on the basis that the defendant lacked the ability to control his or her drives

JUDICIAL NOTICE an evidentiary shortcut, which permits judges or jurors to recognize as facts certain matters which are universally recognized as true, such as State laws, geographical features, the calendar, historical events, etc.

JURY NULLIFICATION a theory that jurors can ignore the law and the evidence, and decide the guilt or nonguilt of the defendant based on the jurors' individual predilections

LEADING QUESTION a question which instructs or suggests to the witness how to answer, or puts the questioner's words in the witness's mouth; only permissible in limited situations involving "cross-examination", or "direct" or "redirect" examination of a hostile witness

LIBEL defamation expressed in writing, pictures or signs—distinguished from "slander" which is oral defamation

MISDEMEANOR a less serious criminal offense than a "felony," generally punishable by fine, penalty, forfeiture or imprisonment for a short period (less than a year) which is not in a state or Federal penitentiary

MOTION a request to the judge for the purpose of obtaining a ruling in favor of the person making the request

MURDER IN THE FIRST DEGREE a willful, deliberate, premeditated killing, or one committed during the perpetration of a serious crime such as rape, arson, burglary

MURDER IN THE SECOND DEGREE all murder which is not in the first degree; murder is homicide committed with reckless indifference to human life, but without premeditation

OBJECTION a legal argument raised during the course of the trial that certain statements or evidence should not be presented to or considered by the jury

OVERRULED a judge's determination that an "objection" is not valid, and that the statement or "evidence" can be presented to the jury or remain a part of the record the jurors may consider

PEREMPTORY CHALLENGE removal of a juror arbitrarily by either side even though the juror cannot be removed "for cause"; challenges are limited by state law or judicial rules; cannot be used to remove jurors based on certain factors, e.g. race, sex

PERJURY the willful assertion of a fact, opinion or belief which the individual who is testifying, or who is submitting an affidavit, knows is false

PLEA-BARGAIN an agreement between the prosecution and defense that the defendant will plead guilty to a particular crime, on the basis that a more serious charge(s) will be dropped

PRIVILEGED COMMUNICATION statements which the law protects from forced disclosure on the witness stand because the law wants to encourage open communications between two parties, e.g., husband-wife, attorney-client, priest-penitent, doctor-patient

PROBABLE CAUSE (1) for arrest, or search and seizure, reasonable grounds to believe that the person should be arrested or searched; (2) reasonable grounds, not mere suspicions or beliefs, but facts and circumstances which would lead a reasonably prudent person to arrest, or search and seize

PROBATIVE VALUE tending to prove, or actually proving

REBUTTAL "evidence" given to counteract, explain, or disprove evidence submitted by the other party

REDIRECT the examination of one's own witness after the witness has been "cross-examined"

SEQUESTERED to separate or isolate; of jurors, to separate and isolate them from the public, from external influences, and sometimes from friends and family, during the course of a highly publicized trial

SERIOUS FELONY a crime of graver and more serious nature than a "felony" in California; federal and State governments may classify felonies (such as Class A,B,C) or by degrees (first, second, third) to designate kinds of felonies and sentences for each class

SIDEBAR position at the side of the judge, where trial counsel and the judge discuss matters outside the hearing of the jurors

SLANDER an oral "libel," a defamation of the individual

SPECIAL CIRCUMSTANCES provisions in the law which allow a more severe penalty to be imposed than would a mere finding of guilt, e.g., in California, conviction of murder would require a finding of "special circumstances" before the defendant could be sentenced to death

SPEEDY TRIAL Constitutional right (6th and 14th Amendments) guaranteeing person arrested and charged with right to a trial without undue delay; states, such as California, have specific time limits which must be met or the charges will be dismissed

STIPULATION an agreement between the prosecution and defense that a certain fact(s) is undisputed and therefore is true, and so there is no need for any proof to be introduced

SUBORN PERJURY to cause or encourage another to commit "perjury"

SUSTAINED to affirm, uphold, approve, as when a judge agrees with a party and upholds an objection made by the party

TESTIMONY "evidence" given orally, under oath, at a court proceeding or hearing

THREE-STRIKES-AND-YOU'RE OUT increased penalties imposed on third time criminal offenders, in some cases leading to life imprisonment after a third conviction

UNDER PENALTY OF PERJURY a statement made acknowledging that a willful misstatement could subject the person to conviction for "perjury"

VOIR DIRE to speak the truth; the examination of prospective jurors to determine whether they are qualified to serve as jurors in the particular trial

VOLUNTARY MANSLAUGHTER unlawful killing without deliberation, premeditation or malice, as in the heat of passion

WEIGHT OF THE EVIDENCE the quality of the "evidence" and not its quantity

INDEX